SPIRITUAL LETTERS

SPIRITUAL LETTERS

SISTER WENDY BECKETT

ORBIS BOOKS
Maryknoll, New York 10545

ORBIS BOOKS
Maryknoll, New York 10545

Fathers and Brothers
MARYKNOLL

Founded in 1970, Orbis Books endeavors to publish works that enlighten the mind, nourish the spirit, and challenge the conscience. The publishing arm of the Maryknoll Fathers and Brothers, Orbis seeks to explore the global dimensions of the Christian faith and mission, to invite dialogue with diverse cultures and religious traditions, and to serve the cause of reconciliation and peace. The books published reflect the views of their authors and do not represent the official position of the Maryknoll Society. To learn more about Maryknoll and Orbis Books, please visit our website at www.maryknollsociety.org.

First published in Great Britain in 2013 by Bloomsbury Publishing Plc
50 Bedford Square
London WC1B 3DP

First published in the USA in 2013 by Orbis Books
P.O. Box 308
Maryknoll, New York 10545-0308

Manufactured in the United States of America.

Library of Congress Cataloging-in-Publication Data

Beckett, Wendy.
Spiritual letters / Sister Wendy Beckett.
     pages cm
  Includes bibliographical references.
   ISBN 978-1-62698-051-8 (pbk.)
   1. Beckett, Wendy—Correspondence. 2. Carmelite Nuns—Correspondence. I. Title.
BX4705.B2675A4 2013
271'.97102—dc23
                        2013005207

Contents

PREFACE BY SISTER WENDY

We all know the Chinese curse: 'may you live in interesting times,' and those who were born in 1930, as I was, have indeed known the affliction of living through times of terrible and sinister interest. Yet, I feel, though I have lived through these times I have somehow escaped the curse of them. This is not to my credit, because the tragedy of these years must have purified and ennobled those who were willing to accept suffering as the Cross of Christ. We all have a cross, the cross of who we are and where we are and when we are, and in carrying it with Jesus we are drawn into His redemption. Somehow these big and painful events passed me by. My life has been a very sheltered one, with hardly any 'events' to provide much of a narrative.

In this unimpressive life of mine, I can distinguish only two significant choices. The first, which formed itself in early childhood, was to become a nun, and this I was able to do just before my seventeenth birthday. I wanted to become a nun, because that was the only way I could see to belong totally to God. I understand now, of course, that every way of life can be given to Him, and that a nun is no more potentially holy than a bus driver or a dentist. But subjectively, in personal terms, to become a nun was necessary for me. I have come to the conclusion, looking back, that a bus driver or dental Sister Wendy would have fallen pathetically by the roadside. I would not have been strong enough to accept the Spirit of Jesus drawing me to the Father, without the framework and support of the religious life. When I thought of becoming a nun, (which I imagined would solve all my difficulties), I thought essentially of having time to pray. It never occurred to me, idiotic child that I was, that I had asked to enter with the order where I was at school, the Sisters of Notre Dame de Namur. This is a splendid order of devoted apostolic women, heroically living by the spirit of St. Julie Billiart, dedicated to education, particularly of the poor. Such a life of happy sacrifice is not possible without a deep spirit of prayer, but part of the sacrifice is that the time for prayer has to be limited. The generosity of an SND makes that limited time fruitful throughout the day. I chose well, in that I entered a loving community of women, who would teach me the basics of religious life, so that I understood the vows of poverty, chastity and obedience. These vows set the nun free to live for God. I was too spiritually weak to live in this freedom without more time on my knees, and asked regularly if it would be possible to transfer to a contemplative order. I was told that my work with the students was needed, (and after all, the Order had paid for me to go to Oxford, a blessing for which I have always been grateful and which I felt obligated to make use of for our students). But, when one makes a vow of obedience, one cannot disregard it because one does not like what one is asked to do. The pain of submission is a way into the Passion of Jesus that all nuns find profoundly redemptive. Actually, nothing could have been better for me, monolith of selfishness that I was; the life of a teaching nun is deeply purifying. Finally, however, my health gave way when I was 40, and the Order itself, very generously, suggested that I should try the contemplative life.

This was the second and final change in my uneventful life: I came to live in solitude. A Carmelite Monastery agreed to let me live within their enclosure, and bought me a caravan which stands within a small copse of trees. The Bishop allowed me to take the vows of a Consecrated Virgin, living under the protection and guidance of the Carmelites. The prioress of the monastery is my Superior, my prioress, and the sisters care for me. I do not speak to them, except to the sister who is my official and beloved 'guardian'. There is no blueprint for the kind of life that I am now privileged to lead. I had to make out my own horarium, which included seven hours of prayer, seven hours of sleep, two of work and so on. I had to decide on how to simplify all I did, so that my attention could dwell uninterruptedly on God. Hence the need of a religious habit, so as never to have to think of what I was to wear, and of daily simplicity of meals, so that I would not have to think of what I would eat. I did not want to waste time on these things, and the Community undertook, in their goodness, to provide me with cooked vegetables cold, and milk and whatever a healthy diet demanded. Because they have taken on this burden of love, I am able to devote myself to prayer, which is the greatest of privileges and the most demanding of responsibilities. I had read about people living a hermit or semi-hermit life, who spent prayerful hours gardening. I value this in theory, but in practice I am a sadly sedentary woman. For me gardening would be a penance that I would actually find distracting. The other activity of the solitary seems to be what is known as the apostolate of the letter. Again, I admire this and have read such letters with delight and instruction. The Spiritual Letters of Dom John Chapman OSB was one of my favourite books as a young nun. But it is not an apostolate to which I have ever felt drawn. When I came to live in solitude I made it clear I would not be writing letters, except out of duty. This meant a fortnightly letter to my mother, and the occasional letter of thanks to friends and benefactors. But one cannot limit duty to what one would like. There were people who had helped me when I was a teaching nun and there were sisters in the Carmelite monastery who occasionally asked my opinion, for what it was worth. I had no idea of how many of these 'helpful letters' I had written, still less that the nuns to whom they were written, had saved them. It seems an impertinence to write a preface to letters that I have not re-read, but

I simply cannot bring myself to do so. In fact, I do not think I have ever 'read' them, because I scribbled them off (in my illegible hand), and sent them off without ever reading what I had written. It is difficult to imagine that there is anything worth preserving in them but, by not re-reading them, I am saving myself from the embarrassment of finding out how painfully true this is (is this shameful?, oh, perhaps ... but I *cannot!*).

Sister Gillian Leslie, the librarian to the monastery, has been kind enough to agree to edit whatever letters have been sent to her and to provide an introduction.

INTRODUCTION BY
SISTER GILLIAN

This collection of notes and letters, brought to light for the first time here, reveals an aspect of Sister Wendy about which few who do not know the religious life from within could have much idea. The nun who faces the camera and talks so knowledgeably and wittily about works of art has become a familiar sight, and articles and interviews have detailed again and again the solitude and hours of prayer that support this spare and now visibly aged figure. But to read someone else's account, often polite but uncomprehending, is one thing; to overhear the voice of one who is speaking intimately out of the heart of the spiritual sources that sustain her is another. It is something like this to which these letters expose us and, in doing so, help us to understand what drives this life lived so uncompromisingly for God.

All but two of the letters quoted in this collection pre-date Sister Wendy's emergence as 'the Art nun' and fall within roughly the same time period: the sixteen or so years immediately following her transfer from the life of an active, teaching Order to that of a hermit, a woman consecrated by the Bishop of the diocese for solitary prayer on behalf of the Church. Because they frame her at such a vital and sensitive the full implications of the Fatherhood that Jesus has revealed, we should not tread timidly for fear of his disapproval but would step out boldly, uninfluenced by any other consideration than how to serve him more effectively and purely. The fact that we find it so hard to let go of patterns of life we find safe, because familiar, is a sad reminder that even the faith of 'religious' people does not necessarily go very deep. It is at the level of spiritual insights such as these that Sister Wendy's letters transcend their original, somewhat limited context and have something important, indeed vital, to say.

At the time these letters were written this need to encourage a robust, faith-filled spirituality was probably the one to which Sister Wendy returned most often. Nothing dismayed her so much as unreality in otherwise good people, an unreality that was still associated in many minds with religious piety. To a nun whom she knew well, she wrote:

> 'I fear people expect nuns to be 'different', special, rather remote spiritual beings, that's why I hesitated over any suggestion, however innocent, that we were actually living that 'perfect love' that we all *long* to live. Our goal and desires they can understand, as long as they understand that, just like them, we are striving – not reposing blissfully on the clouds of achievement!'

This assertion is as typical as it is deeply felt; art the means by which, as often as not, she found a way to express it. Art was by no means just an aesthetic experience for her but an opening into a universe of human experience and emotion, of self-knowledge and spiritual understanding. In addition it had given her a means of communication with which she felt comfortable. A number of the notes published here began as, or included 'picture commentaries': reflections on reproductions of works of art that had something apposite to say to the person for whom they were destined. While the occasion for which they were written was frequently very specific, the reflections themselves can speak to anyone, as has been shown by their evolution into her many published collections. Ann herself had already discerned their potential during the years covered by this correspondence and it is interesting to learn that she had been one of the first to encourage Sister Wendy to find an outlet for their publication.

If pictures fed Sister Wendy's contemplation, books were her relaxation. Here, too, Ann was the indispensable benefactor, sending regular packets of books to celebrate various feasts and anniversaries and receiving comments in return that indicate the depth at which Sister Wendy habitually read. An astonishingly wide and perceptive reader, she was a great contender for using literature to broaden and stretch the mind and, even within the relatively narrow compass of these letters, we are introduced to a reading list that covers the spectrum from detective stories and novels to the latest and most up to date art books. Indeed, the solitude to which she believed she was called did not prevent her from keeping abreast of what was going on at the time, whether through books or on the wider stage of current affairs. This, to her, was not a betrayal of her spiritual commitment but an essential component of it. That she should have come to understand the workings of the human heart so well, its spiritual hunger and emotional vulnerability as well as its evasions and self-deceptions, has a great deal to do with this incorporation into her regime of the great variety of ways in which writers of all kinds have described the world around them and the people within it.

Letters to Ann come to a natural end with the conclusion of Ann's term of office both as Religious Superior and as a college Principal. Aware of the void and danger of depression that can follow on the loss of a responsible position, Sister Wendy had encouraged her to follow through her intention to take a sabbatical in the United States and follow the course in spiritual direction to which she felt drawn. Ann seems to have entertained the idea of starting a retreat house when she returned to England but events forestalled her. At the end of her first year away the religious obedience to which she was bound called her back to her community and other forms of service. Throughout this eventful time in Ann's life Sister Wendy's letters show both sympathy and firmness, encouragement and complete openness to the manifestations of God's will. In fact one might say that, even as Ann was studying the technique of spiritual direction, she was herself being quietly directed through the medium of this correspondence.

The second group of letters in this collection has a completely different origin. It consists entirely in the exchanges of notes between Sister Wendy and some of the nuns of the Carmelite Monastery on whose property she now lives. Here there is neither particular sequence nor thread, each note consisting in a response to some question asked or reflection shared. As with the *Letters to Ann*, however, the same preoccupations, the same desire for the highest spiritual ideals shine through.

When Sister Wendy came to Quidenham in 1971 to take up her life of solitude it was clearly understood by the Carmelites that any contact between them would be minimal. The seclusion of the hermitage was strictly respected and, since no occasions arose for personal contact, no conversations were possible. Nevertheless, since the nuns were now responsible for Sister Wendy's well-being, a certain arrangement had to be put in place whereby her daily needs would be catered for. This led to one of the nuns being appointed to take care of her few daily needs, providing her with a lunch basket and looking in each day with mail, books and – with increasing regularity – notes. For Sister Wendy's physical separation from the community did not in any way imply lack of interest or concern. To the contrary, it soon became manifest that she had much to offer and the community much to gain from her presence. It was not long before she began to be invited to give spiritual conferences to the young Sisters of the novitiate and these, even though infrequent, generated questions and personal confidences to which Sister Wendy would unfailingly reply. As the volume of correspondence grew so did the collection of responses out of which the present selection has been drawn. These were written on odd slips of paper, the backs of envelopes – anything on which there was space to write. Many were accompanied by the kind of picture commentary that, as has been noted, was her preferred method of making a point.

The majority of notes in this collection have been grouped according to their recipients who, as it happens, represent the various age groups in the community: from the young Novice, just beginning her religious life, to the mature nun appointed as Novice Mistress and the elderly Sister whose task it was at that time to see to Sister Wendy's needs. Each of these was among the number of Sisters who turned instinctively to Sister Wendy at various times over the course of their religious life, whether to ask for an opinion, to seek out spiritual advice or simply to share a book or picture. The notes, for the most part, stand alone and have no connection to one another. What they do have in common, of course, is the voice of their author, always consistently calling to a more humble and realistic estimation both of oneself and of the demands supposedly being made on one, while emphasising, again and again, the complete confidence we can have in God's unfailing desire for our good. In their own way, and certainly unintentionally, they follow in the long tradition of questions and answers between the spiritual master and the disciple. At times they are charged with an emotion that springs from a deep-felt longing that God be better known and understood. If their publication can better serve that end, it will have fulfilled its purpose.

LIST OF ILLUSTRATIONS

1. Christ Discovered in the Temple (egg tempera on panel), Simone Martini (1284–1344) / © Walker Art Gallery, National Museums Liverpool / The Bridgeman Art Library

2. The Polish Rider, c. 1655 (oil on canvas), Rembrandt Harmensz (1606–69) / Copyright The Frick Collection.

3. The Lacemaker, 1669–70 (oil on canvas), Jan Vermeer (1632–75) / Louvre, Paris, France / The Bridgeman Art Library

4. The Sleeping Shepherd, 1834 (tempera with oil glaze on paper, laid on panel), Samuel Palmer (1805–81) / Private Collection / Photo © Agnew's, London, UK / The Bridgeman Art Library

5. The Egyptian Curtain, 1948 (oil on canvas) Henri Matisse (1869–1954) / Philips Collection, New York. © Succession H. Matisse / DACS 2012 / Photograph © Archives H. Matisse

6. Ad Parnassum, 1932 (oil and case in paint on canvas), Paul Klee (1879–1940) / Kunstmuseum, Bern, Switzerland / Alinari / The Bridgeman Art Library

LETTERS TO ANN

1970–1975

August, 1970

... What we cannot accept is that we are the beloved, or, to put it more concretely, speaking as Everyman, that *I* am the beloved. God longs for me, He presses on my heart with a tender, humble, hunger for me. He wants to possess me: when I let Him, it is prayer. Always His love drives Him to possess – one might call this the prayer of living? And when we have time, He enters into His own like a king – what one might call pure prayer. The pain of prayer is frustrating His love, and the joy is assuaging it, however feebly. To be so loved and so wanted is so terrifying and so awful that we can see why we shrink from believing it.

Another thing we are chary of believing is that prayer is gift. We don't choose our own prayer (or it might be different!). God is the prayer, the Pray-er. All He wants is that we accept, suffer, be involved, be left defenceless. I think one might easily die of it, yet what could be simpler?

No other letters survive from this early period. On June 1st 1971, after briefly testing her vocation as a Carmelite nun and discovering that this was not God's will for her, Sister Wendy took up residence in a hermitage situated in the grounds of a Carmelite Monastery.

20 May 1974

You have come often into my thoughts, (prayers),
so in one way your letter was a joy, but in another it
has tended to confirm the fear that I was too rough
with you! There was so little time,[1] and I feel that
all the shades and grades of meaning had to be left
to take care of themselves – never a safe thing to
do with your kind of person, who is only too ready
to believe all is as bad as her secret fears suggest! I
often feel that God could hardly have picked a worse
spokeswoman for Himself than me. It seems to me
sometimes that He is showing me His own view of
a soul, and He makes it quite clear whether she is
ready to hear or whether her heart is just unable, yet,
to let Him in thus far – but as to how the message
is to be delivered, that He seems to leave to me. All
I can do is to fix my whole attention on Him, take
what words come to me. But coarse, crude woman
that I am, I fear the words are so often too violent,
and I distort what He wanted said. So in your case.
I do not think you are a failure, and certainly didn't
mean to make that the dominant impression left on
you – and all the same, I do feel that the grain of
wheat never dies until, or unless, it accepts to fail.
More than just accepts, goes down contentedly into
those bitter waters, putting all its hope, now, in Jesus.
I think that even He *had* to fail, as it were – 'was
it not fitting that Christ should die …',[2] and that
luminous text, 'He learnt obedience through what
he suffered'[3]. What I am trying to say is that all is

very well with you – God is detaching you, in the only way He could ever do it, from your deadly grip on your own 'justice'. I know that's an unfair way of putting it, but your trembling insecurities are kept in balance by a sort of hidden self-reliance that you intellectually repudiate, and would indeed practically repudiate, to the best of your power. But these deep, deep clingings are beyond our own power – they can only be broken by the mystical action of the Spirit, as St John of the Cross never tires of insisting. Dark Nights and Mystical Deaths sound so beautiful when we read about them, or have the privilege, as I have, of seeing them in another – but they are the reverse of beautiful to experience. As long as you have a sense of Him to sustain you – as long as you feel that your prayer is achieving something in you – or even that you are a happy and fruitful woman – let alone the question of external recognition and success, which means much to you precisely in its implicit 'approval' of your spiritual course – well, as long as there are even some of these supports, you can never be thrown wholly on God, however earnestly and sincerely you desire it. All you can do now is hold your poor barren self constantly before Him, thanking Him for loving you, and believing that all you suffer *is* love.

Two more concrete suggestions: part of your state is sheer fatigue. Please force yourself to relax, take time off to read, etc. And admit the element of compulsive perfectionism in the ideal of the ever-open-door, and have times when it is firmly shut! The other comes from seeing how inadequate was our hour together, and moreover, you missed Janet, so like you in many ways, a most nervous, sensitive creature, riddled with insecurities, (though now she has come to terms with them and entered upon a lovely freedom) and always more sought after than seeking where others are concerned. (I asked her permission before saying all this!!). Now I've also asked her if you couldn't come again, by yourself, for, say, a week, and really relax here, away from it all, and talk things out at leisure. Would you like to? Or find it possible? ...

I laughed, dear Ann, at your claim to 'love' me – would that you did, though it would be rather wasted on me! A good overwhelming love for someone would be ideal for your nervous tone! Which doesn't need psychiatric assistance, in my opinion ...

I don't know if this is any help, or only makes things worse. I feel *very strongly* that you are drawing very near to God, that He is taking you deep into His mystery – but you must endure and *want* to endure the pain of it.

1   Sister Wendy had received a visit from Ann.
2   Cf. Lk. 26.24.
3   Heb. 5.8.

24 September 1974

I know you won't misunderstand a silent kiss of welcome![1] ... I hope very much you'll find her helpful.[2] She's close to God, and in some respects like you – fine-grade porcelain, the pair of you!! I know your sole purpose in coming is to become more united to God, and it seems to me impossible that He won't fulfil that desire. But it means, you know: 'knowing nothing but Jesus Christ, and Him crucified'.[3] You remember the bitter realism of Isaiah: 'Without beauty, without majesty: we saw Him, and we turned our eyes away'.[4]

Poor Ann, what a welcome! But it's what I pray for you, with all my heart's affection. I hope you'll rest while here, but I promise not to do any eyebrow lifting if you really want to come to Lauds etc.![5]

1   She means that, due to her seclusion, this note must substitute for a greeting in person.
2   Sister Janet, at that time prioress of the monastery.
3   1 Cor. 2.2.
4   Is. 53.2.
5   Morning prayer (Lauds) for the Carmelite community was at 5.50 a.m.

28 September 1974

... If you think about it, my dear, you have listened to God's Word with all that is in you, as total a listening as you could, and the Word called for a response from all that is in you, a response so total that you really haven't room for any more, have you now?

This is mostly just to say a very loving thank you, above all and primarily, for the joy you gave me in your openness to Jesus-as-He-is, the poor Jesus who takes us into His poverty, which alone can have the capacity to receive the Father's love from the Spirit. And then, on another plane, for the beautiful books which will show something of His Beauty to all who look on them. I feel so sure that art keeps us alive to God in a way that no other human activity can measure up to. And music especially, perhaps. I know the community [here] do have a recorder and tapes, but for me the apparatus-y angle, and also silence, and time-spans, make art the one form of this kind of prayer I can allow myself . . .

Certainly don't feel anxious about yourself, your past or your present. The only real criterion of the past is: where has it brought us? And yours has brought you to His Heart. And all the present demands, (all!!) is to keep lovingly, longingly, close to that Heart until Its Love beats within your own.

Goodbye for a little stretch of time that only unites us in surrender to Our Blessed Lord.

20 December 1974

I thought I would have to sacrifice a direct 'thank you', but at the end of prayer this morning, it struck me (very happily) that I can't do it [*through anyone else*] without tactlessness! I won't elaborate on how I appreciated every detail, but truly, both parcels were a joy to open … As for the books, they made me sigh with happiness! Think of me, after Lauds each morning, just looking at one picture, until the impact of the glory it gives to God forces me to shut my eyes. And our dear Angelico still to come![1] I know well these books are not 'mine' (and I wouldn't want them to be) and part of the delight is handing them over. On great festivals I ask for a loan – and, in a way, this seems to me the condition of loving the world's beauty: the whole sweetness is ours as long as we don't possess it. Then, through it, God can possess us, as was always His intent.

Your card is before me – and will be there for a long time, (non-sentimental reasons, need I say?)[2] and it strikes me that one could think of the upper panel as my life – the Virgin alone with the angel, and lost, unaware even of him, folded hands, open book forgotten, cloak slipping from her shoulders – and the panel beneath – might it not be yours? The Virgin surrounded – kings and servants and camels, not an angel in sight, (though she has St Joseph and a star!). Her cloak is firmly tied, her hands are fully occupied, but oh, Ann, with what? How gently, lovingly, self-forgettingly, she holds out to the crowd the little Jesus. One, Mary holds Him to her heart; the other cannot even see His beloved face, turning

Him as she does, to those who come near her. Yet it's the same Mary, and the same love. Never think He has done for me what He has not cared to do for you. If there were any way in the world to possess your heart more powerfully, He would take it – and it is so clear to me that, for you, this painful, unsuccessful life, this constant striving to love with His love, and seeing more failure for your efforts, is infinitely precious to Him. I understand well how you feel with regard to your community – and I do pray, and for all the province, of which it is a microcosm, – but since the only happiness is to be at His disposal, I can't wish for your release, or change, or anything but a deepening love. Your letters, though they go unanswered, have not needed any response from me. With God to teach you love – *and He is doing*, I see the growth – you don't require any tootlings from my little flute!

1   Fra Angelico (c. 1400–55), a Dominican friar and one of the earliest artists of the Italian Renaissance. She is alluding to the gift of a book about him that had not yet arrived.
2   That is, Sister Wendy will keep the picture in front of her as a focus for her prayer and not simply because Ann has given it to her. The picture itself, no longer preserved, would probably have been a Nativity scene by one of the great Masters, printed on a Christmas card.

20 January 1975

… What I feel is holding her back is fear[1]: partly fear of what people will think, but mostly the fear that comes from an achievement-relationship with God. To be a nun – to belong to His élite – these are the signs of His favour ...[2] So she simply can't afford to leave as long as she feels it is a step down, and hence, spiritually, a step away. What she has to be shown very forcefully is that she is in fact being asked to step *up*, to follow God's call to a higher plane, where alone true maturity and happiness await her. Until she sees it as a finer thing, she will fall ever backwards, as she is doing, to maintain her footing and prove she is not a 'failure'. And nobody will be able to convince her that the failure would be to ignore the signs of God's will that she finds within her own heart, unless she accepts that person as a spiritual woman – and I feel she does accept you as one ... But also she will have to feel certain that you – or whoever it is – regard *her* with respect as also a 'spiritual woman'. Any trace of lowly assessment, and she will instantly feel she is being fobbed off onto a second-class vocation because not thought up to standard. I must add, too, that I think possibly some exceptional step should be taken ... something to emphasize both the urgency and the value you place on her. If it just emerges, as it were, she may well feel that it reflects lack of interest or failure to value her. Oh dear! – you won't be too pleased with all this, I know, nor would any humble soul be! Nothing more painful than to step into the sanctuary of another soul, specially uninvited. If you *are* uninvited – I know you'll be truthful here – then, of course, the Spirit is asking something else of you. But I only write *in case* you feel God is inviting you … Whatever you do, I know will be done looking at Him, so please don't take this as a push!

I treasure the Angelico card, and truly, want no more! I know it is to the Lord you are giving, through me, but the most infinitely precious of all your generous gifts, is what you show me of a soul being ever more steadily drawn to His Love. That was a lovely letter. I was going to say: open your heart ever more totally to the Suffering Servant, and I do still say that, but in the cramped confines of a letter, it could sound over-precise. Because what He wants is for you to see 'nothing but only Jesus' – whether He comes in glory or in humiliation should hardly impinge – and yet I deliberately say 'Jesus' rather than 'God', *because* He is the Man of sorrows, crucified in weakness – the Jesus we see in Hebrews, 'crying aloud'[3], and in John, 'greatly troubled'[4]. 'God' can sound as if holiness took us into glory, whereas it takes us, with Jesus, into the garden and on the Cross, *conscious only* of the Father. Hope you can make sense of my poor stammerings.

1   The whole of this paragraph concerns the future of a nun who, in Sister Wendy's estimation, did not have a real vocation to religious life and needed to be kindly and lovingly helped to see this for herself. As Superior in the same convent, it would fall to Ann's lot to make the attempt.
2   This statement is not meant to express what Sister

Wendy believes. She is trying to convey what is going on in the mind of the person concerned.
3   'In the days when he was in the flesh, he offered prayers and supplications with loud cries and tears …' (Heb. 5.7).
4   Cf. Jn 11.33.

Easter 1975
A brief, (I'm sorry if also disappointing) rejoinder to your recent letters, and your generosity.

About the future: you should know that God shows me nothing specific, only that the future is pure Love, is Himself. So, *pace* your private pythoness, I'm not 'preparing' you in the usual sense. But what comes home to me very strongly is that now *is* the future; no link in the chain is subordinated to another. All God wants is to give Himself now, and it is this moment that makes the total gift still to come possible, or not. I think we can lose momentum by unconsciously regarding His great designs of Love as being somehow 'in preparation', and they are not: in Jesus they have come. And they have come, most surely, for you. When I look at you in him, I get a great sense of God beating down on you. He has given you a painful vocation, both in its setting, geographical and temporal, (oh, how deeply your Congregation went with me into the death-and-resurrection of this week!) and also in the demands He makes on you in Himself. But believe me, my dear Ann, there is no other way of setting you free from your selfhood. You have a deep grasp of this selfhood – the very characteristic that makes it possible for God to enter into full triumphant possession – but as yet, no longings or strivings of your own can prise loose that grasp and let God take! But *it is being done* – God is doing it exactly in the sort of – I won't say 'life' – but in the day He gives you.

I liked what you said about daily bread. Only for you it may taste like ash-cake, moistened with gall.[1] Oh, but what it is achieving in you! – I can see such growth in liberty and sweetness! Turn your mind, often and eagerly, to the way He gives Himself to everybody. All are infinitely dear to Him, really dear, worth dying for. That's still your most rigid area. I don't know whether I do need people, strictly; but He has shown me, more and more that, in Him, I need them to my depths. We need them because of His need. The heart of Jesus broke because He could not bring all His brethren into His Father's house; He was not Himself, not fully and wholly Jesus, until He had made that homecoming possible. Open your heart, dear Ann, to receive from the Spirit this glad, agonizing, self-forgetful Love of Jesus. Then one day you will turn round and find your own imprisoned self has vanished and there is only God's love keeping you alive. He gives it when we want it enough, and all it means. You are so near, I pray constantly and very happily.

You know what blessed Angelico[2] means to me; nothing could give more tranquil happiness. Yes, the eyes and the movements that express an inward grace. What is silently in my heart this holy day[3] seems externalized there before me. A deep, loving 'thank you' – and how beautifully you wrapped up the other parcel. I intended to give most of it away, but the Lord told me not to be ungracious! The Chartreuse doesn't have to be recommended by its tonic properties either! ...

I look forward to the promised Paschaltide letter.

1   Cf. Pss. 102.10; 69.21.
2   Fra Angelico, *see n.1, 20 December 1974.*
3   Easter day.

18 June 1975

I was so glad to hear from you, and nothing in your letter was unexpected: you have been much on my heart these last weeks. I knew you were intensely wretched, but felt I should wait until you yourself had found the ability to set it down. Dearest Ann, that loveless slum you see in yourself is quite truly you – I won't pretend otherwise, but it is you seen *in the light of God.* The 'you' that He passionately loves, that He chooses to be most intimately possessed in a love-union – that you is the poor thing you experience as your true self. So, despair is the last thing to feel, rather a blazing surge of hope and gratitude that His love doesn't depend *at all* on our beauty and goodness. But there is even more joy to it than this, because we just can't see our poverty unless *He shows it*. (Forgive all these Victorian emphases!)

So to see it is clear proof that He is present, lovingly and tenderly revealing Himself to you. It's the contrast you are experiencing – can you understand? How do you know you are weak and unloving? Only because the strength and love of Jesus so press upon you that, like the sun shining from behind, you see the shadow. This is the surest way to *Him*. These are the only two essentials the soul can see – in this life we can't encompass both. Either we see all in the light of Him, and primarily self, or we see only Him and all else is dark. Same grace – what Ruth Burrows calls 'light-on' and 'light-off'[1]. But it is up to you to accept His grace; only you can thank Him for it, and let it draw you, as it is meant, to long constantly and trustfully for His purifying love. Nothing so makes us live the parable (do you remember it?)[2] than what He is now showing you. It means we lose ourselves in Him – or die – nothing else really has been left.

I do so hope you can believe me. Please write and tell me if anything is obscure – I know how very much He wants you to accept this, but I can't find the luminous words that reveal Him …

Much love, and praising God for your temperament!

1   See ch. 4, *Guidelines for Mystical Prayer*, 2nd edn, Burns & Oates [Continuum], 2007).
2   Ibid.

26 June 1975

I am writing again, because I'm not quite sure if my last letter was any good to you. My dear, I *do* believe all you say about your state, and I both compassionate and congratulate you – in the Latin sense, suffer with you and rejoice with you. Because in your heart, where you can't see Him, Jesus rejoices: He is more you than you are yourself. But the experience of this is exactly back-to-front: precisely because He is there, so close, we see ourselves in all the agonizing truth. How the human heart longs to see beauty and grace in itself – to be 'as god' in some way – believing this is so as to become more receptive of Him, to be our own support – and in His passionate love for you, He *will* not let you have any God but Himself. Can you see that, if you could *feel* this, could joyously write off your sense of sinfulness as proof of His nearness, then it would fail of its kenotic power? You can't feel it, but you can live by it, which is all He wants. You can tell Him that if He is pleased, you are pleased – and that you trust in His love so completely that you *know* He would always let you know if there were something practical He wanted you to do. When He wanted you to appreciate your lack of true love for and interest in His children, He asked me to speak for Him and this is something

His own fidelity will always see to. You were going to come in June – He has made it necessary to wait. And when, at His time, you come, be assured I'll tell you if He has any specifics to be done or endured. But at present He says: Be comforted, be comforted, my darling child.

That sense of being alien is not really caused by the Order, – it is a sign of 'I live, now not I'[1], though we think that a change of context would dispel it. Janet feels the same about Carmel, a not-belonging-ness, an out-of-tunedness, with nobody sharing her deepest ideals. You would find the same. Life must press like this – it did on Jesus, ('how long a time must I suffer you, how long a time must I be with you?').[2] And don't think either, that you hesitate or grudge Him. You do neither, but you are truly learning for the first time at depth, what love means and how helpless we are, of ourselves, to respond. When you know this to your inmost core, Jesus 'takes over'. So I do indeed rejoice in your temperament and in everything else that exposes you to Him!

P.S. There is a true sense in which I don't suffer and pay no cost because it all comes from God.

1   Gal. 2.20.
2   Cf. Mt. 17.17.

20 July 1975

How strange that you too should have been drawn to the image of the Entry into Jerusalem! It has been in my mind these past days in these two aspects: that for most, their enthusiastic acclamation of Jesus as Messiah disguises from them their repudiation of what that messiahship means. As soon as it involves, not just death but degradation, to be driven 'outside the camp bearing His reproach',[1] they reject Him. They cannot believe that holiness is without beauty and majesty. And Jesus knows they can't. This aspect is so poignantly portrayed in your picture – the grave tranquillity of the still centre where Jesus sits, amid the threatening swirl of friends as well as foes. He understands our heart and how little able it is to realize truth and adhere to it – and it is this clear vision that gives His love its aching utterness. Whoever has been as lonely as Jesus, perhaps lonely in proportion to His total love? We can so easily think that love brings us into a warmth, an emotional companionship with our sisters – and I think this is not so. It is the sacrificial reality of love that they are looking for.

No one ever came to our dear Lord without knowing that here was Someone to whom he or she mattered, who would gladly die on their behalf – and I think that is what we must ask Him to achieve in us. And the cost of coming so close to Him may well be an increasing sense of isolation from the stream of life around us.

Thank you so much for the letter and prayers and just-right presents – you never 'overstep' (hallmark of the genuine porcelain!). The raw passion of Rouault's protest will be valued in the community.[2] I used to love him, but now I find his intensities, like those of Goya or El Greco or van Gogh, lead me to where I already am. So I succumb beneath a double weight. What I want now are proclaimers of the Risen Lord: Raphael, Vermeer, Botticelli, Rembrandt. I am rested and strengthened by the mysterious beauty of Leonardo or van Eyck, or the tranquil power of prayer in Fra Angelico, bless him, or Giotto. Landscapes, too, like Canaletto's or the marvellous five months of Breughel.[3] (One is in this book, but too small.) Forgive me if this seems off the point, but it isn't really. In a cumbersome fashion, because I am speaking in the context of your remark on being a woman rather than a child. Art is a form of prayer I value because it deepens in me my womanhood. It makes me more 'there' for His possessing – and, within the ascetic stringency of my vocation – and yours – this is something we need. But the more 'woman' we become, the more the possibility of becoming 'child'. We are not his 'mate': woman to His man. His love must always be protective – and He cannot 'protect', use love's diminutives to us, if we are still undeveloped. He has to 'leave us alone' to let us grow. 'Child' is a term of weakness when it means immaturity. He can only use it in tenderness when it is the love-title of an achieved humanity. 'Unless you become ...'[4]: something we have to strive for. Not so??? ...

I feel very happy about you, confident that God is drawing you to Himself by all within *and* without ...

1   Heb. 13.13.
2   Georges Rouault (1871–1958), French painter. He frequently took as his subjects the despised and rejected of society, such as prisoners and prostitutes.
3   Pieter Brueghel the Elder (c. 1525–69) painted a series of five works depicting the seasons.
4   'Unless you become like little children, you shall not enter the kingdom of heaven' (Mt. 18.3).

October 1975 (undated fragment)

I suppose what's really behind this letter is this: that I don't see any chance of spreading the message casually or in conversation. It's too deep. To understand it requires time and attention: a full-sized approach making evident the total demand ... in other words, it will have to be preached – proclaimed – or people will inevitably take it as just another 'adaptation'. You – and your group – will have to put your neck on the block quite deliberately and unmistakably – it won't just 'come'.

'This is a hard saying and who can hear it?'[1] Those who truly want Him can – and want Him with all the consequences that must follow. O dear Ann, do you know what I mean? Jesus will do it, longs to do it, so you've nothing to fear. Is it Oct. 3rd you leave and 17th return? Laden with sheaves, I know, and the best sheaves.[2]

1   Jn 6.60.
2   Cf. Ps. 126.6.

October 1975[1]

Oh, thank you for your three feast day gifts!

The child-image made me happy, because I feel very profoundly that a birth is taking place. Yet, mysteriously, you are also the woman who is giving birth – or, equally, it is true that Jesus is the Child, and it is He who gives birth, too.

But, dear Ann, you are not greedy. If you think about it, every initiative has come from me, which means from the Lord, as I hadn't envisaged the way He wanted to do it, as you know.

Think how intensely, how specially God loves you, that he has sent me to tear away all that impedes His taking total possession of you. For how many has He done that? (and how many will let Him, as you do?).

My poor darling, I wish I could comfort you and take away the pain: so how much must the tender Heart of God feel? But He sends it all to do His work. I only wish I had made it plainer to you what sacrifices friendship with me entails.[2]

That loving, laughing little Bambino. That's how He lies in a surrendered heart: – a heart that surrenders even the assurance of being surrendered …

1 Sister Ann was staying in the monastery guest quarters making a retreat. A series of notes was exchanged between the two during her stay. The exact order in which they were sent is not known.
2 It seems that Ann was disappointed at not being able to speak to her as often as she wished.

October 1975 (the same occasion)

I can't find the right words, but what I want to say is: God is always coming to us, as totally as we can receive Him, but *from every side*. He comes in 'life', just as it is. The as-it-isness is precisely how He comes. If we look for Him in certain patterns or forms, we only receive a fraction. Now for you, the natural tendency is to romanticize the way of His coming. Your self wants that, at least: at least *that* glory, the glory of holiness. And He says: No, – I can't give myself, not fully, in *any* way that gives self a foothold. Nothing romantic or beautiful or in any way dramatic; nothing to get hold of, in one sense, because it must be He that does the getting hold. A terrible death in every way, destroying all we innocently set our spiritual hearts on: all but Him. So utter joy, in a sense that 'romance' can never envisage. There are depths of self-desire – innocently – that He must empty so as to fill them; He's doing it and you must set your thinking being to co-operate …

O dear, is this any use? It's all so much bigger than my poor mind can verbalize.

October 1975 (the same occasion)

Oh my dear, *please* don't be grieved about 'not looking attentively enough or looking in the right direction'. Our Blessed Lord doesn't grieve over you – quite truthfully, you are one of the tiny handful of people to whom I can speak without pain. What I am speaking of – so poorly – is the profoundest of human inadequacies, something that is there by necessity in our fallen and non-divine nature – but something that He chooses should be taken away from us, destroyed in us so as to set us wholly free for love. But, and this is the whole crux: He can't take it away until we are sufficiently 'there' to be able to say His Yes. Our own yes can only be partial, with all sorts of secret and unconscious reservations. Only Jesus and His sweet Mother could hear and affirm the Spirit's 'Yes' within them. Now that is what I strive to bring you to. There's no short cut, no gimmick, no price that *we* can take in our hand and assess and consent to. But what we can do is see where we positively – not fail, – but miss the mark. We can align our hearts on His and pray pray pray to be kept in His ambience.

The 'anxious duchess' was an affectionate tease – you looked so dainty and earnest. *Not* serious!! No, the sisters haven't spoken about you, nor have I experienced it, in one sense. I just sense in the Lord that there is a chill, an aloofness, an unwillingness to go down into the marketplace – that impedes ... He loved enough to live in the streets ...

17 October 1975

I'm writing this before morning prayer, hoping it will arrive shortly after you do.[1]

When I spoke of this yesterday your eyes filled and I felt I must keep it 'general', but there was much in my heart about the beauty Our Lord finds in you. If I have only dwelt on the shadows, the unpossessed places, it was solely so that the beauty – His beauty – might shine all the more for Him. Many, many years of genuine labour to be unselfish and prayerful have set your heart wonderfully to receive Him. The very fact that you can *listen* to me – so humbly, so truly – something I only find at such hungry depths in Janet. This alone should show you what a beauty God has formed in you. Now I want you specifically to offer it to Him, His own doing, His own reflection: spread it out before Him and praise Him. What is still to be done – profound though it is – is *His* to do, it's beyond you, as you know. And this grateful, humble leaving yourself peacefully open to His loving eyes, will do more than any anxious depression or soul searchings and flagellations!

Have I ever said out, that I too love you, dear Ann? You are a joy to Him, and so, in Him, to me.

I feel very happy at that inspiration about honouring our dear Lady by contemplating her pictured mysteries. Tell me which you choose. About Confession. I think I'm odd. Janet cannot enter into my approach – but then, I can't understand her shrinking, nor how Fr Henderson could see 'discussion' etc. as 'control'. There's a lot I'd like to say on this; maybe next time??

My deep and loving gratitude for all you gave me, with such tender thought, and all you will be to Jesus, and are and have been.

1   Sister Ann had finished her retreat and was now on her way back to her community.

Undated

I am happy your talks are calling forth evidence of the longing for Jesus that is the sole foundation of religious life. Only He can fulfil the virgin and be riches to the poor – and freedom to the obedient.[1] I feel He has given you words of life to speak: a humbling vocation. All in your life has led up to this, and all in your present life is His chosen context, the setting in which He can more clearly reveal Himself through you. So 'reluctance' to pray is a suffering of apostolic import. I've often felt that my poor words are blocked by people's sensing that all I want is to be still with Him. Far more effective when we speak from human struggle …

1   A reference to the three vows of religious life: chastity, poverty and obedience.

9 November 1975

I'm sorry – only a business letter again – but maybe this is more welcome? It means you seem to me to be growing steadily and sweetly, towards that 'Yes' Jesus so longs to say in you, and that the kickings and screamings of anguished nature are merely noises off! …

Strange how few understand the value of art and literature in a life of prayer. And some who think they do, are only playing with beauty. To use it, as God intends, is a costly business …

… Do you think you 'need' Book 2 before you can accept Book 1 because it guarantees that the shabbiness is really glorious after all? Does it cushion for you the full impact of *nothing* but God, not in concept, where it sounds so beautiful, but in the concrete, where it comes as self-dissatisfaction and immersion in some kind or other of ordinariness? I think that desire to have Him on your own terms goes very deep in you – and it's in the accepting this (as you so humbly do, dear Ann) that it gets rooted out. Since this is almost certainly my last letter before Christmas, I send you a card I've been saving ...[1] both the expression and position may have something to say to you. How far she is from the contemplative stillness, the angelic tranquillity, so often depicted! Isn't she a marketplace Madonna, all alive and sentient? A woman to her depths? And see how she delights in *Him*, quite unconscious of the way He ignores her ... And, ah, how she lets herself be *seen*, lets all who want to look at her, as Jesus is to do all His life.[1]

1   A picture of the Virgin Mary. The picture itself has not survived.

[?] November 1975

My poor dear! If I tell you I'm not worried, please don't think it means any callous underestimating of your pain as 'merely bodily'.[1] Oh no, I ache for you, and with you, but the whole thing comes to me so clearly as a way God is taking hold of you. Just in its dread self, pain always seems to act out, to be a sort of living parable within us, of what it means to be only human. Even with painkillers, we are still 'not in control', cannot ride as master over the terrible waves that can swamp our consciousness and leave room for nothing but endurance. (But I hope you're not too often in that extremity). It always seems to me that my body is letting me feel, then, God's Presence as power. And equally, taking me into the human helplessness of Jesus. In surrendering to

Him in it, in trusting His utter tenderness when He presses so un-tenderly, we come marvellously close to Him, however darkly. It's only those who can't accept this secret grace that cause me anxiety, since pain will all too easily turn them in on self instead of carrying them into Jesus …

1   Ann was faced with the possibility of an operation.

12 December 1975

I am indeed praying, and I know within me how harassed and pressured you are at present, and with the niggle of pain, and sometimes worse than niggle, rubbing away at your energies. And the dread of the gynal couch.[1] But I can't feel anxious. It seems so clear to me that this is pure Love giving Himself in a way you *must* learn to accept Him in. Either you say: 'Come my Love, anyway. You choose'. Or you make it impossible for Him to come at all, except in the few hours marked 'spiritual'. Love can't take hold under these restrictions – and how well I know that He is only doing what your deepest heart wants. You have *never* chosen to restrict Him, willingly. So now He takes you at your unspoken, understood, but intended word. Didn't your insight into Duccio's *Annunciation*[2] tell you that death equals love?

1   Apparently a rather fanciful neologism. Ann was due to have a hysterectomy.
2   Duccio di Buoninsegna (1255–1319), a Siennese artist in the Gothic style.

26 December 1975

A very brief note to say you will be deep in my prayer during your ordeal. A call to you to surrender to His call, though it comes through human and physical channels. So hurrah for anything that makes Him more wholly in possession. Your [*Christmas*] gifts were such a joy. Duccio[1] kept me prayerful company all through yesterday, and now I'm looking at the massive dignity so innate to Massaccio.[2] Will talk at length when you come – do bring your own Duccio for comparison.

1   Duccio, see n. 2 above
2   Massaccio (1401–28), the first great painter of the Italian Renaissance.

30 December 1975

Your letter has just come. O Ann, Ann, now I am crying too, great wet tears to splash my typewriter.[1] My dear, I wanted so to write for Christmas, but what kind of solitude is it if I write to those I love at my own choosing? You may say that you needed that letter. No, Ann dear – He gave you what you needed, a deep entering into the lonely poverty of His own Christmas ... as you know. That suffering, darkened day was the night when angels sang and shepherds came running, but the poor Little One lay in the cold amid the straw. But I did think of you so lovingly, (did Janet pass on the message of what joy and gratitude your gifts brought? Who has ever been so tenderly kind to me?) Yet all I can give you in return is Jesus. I myself am nothing – and if I am to live in that nothingness and offer Him to you, then I can't take what I want. I must keep wholly attentive to Him and what *He* wants. A letter just of 'mine' would bring you little joy – so in a sense, it's for your sake, too, that I don't write except when urged. I have sent a wee note by N to tell you I'll be praying very profoundly on the 5th.[2] I know how you will shrink from the examination – but, O my dear, what a chance to say 'Yes', to let the Spirit say the 'Yes' of Jesus in you, which was always uttered in just that kind of unspiritual circumstance. Jesus lived by choice, or by the Father's choice, (same thing) in the marketplace. I too love de Caussade[3]; perhaps that's where I got my doctrine, though I *think* I learned it direct …

1   Ann had expressed pain that Sister Wendy had not written to her.
2   The date set for Ann's medical examination.
3   Jean-Pierre de Caussade (1675–1751), a French Jesuit priest. He was spiritual director to a community of Visitation nuns at Nancy and author of several works on the theme of self-abandonment to divine providence.

1976

28 January 1976

You have been so much in my prayers, and perhaps as I write you are undergoing your ordeal – yet despite very real compassion, I can't but feel happy about you. In all that matters, it is so unmistakably well with you. I see so clearly, as you do, that all this hospital-business, all the pain and suspicion, too, is doing something within you. Maybe it is leading you deeper into 'the weakness of Jesus'.[1] I am quite certain that is meant to be your home – and it is only to that home that your sisters will willingly come, because only there can they too feel at home. You strike a deep chord in me with your de Caussade quote.[2] I've been thinking on those very lines these last days, only from the other end, so to say. I had been thinking of 'the Living God' – so alive, so living that to be near Him is to burst into life oneself. And that this may be why some find prayer difficult. The dead parts in people are what they want dead – and He stirs them willy-nilly into life, a blaze of vitality that makes the old comfy, manageable life impossible. If we truly pray we will live, with all that means of responsibility, pain, freedom. Yet the pressure of total life overwhelms us. No one has ever come close to It and remained intact except Jesus, the Son. He can face what it means to 'enter into Life', and in Him we can live, too, dry bones though we be. Don't you think the quality of living-ness is the essential Christ-sign? And, like the stigmata, it is both a glory and an agony for us since we have life by 'losing it',[3] i.e. by entering into the weakness of Jesus, 'the Lamb, standing as it were slain'.[4]

As to the Madonna: here is prayer simultaneous with alert and luminous activity. She is a symbolic representation of the state when all-is-prayer. But to get there, we must have spaces of what you call stillness but that we could also call 'direct' or 'pure' prayer – being there for God to do what He likes with, directly. In prayer we open ourselves, like a piano taking off its lid, for Him to play. He can play what He likes – and let Him alone hear it: ours is but to be open, all His. Total generosity in letting Him have us so, makes Him at last so wholly the meaning of our life that, in everything, we can be there for Him. Don't know if I've put this sensibly?

I hope Rosemary rests with you. She is 'sowing in tears'[5] – and probably the real grief is to feel that there is no sowing. But sometimes the tears are the seed.

1   Cf. 2Cor. 12.10 and 13.4.
2   Jean-Pierre de Caussade, *see n. 3, 30 December 1975.*
3   The whole of this paragraph is a web of Biblical allusions: cf. Mk 9.42–48; Mt. 10.39, et al.
4   Rev. 5.6.
5   Ps. 126[125].6.

17 February 1976

The flowers are from my garden, (my wilderness),[1] a reminder of the unshadowed joy God must take in a creation that makes no claims, just 'is', and seeks no defences. Your letter gave me unshadowed joy too; you have changed so deeply. I don't mean overnight, but the change that God is working in you grows steadily more apparent. But I can see that the hospital unselfing has had its effect, and so much, also, of your own repeated endeavours to let Him take you into His weakness. You've been very much in my prayers of late, partly because I was anxious about your poor body (hope the robust tone of that letter wasn't unfeeling??) but mostly because I could feel the preciousness of your present opportunities. Abdication at some levels, balanced and made possible by a reckless disregard for safety at others. He directs your mysterious way to its unimaginable end – which is to be possessed by Jesus ...

Art is a great gift, isn't it? It says to us: if this is true, what does it ask of me? Or better, what is God here pressing upon me, since He never asks from us, only to give to us?[2] More and more it comes down to truly wanting: we get *exactly* as much as we desire – no subterfuge in prayer. I am always glad to hear of Claire. All this pain is her way to understanding. Great trust is being demanded – i.e. given, if she will take it.

1   Wild flowers from the thicket around her hermitage. Sister Wendy was not given to gardening per se.
2   That is, God does not ask us to give to Him but asks whether we will allow Him to give to us.

25 February 1976

Business letter – but first let me tell you what a joy the birthday book is, a joy almost painful, (but that's the way of it, isn't it? The more He is there, undisguised, the more His presence presses. You are right, that is the verb I instinctively grope for).

... My dear, tension is not an academic word for you, is it? But, O Ann, the empty weariness that underlies your letter: this is Jesus. We could think that it would be well with us if the pettiness of life were absent, its complexity, its undiagnosed, let alone unhealed, ills. Yet it is in abandonment, there, precisely there, that we become His possession. 'Now is my soul troubled (= tense, distressed, weary) and what shall I say?'[1] This is Jesus tasting to the full our human ignorance, not even knowing 'what to say' to His Father! Dear Ann, you are being taken deeper into His stark 'Yes' every perplexed day.

1   Jn 12.27.

Holy Week 1976

My poor Ann – and *blessed* in sharing the poverty of Jesus. I send this for you to pray over.[1] My little note will have told you that I knew you were suffering, and offered it to the Father in the pain of His Son. Today it struck me this might be a help for you here, especially in the second half of Holy Saturday. It's my 'translation', but only in that this is what the Church *wants* to say in that stilted Latin. I have been thinking much this Lent of Our Lord's words to Julian of Norwich: 'It is a joy, a bliss, an endless liking to me that ever suffered I passion for thee'.[2] The immense, unfelt joy of Jesus to know that what came to Him as agony was bringing all His fellows into the Father's arms. And that is what we must live to validate that joy of His: we must not make His passion appear wasted. The joy of Jesus in having 'done' it, ('consummatum est')[3] demands that we *let* Him do it, and take his joy into our own actual living. So all the heartache, dearest Ann, the failure and weariness, all are the condition of His joy, in us as in Him on the Cross.

Blessed entry with Him into the Passion and its Easter flowering.

1   Sister Wendy had composed the following verses, still in use today by the Carmelite community at Quidenham. They are a free translation of the hymns used in the Divine Office for Holy Saturday:

At Matins

You left the joy of heaven, Lord
Your lost creation to restore,
And gave yourself upon the cross
That mortal man might die no more.

Achieve in us, O Christ, today
The triumph of your victory,
So all the world may come and pluck
The blossom of your sacred tree.

God's holy Lamb, to make us pure
You gladly paid the bloody price;
You took your strong and gentle life
And laid it down in sacrifice.

And now no more our own, but yours,
Within your death we too have died,
And rise to sing the Father's praise,
Within your glory glorified.

O keep us ever one with you,
Our King and kingdom, perfect Son,
Where, through the Spirit utterly
The Father's holy will is done.

At Lauds

You died a bitter death, dear Lord,
To break our sinful slavery;
Ungrateful still, yet with what grief,
We beg again to be set free.

Upon the cross with bleeding hands
The ancient enemy you slew,
So on our brow we bear that sign,
The proof that we belong to you.

Around our weakness evermore
Is set your strong protective arm;
So held within your holiness
What evil foe can do us harm?

Your love for us came leaping down
Where, in a dark and lonely place,
The dead were waiting silently
For you to come with life and grace.

And each of us will wait at last,
When you have ended time and place,
to see your beauty unconcealed
And read our judgement in your face.

Your wounds of love will heal, O Christ,
Our wounds of sin, and make us strong
To praise, in you, the Father's power.
And cry the Spirit's triumph song.

2   Julian of Norwich, *Revelations of Divine Love*, ch. 22.
3   'It is finished' (Jn 19.30).

May 1976

I hope you had no feeling this morning[1] of being
pushed further than you wanted to go. No, I do
feel, in the Lord, that you can only be bread for your
community at great cost – in weakness, exposure
and poverty – but *how* is another matter. In these
things we can only go by what we *see* ... It's just the
direction, the timbre of the years ahead, I wanted
to emphasise. But none of this is frightening or a
weight. God isn't making *any* demands: He only
wants to give. I feel very happy about you and your
new simplicity before Him. So I scribble this in case
the weariness I could see was from within – or of my
making. It's all comfort and closeness on His side,
dear Ann.

1   Sister Ann was visiting Wendy over Easter.

May 1976

Didn't we have a happy time? At least, I did! Oh dear
– how hard to find the true words for what fills my
heart about the points you want in writing!

'The Window': what nearly everything Vermeer
paints seems to body forth – mysteriously – is
the essential nature of Light. Outside (where the
Impressionists sought for It),[1] It can't be truly seen;
It is diffuse and only Its effects are visible. We see by
It, but do not see the Light Itself. But Vermeer says[2]:
do as Christ bids, 'Go into your room and shut the
door'[3] – and to the enclosed person, shut within four
walls, Light comes through the window. Now we not
only see by It, but It becomes the main character in
our picture ... God seems to be found in freedom,
in experience, in openness – but the true finding
is in sacrifice, in deliberate renunciation of other
possibilities. He comes to be seen through His Jesus-
window, when we have gone into the enclosed room
of our own truth and let Him shine as He pleases.

(Not well put at all, but maybe you can fill in the
gaps, dear Ann.)

The Transfiguration: even with holy people, who by
definition love us and come out to embrace us, we
always feel the inner direction of their whole heart

to God. This is the true trait of the saint, surely.
And so par excellence with Jesus: how profoundly
the apostles must have felt His attention was on His
Father, and that, mysteriously, ('I have meat to eat
that you know not')[4] He was drawing from Him
His life and radiance. This was constant, just as the
assault of temptation was, too. And both these things
are externalized in the only medium open to them:
a story. And they add the final touch that must have
characterized the personality of Jesus: this sense of
always being in the presence of the Old Testament
awareness of man's vocation to suffering. 'Christ
had to suffer,' said the Risen Lord.[5] Whether He
expressed it or not, this consciousness never left Him
– because this is the destiny of us all – and this, too,
was externalized and given story form. (How this
sense of the coming 'lifting up'[6] must have antago-
nized Judas).

1 The Impressionists were a group of painters in the
   nineteenth century who transformed the direction of
   contemporary art with their attempts to capture the
   'impression' of the object as seen by the eye, rather than
   the realistic canvases composed by their predecessors.
   Sister Wendy capitalizes the word 'It' throughout this
   reflection to indicate that the Light in this instance refers
   to Christ.
2 Johannes Vermeer (1632–75), Dutch painter, a master
   of domestic scenes in which the light from a window or
   other source enters almost as another character.
3 Mt. 6.6.
4 Jn 4.32.
5 Lk. 24.26.
6 That is, Jesus' crucifixion (cf. Jn 12.32).

May 1976

I do so hope you both[1] have restful and happy times, with the burden lifted. Of course, when Our dear Lord lifts it off, it's only so that we can bear the Weight of His own burden, – which is essentially the only one – the weight of unwanted Love. You both bear that burden continually, but it can appear to be a rather secular and 'distracting' burden disguised, as it is, in our complicity in lovelessness. When we are left free and can look long at what He is doing with us, we see through the disguises ...

1   That is, Ann and another Sister, who was accompanying her to spend a time of retreat at the Carmel.

2 June 2, 1976

... No, not a slow learner, dear, but a true one! ... I'm so happy about Morna – how our dear Lord longs to bring her into flower. And for you, dearest Ann, remember that His total desire was only for the Father: His 'Yes' to suffering was – had to be – fearful and was experienced as reluctance. Oh, the weakness of Jesus that alone could receive the strength of Love! Let Him receive it in your surrendered heart and praise Him for what He has done already.

P.S. I won't of course see the cardinal[1] – but how we must pray for men and women who have *power*. It can so insulate against God.

1   Cardinal Basil Hume, Archbishop of Westminster, was
    due to visit the Carmel.

10 June 1976

I would love to write a proper thank you, but I must
leave that to the Lord. I thought M's letter was
beautiful, and an objective proof of this sense of mine
that our dear Lord is preparing her for something
... One could use other images, but the essence of
his message is that God is a Father, and in Jesus, our
Father. So those are the three notes that to me always
spell authenticity – Godhead – Fatherliness – mine.
They are very clearly marked in what she writes. More
even in her tone than in her words. The incredible
'mineness' of a grace, however humbly described, so
often masks a secret and subconscious ego-boasting.
Only the terrible 'Godliness' of God disinfects human
conceit and lets His intensely protective and concerned
love appear in its stark purity. It is a wonderful joy to
Him when He is *able* to do what He constantly longs
to do, and let someone have a glimpse of how He
loves them – and what this implies. Has she any ...
definite prayer or reading time? This might be a need
for her. (Just between ourselves, I was also struck by
her loneliness, greater than she's aware of, I would
guess. All part of the pattern: His way of preparing
her heart for Him) ...

Regarding Rosemary's critique of *Before the Living
God*,[1] would you say, if occasion offers, that in my

mind, the author's emotional style and introspection is all part of the message – very much so. Perhaps the sternest test of our desire for God, and our willingness to *let Him be God* is whether we, in practice, distinguish between elements in me that impede transformation in Jesus, and those that are human, morally neutral matter, for transforming but not for eradicating, without lessening my full womanhood. Think of the nuns we know who have emasculated themselves (if a woman can make use of this useful word) and who aren't really 'there' any more. This isn't virtue, this is disguised playing-safe. But all *God* does makes us more personal and sharpens our human flavour. The more we are Jesus, the more we become us! But this is terrible for human pride, and hence the prettying up of the saints and the wholesale construction of a holy 'image' that gives reassurance both to ourselves and to lookers-on (St Paul's 'law' back again[2]). Janet doesn't meet the test of the virtuous image. But she does meet what I am sure is God's test: a loving self-abandonment that she has worked out within the limitations of her own personal nature. The limitations aren't transcended – God never meant them to be – they are accepted and offered to Him. So I do truly feel the book is basically saying almost more in its imperfections (none willed or in God's eyes any obstacle) than in its 'beautiful' passages. The Cardinal[3] expressed his great interest, I hear ...

Sister Ann's religious Order was in the process of renewal and 'aggiornamento' according to the requirements of the Second Vatican Council. Some of her Sisters were unhappy with a certain direction of thought within the Order and, through Ann, had sent a copy of the proposed programme of renewal to Sister Wendy with a request for her comments. The letter continues with her reply:

Consecrated celibacy: yes, this paragraph is fine, but there is a subtle elitism about it. 'Love is to be given to others' etc. but no mention of the human impossibility, for the ordinary person, of living without *receiving*. All the stress is on receiving from *God*. No, a saint can live like that, but it warps the average woman, makes her either a complacent mother-figure or else cold and frustrated. This is one of the real existential problems in all communities, and here it is just glossed over as if this kind of love is simple. This ignoring of what are in fact the real issues, and substituting lovely expressions, is the fundamental flaw of this whole statement. And it's what makes it sound *false*.

Poverty: the same unconscious insincerity. The essential of religious poverty is that we don't *want things*. Talk about availability and openness and generosity etc. is fine, but it can well coincide – and does – with a desire to have. The only safeguard is not wanting. There is no mention of this attitude here, but rather a description of what could equally be a way of sharing in this world's materialism.

Obedience: 'Listening to the voice of God ...' is *Christian* obedience; the religious Sister specifically adds a context where He speaks – as is not the case for the layperson – and that is in the voice of another human being. Once again this is the real problem today, this listening to God in my superiors, and it is hidden away and played down. But pretending we haven't got superiors doesn't solve the problem, just makes it insoluble! So once again, I feel the statement is cheating and playing the saintly ostrich.

Prayer: 'We need to be willing ...' etc.: this is the whole approach, '*willingness*'! But the religious should *hunger*, be absolutely dependent on keeping close to God in prayer. This 'one-among-many good things' attitude is dangerous.

'... **eliminate human suffering**': a noble humanist aim, but certainly not that of your Foundress – or that of Jesus. They wanted to teach us to understand suffering, to use it. Your Foundress wasn't at all concerned with social justice; she craved desperately to make those children[4] understand what Jesus was and how their lives made sense in Him. And since suffering is our biggest difficulty, she wanted them to sanctify their suffering. But all the emphasis here is on fine things that are not, and never have been, your vocation. We can't be everything; human beings have to choose. And this crude fact the statement doesn't like to face up to. So in the end nothing will be done and God's time wasted, 'nobly'.

1   Ruth Burrows, *Before the Living God*, Burns & Oates [Continuum] 3rd edn, 2008.
2   Especially in the Letter to the Romans.
3   Cardinal Basil Hume.
4   That is, the school children taught by the Sisters.

24 June 1976

I take you with me in my surrender, and will offer you at special depth during the retreat. It seems to me the happiness of the last months has carried you far on your journey – you have been given a strength and a certainty that is new, and, my dearest Ann, I see you at last taken into joy, which is the sole desire of the Heart of Jesus. You are taken, and kept: believe this even when all 'evidence' tells you otherwise. *This* is what it means to live in Jesus, and to live by faith. The whole world is different, and yet drearily the same. But now we *know* ...

13 July 1976

Happy birthday, my dear: happy re-acceptance, conscious now and willing, of what it means to be alive. May this New Year in your life-cycle be more intensely alive than any that have gone before – and, dearest Ann, that isn't a prayer I make in the void, hoping, but with certainty. I *know* God is going to do it, to draw you deep into Life, into Jesus, this birth-year of yours. You must also be aware of this. Your last two letters, especially, were such a joy, with their evidence of Jesus progressively taking over and setting you free for others. But that must be experienced, on our side, often enough, by a sort of death – 'martyrdom' in its emptying, God-centred aspect, (not martyrdom as it looks to spectators). 'To belong totally to the Father', 'living in Jesus', weak, 'through the Spirit's power': ah, my dear, He will grant this prayer *in full* if you truly desire it – but then you enter into the state of 'without beauty'[1] ... the only state worth our desire, the state Jesus chose as His own, and through which He redeems His poor lost world.

I hope you like the little bird. He's been my paperweight, not great art certainly, but so small, so hopeful, with his trustingly upturned beak and breast, and the insouciant tilt of his tail feathers. It comes with all my love, rather a pathetic recompense for your great and sensitive generosity to me, but all I have! ...

I'm afraid this letter may disappoint you, as too short etc., but these are all the words, however poor, that the Lord puts into my hands at present. The beauty, the value of our contact, is that it is He who speaks in it, and I must be faithful to that, at whatever cost. It is a cost, too, when I know you would like me to write at greater length – but if it was just me, you wouldn't be able to 'feed' on it, if you know what I am so clumsily trying to say.

1   A reference to the 'Suffering servant' passage in Isaiah 53.2: 'Without beauty, without majesty, we saw him / No looks to attract our eyes ...'

22 July 1976

Poor, poor Helen, she is, as you say, quite unaware of the spiritual elitism that lies behind her words. I have put before her with all my power (His power), the truth that the Sisters will listen to what we preach in the proportion that they *see* us to be sweet, loving, happy women, free, fulfilled, Jesus-centred. But she has to live out the truth of this, not just 'accept' it ...

(*referring again to the matter of the Order's renewal discussed in the letter of June 10*):

... Your big question I've left to the end, and still feel unwilling to cope with it in writing. Would rather talk it out, and since [*the next meeting of the Order*] is next year, will we not have a good chance to do so? It is, as you rightly say, crucial, and I can recall a momentary pang when you did not seem eager to take it up. Maybe I put it too baldly. But I think it is He himself who is niggling at you! So much fine talk and resolutions and committees, but none of the real problems, the things Our dear Lord *must* have changed if is to be what

He intended, none of these are even touched. All swept under the carpet of idealism. The things I am thinking of are the absolute fundamentals, but there is a fear of really looking at them. Foolish fear! They won't come right of their own by magic; no, only in the agonies of the human hearts that must tackle them. And the first is: what is the direction of the individual Sisters' lives? There are three kinds: those who desire to be totally God's; those who would desire this with help and guidance, but cannot under their present circumstances; and those who have never wanted this at all, those who have only wanted to lead religiously oriented lives, doing 'enough' ...

All this is very poorly put, dear, but it's essential to the question of community, and why you live in it, and what its function is. And I would distinguish between 'ideal function', (and, for once, not using this word pejoratively, but as what God intends), and actual here-and-now function, which is as you describe it. But all this *needs* to be talked out. If absolutely essential I could reluctantly write, but am stupid with hayfever at present, apart from other considerations. Please tell me if this is all right with you.

Dull letter, I fear, but my prayer, being not mine, is a fire that makes my poor words unimportant.

9 September 1976

The enclosed is practically worthless[1] – nothing that we didn't speak of with more force and depth. Yet, as it might as well go into your wastepaper basket as into mine, I send it in any case ... I am very, very happy to hear of the Sisters' reactions, and your wise plans. I do see your point about questionnaires, but I would still stress very urgently the need to have all of them actively engaged in a true searching of the heart, and a true acceptance of vocation. Stress that this is *not* just another way to work the same old machine: God intends it to be a real rebirth, and anything imposed passively from above, though far from valueless, will fall pitiably short of the possibilities.

[I] feel I must accept gratefully the book of Modern Art, though I agree with KC[2] that a work may fully express its age without thereby becoming major art. I feel the moderns give us the raw material of art. They look at the world's mystery (Romanticism) and fear it; they look at the world's order (Classicism) and scorn it. So the truest joy of art, which is to force recalcitrant matter into the beauty and meaning God gives it, is almost wholly absent. Klee and co.[3] please because they play; and the rest, even the vastly gifted Picasso[4], trouble me with their refusal of the creative burden.

P.S. Oh, Ann, how totally God will possess us if we *want* it.

Community – Suggestions towards renewal

1. (a) All persons are made for community – it is not the prerogative of the religious life.

(b) What distinguishes religious community is that it is a deliberate banding together of those who share the same ideals spiritually.

2. (a) Hence religious Sisters *want* to live together, they choose it from the deep conviction that to surrender wholly to God's call is too much for them unaided.

(b) But their weakness will be supported by the help and example of others, called just as they are and likewise expecting support in their own weaknesses.

3. So community is not intended as a penance; its aim is not to provide friendship either: it is essentially (though these other elements may well be present) an indispensable human means to fulfil God's will for the Order in each sister.

4. But this support depends entirely on *shared* ideals. The Sisters *are* sisters precisely when they understand

God's call in the same way, though inevitably at different depths.

(b) We have to face the truth that in many 'communities' this shared depth does not exist.

(c) This is not a question of conservatives and radicals, still less of good Sisters and the 'difficult' ones: these mostly depend on temperament or on the secret response to grace. This is only a question of what we understand religious life to be and what structure we would choose as best fitted to establish us in that consecrated mission.

5. (a) So any renewal that starts from block grouping (provinces or houses already constituted) is evading the essentially individual character of the problem. Ideally it should not be so, but we have to deal with what is, not, as yet, with what should be.

(b) The primary need is, then, to ascertain what each Sister sees before God as His call, and to regroup the province on this interior and wholly spiritual basis. This really calls upon each Sister to make a new beginning in Christ, to enter deep into her heart and express to herself – and to others – what her ideals truly are. She may find: (i) that they are not compatible with the spirit of their foundress: that Sister must then see that she would be happier and *holier* if she left; (ii) that she has been unfaithful; (iii) that she will always be unfaithful *unless* hcr life-style changes. All this requires great honesty, courage and openness to the Spirit, Who calls us to the Father to express to others the redeeming love of Jesus.

1 A reference to the notes on community life that follow.
2 KC: the art critic Kenneth Clark (1903–83).
3 Paul Klee (1879–1940), a prolific painter; born in Switzerland of German parents, he established himself in Munich as an artist in the avant-garde, Bauhaus school.
4 The Spanish artist, Pablo Picasso (1881–1973), founder with Georges Braque of the Cubist movement. Although generally considered the outstanding artist of the twentieth century, whose work has had an incalculable influence over the development of modern art, Sister Wendy had private reservations about what she felt to be his essential lack of seriousness.

16 September 1976

I feel that all depends on a full, detailed explanation, with discussion coming *after*, of the essential points[1]: (i) that living in community is designed solely to support our deepest responses to God …; (ii) that there is a truthful acknowledgement of the various ways in which the Sisters see this response – not so much in its outer manifestations (*not* 'lifestyles') but in its inner intensity; (iii) that the need for a radical change at depth is accepted – a very good point of yours about 'playing with adaptation and calling it "renewal"'. But all this requires teaching so as to lead to real conviction …

There's a new Penguin, *The Puritan in Africa*, which sounds as though it might be a wise read before you go?[2] May the Lord use you to show the Sisters there what He wants of them – implores of them – and may the experience be for you rich and lovely. Hope you can wander off into the bush near Embakwe – the veld is made for prayer, in its space and sweep and its infinite delicacy of no-colour.

As you say, KC's *Rembrandt*[3] is less than *Landscape*[4], (only ordinarily superb, I suppose), I think I'll read that first and keep the other for the Presentation[5], which is always a rather nostalgic day for me. I don't know when there will be cause to write again, but you know that you and your vocation are always in my heart, and not writing never means lack of love. I know God is mightily moving you to the abandonment of total love – moving both your heart and (literally) you yourself, and so I cast you with myself into that strong, holy, terrible love. Thank you for so much.

1   This letter begins by continuing Sister Wendy's reflections on the renewal programme being carried out by Sister Ann's religious Order.
2   Sister Ann was about to pay a visit to the houses of her Order in South Africa.
3   Kenneth Clark, *Rembrandt and the Italian Renaissance*, John Murray 1966.
4   Kenneth Clark, *Landscape into art*, John Murray 1949.
5   The feast day of the Presentation of the Virgin Mary in the Temple, celebrated in the Catholic Church on 21 November.

Undated

Welcome home, love[1] – 'He is our homeliest home',

as Julian says, and only where He chooses for us can He be wholly at home in our hearts and ours in His. But I send you this regal African bird and the exquisite eastern catalogue pictures, partly to give you pleasure (I hope?), and mostly to remind you of the great worlds of sun and space and mystery that you sacrifice for Jesus – and not *in vain*. All that you dimly and secretly yearn for simply opens new depths within you for Love, makes you more 'home' to Him, since you choose to find fulfilment only in a death to all but what He puts before you ...

Kenneth Clark, in that beautiful Rembrandt book, says of his *Jewish Bride*: 'it embodies certain universal and enduring truths: that we need each other, that we can achieve unity only through tenderness, and that the protection of one human being by another is a solemn responsibility'. Tenderness is closely akin to what I mean by weakness – a loving self-forget-fulness. And that solemn responsibility for all others, individually, is essential to our religious vocation. We are called to protect and cherish God's little ones, being first convinced that we ourselves are the least. This is it, isn't it?

My mother is so excited as she expects her present. She evidently feels awed at your kindness – as do I! Do let me know what you'll make of the book, which you'll have by now.

A dull and hurried letter ... but with true love. May Jesus give Himself to the Father ever more totally in you.

1   From her trip to South Africa.

19 November 1976

You have been much in my heart, as one suffering, but I could see, too, that the pain 'didn't matter'. I can say that to you without seeming heartless, as you'll understand: it is the pain of being human, living as a bodily creature who vibrates to life's unpredictabilities and enters, with Jesus, into its mystery. Woe for one such as you if you didn't feel any anguish ...

I can imagine how much you would tell me of South Africa and other affairs if we could talk, but Jesus will give us a time when you need it. All you need at present is to surrender to dark Love, letting Him have it all and accepting to be without achievement before Him. (No Alps, no veld, not even almond blossom under Fujiyama: just smog and sweat and lack of appreciation, and *no arbours anywhere*). Oh Ann, 'crucified with Him'[1] sounds so clear-cut, somehow; yet it is what drab life does incessantly if we look at Him.[2]

1   Gal. 2.20.
2   She is trying to say that it is ordinary life, rather than the

exceptional sufferings that sound more romantic, which assimilate us to Christ crucified.

10 December 1976

How grateful I am to you – for too many things to be listed. But there is nothing you do for me that I don't hold up to God as a sign of your desire to be possessed wholly by Love. You lace my sandals for me,[1] but it is His Feet, (pierced and glorious) that wear them. I enclose dear Frances' last letter for you to read and share with anybody else you think. It breathes to me what seems her characteristic, and that is an unpretentious goodness, a wholesome earnestness that knew only too well that it was not 'excellence', and longed shyly to become better. I've thought several times since her death that, seeing me now, she must feel great disappointment, or rather would feel it if it wasn't clear to her that this only highlights what God did for her: any old, cheap rubbish can become luminous in Him, if we are willing to accept Him thus. And this is even more true for you, dear Ann, isn't it? ...

I hope when next you have time to write that your sadness will be less intense. There is a sense in which our martyrdom is precisely in not having a martyrdom, just living on and on with 'nothing to show for it'. Ah, but it is His eyes that see what shows, and His life we want to live, not ours, which *must* mean a death to all that would glorify self.

1   Cf. Jn 1.27.

Christmas 1976

All through Advent I have held you in the Messiah, Whose presence is salvation, and Who comes to us precisely and *only* where we are. Solitude or hubbub: both are Bethlehem. I am always struck by the actuality of this feast – the whole mishmash of circumstances and accidentals and human blind-nesses that provided the context for our Salvation to come to us. Not only didn't He wait for the ideal or romantic, He almost seems to have emphasized the need of one thing only, Mary's surrendered heart, which means, in practice, that stable or census or Herod or great clumsy shepherds or whatever, all just drew her deeper and deeper into Jesus. May all be that Jesus-window for you, dearest Ann, so that you live in the Light and advert only to that. Ah, but I haven't said what I really want to ... and can't find any words other than these poor ones ...

1977

January 1977

Jesus shares our wine, and makes every feast a Cana.[1]
And when our wine is gone, He will take our water,
if we give it to Him, and change it too into wine. But
the essential thing is that it is all Jesus. His Presence,
His Action, decides what is wine for us and what is
neither wine nor water (potential wine) but simply
non-potable, an obstacle to life. We must look at
Him, not at things-in-themselves. Whatever Jesus
gives us is wine.

1   This short note comments on a picture of the *Marriage
Feast at Cana*, which Sister Wendy had sent to Ann.
As the original card no longer survives, it is not known
to which of the many depictions of this scene she is
referring.

21 January 1977

My dearest – a hasty word to say that Elizabeth died
during the night. How beautiful that you and I saw
Him summon her and were privileged to go a few
steps down with her into the dark waters … Thank
you for the note and the exquisite paper and all else.
But – as you suspected I can't 'take' Grunewald[1]:
all the anguish raw, without its meaning: seen from
without. In Jesus, where we live, pain and death have
been transformed into a redemptive beauty. Ah, but
I can't express it.

Somehow I feel this meeting had a deep meaning. Certainly it has deepened my love for you and my joy in what God is achieving in your offered heart.

1   Matthias Grünewald (ca. 1480–1528), German painter. A reference to the artist's famous Isenheim Crucifixion: part of the altarpiece in the chapel of the Isenheim plague hospital.

12 February 1977

I was so pleased to get your letter – and don't laugh, but this is *my* fourth day with a feverish cold![1] Too slight a fever to need bed in my case, but after Mass I've stayed peacefully in the hermitage all day.[2] Hope you are better, love, it doesn't matter much about me, but you're another matter … That famous, never-to-be-repeated day in bed didn't work, so had a negative value. Deep within me came a summons *away* – hard to describe, but I see that I need solitude and silence, and to be 'in' the community is the wrong place, even bodily.[3] The joy of coming home to the chill, silent, stillness of the caravan …!

Margaret Mary: here is a classic example of the almost impossibility of translating a vision into human terms, not just for others, but even for oneself.[4] I'm sure she 'saw' the longing Love of God, and nearly died beneath its pressure – and her subconscious provided her with an image to cling to … But *that* wasn't what he told and showed her, and her words are even further removed from it … Needless to say, this poor shabby creature[5] can't compare for goodness, but I'm far better *read* and more sophisticated intellectually, probably more sceptical by make-up too, so I can avoid pitfalls. The dilemma still remains, if one thinks the Lord *wants* something shared and one has no vehicle. This is almost beyond enduring, and one does seize at anything. At least St Margaret Mary could find some external that her age could use.[6]

Religious Order: Ann, my love, remember always that the Spirit of Jesus found only one perfect expression, and that was Jesus himself. And following comes his dear pure Mother, as proof of what Jesus will do in a surrendered heart. Only He could *receive* the Spirit wholly from the Father, but Mary and the saints are in their degree wholly *given*. But only these wholly given ones can show forth anything at all of the Spirit. Think of the Church, which Jesus loves, which is himself, in a mystical sense, and think of the vile, shameful things in her history, and of the bitter tears we still shed over her image and actions today – the complacency, materialism, lovelessness – the sheer non-Jesus face she shows the world and drives away from Him, the honest but ignorant. Ah, but it is still his beloved Body, and to reject her would be to reject the disfigured, suffering Christ. Well, Ann dear, just as love of Jesus means love of his poor, faithless Church, and she can only be made faithful to the extent that His lovers are a force within her, so with one's religious Order. Never say or think you

are alien to her; what you are alien to is the dead and
crippling elements that disfigure her and conceal with
their spittle the lovely Face of Jesus. It is what is *not*
authentic you shrink from, what is false and contra-
dictory in her. I can't bear to hear you think it is the
Order 'in se' you don't want, but in this life, as Jesus
knew in His blood, the image must be continually
cleansed. You, and how many more of the Sisters:
you are your Order, though never fully, and it is for
those who share your Foundress' love and vision to
keep it from obscurity. But you can't do this *alone*
– hence the vital importance of community. And
finding those who think the same and can support
each other is your present task. O Ann, once again
I feel how badly I've put all this, and can only rely
on that inward echo of yours that 'hears' what He is
saying, however blurred the human instrument . . .

Rembrandt and Piero and Vermeer are filling my
artistic horizon at present.[7] O that lovely Vermeer
– pleasure is too small a word! Wish there were
some more coloured illustrations in it . . . Berenson[8]
says black and white are best, though – and how I
am relishing him and the vast array of illustrations.
Am struck by how art criticism uncovers a person's
soul. He sees, quite profoundly, that, say Crivelli is
an important and original artist, but his comments,
'tender piety' etc., are fantastically wrong. Bernard
Berenson simply hasn't the spirituality to see why he
likes the man. But our dear Kenneth Clark sees from

within. Notice his passing comment in *Landscape into Art* that Rembrandt and Michelangelo[9] are the two great Moral painters. How true – and how they are complemented by Vermeer and Piero as the two great painters of interior order: Vermeer does it by light, (could write a treatise here), and Piero by dignity. Talk about this when we meet!

The books you give me are such a source of spiritual happiness. I can't say that I 'need' them but they are a way of praying very precious to me and I come from them to my own fathomless prayer with more capacity and receptivity. No, that's not quite it. They are more than a relaxation, far more, yet the worlds they open to me, His worlds, support me in the uninterrupted and unimaginable … No use, dearest, I'll have to stop in helplessness.

1   Sister Ann had written to say that she had been bed-bound with 'flu.
2   At that period Sister Wendy would normally have attended the Choir Offices in the monastery church with the Carmelite Sisters. Her fever has prevented her from doing this.
3   Because of her sickness, she had been put under pressure to allow herself to be cared for in the monastery infirmary, but the experiment had not been a success.
4   Saint Margaret Mary Alacoque (1647–90), a Visitandine nun who received visions of the Sacred Heart of Jesus. Ann had apparently asked Sister Wendy's opinion of this type of visionary experience.
5   That is, herself.
6   Saint Margaret Mary's vision took the form of a human heart surrounded by flames, indicating the intensity of

Christ's human love for us. Sister Wendy always insisted on the relative value of such symbols, pointing out that they are, to a large extent, culturally conditioned.

7   She is referring to books about these artists. Rembrandt van Rijn (1606–69) was a Dutch painter and etcher who devoted numerous works to the depiction of Biblical stories, personalities and scenes. Piero della Francesca (c. 1415–92) was a painter of the Early Italian Renaissance. For Vermeer, *see the letter of May 1976*.

8   Bernard Berenson (d. 1959), American art critic.

9   Michelangelo (1475–1564), Renaissance artist and polymath whose influence over Western art has been unparalleled.

9 March 1977

I'm afraid just another wretched 'postage-stamp-sized' note to say: (a) The questionnaire, if it turns out to be right, would be the final stage in a process of self-discovery. First: the confession that we don't go on as we are; then, the recognition that 'community' is essentially 'support'; and then that this support must spring spontaneously from shared ideals and resolves; and then the painful decision to admit divergence here ... Only then the actual work of finding out what individuals live by and the use, among other instruments, of a questionnaire. The difficult, delicate part is all in laying the foundation, and it will be strong in proportion to both the quality of those who agree [to it] and their number. You may find it takes years ... but the small, unsatisfying steps you take now lead there.

So very happy to hear that Claire is growing in womanhood. She has the woman's strength, but now may be given her dependence and sensitive awareness of 'need' – which men don't have, poor fellows! No, dearest, when we first spoke I saw you lacked something, and it could have come through falling in love. But God, in His beautiful thrift – our frugal God – used matter to hand, and the lack is a thing of the past: merely a foundation now for deeper self-giving.

You are very deep in my Lenten prayer – which is only a sharing in the overwhelming hope of Jesus that His triumph should not be wasted. No, not a sharing: it is all His – but oh, how He yearns that it should truly and literally be 'consummated', handed over to the Father, the work of the Spirit of Love achieved. If we only let Him, with all that it terribly implies, He can't but 'do' it. And this applies very specially to the community situation. Lie, pure and open-eyed, in His wounded Hands, even if you 'see' only darkness. He sees. He will do it through your very blindness if your eye is pure and attentive.

March 1977 (postcard)

You are the one having the hard Lent[1], and all the more in that the pain seems less 'pure' than mine. But it is all from Him: His chosen context in which He longs to give Himself to you and through you to the world. You're deep in my prayer, and the despondency and frustration are only modes of Love.

How hard it was for Jesus, Ann dearest. How blessed to share in His overthrow.

1   Ann had commiserated with Sister Wendy, who had a sinus infection at the time.

22 March 1977

Just another postage-stamp-sized note (it hurts me to write them, but it has to be so, love … It isn't *all* His unless I pare myself, in Him, to the bone – the bone of *my* vocation, as you must be pared to yours, and *are* pared …) Only written to assure you that my ailments are essentially trivial: I would unhesitatingly call myself well, in the best sense, and nada, nada, nada is the answer to what I need.[1]

But no, Ann, *The Polish Rider*[2] could *never* be the prodigal son: that ethereal steed, that noble, searching gaze, the whole atmosphere of a doomed and *willing* hero who searches for his unknown hour of sacrifice. Innocent and ardent: a very Paschal picture … I feel it tells us something of the longing heart of the Lamb of God. Lonely Lamb whose death is our joy. It's his triumphant Love I wear as my cloak and gladly share with you …[3]

Oh dear: can you read it? You're deep in my heart which He makes His.

1   Ann was unfailingly generous to Sister Wendy and frequently volunteered gifts of books and other items.

The word 'nada', Spanish for 'nothing', is an allusion to a saying of the Carmelite saint and mystic, John of the Cross (1542–91), who founded his spiritual teaching on the way of nothingness (*nada*) and self-denial.

2   *The Polish Rider*, a mysterious painting generally ascribed to Rembrandt (see Plate 2). Apparently Sister Ann had hazarded that it might represent the parable of the Prodigal Son.

3   The last sentence represents Sister Wendy's entering into the words that, in her imagination, might have been spoken by the *Polish Rider*. On another occasion she would write on the back of a reproduction of this picture: 'The Christian warrior whose life is never "of this world" though he lives and shares in it. He bears and can use hard steel but is himself all gentleness, all vision, all acceptance, and he rides a horse of poverty. His gaze is fixed on the eternal Truth bodied forth in the secular.'

3 May 1977

You have been kept so close to my heart these past weeks – I longed to write knowing how ill and depressed and hopeless and abandoned you were feeling, but it was *feeling*, dear. Jesus shared with me His own compassion, but He also made it clear that essentially it all didn't matter. Nothing was dead – you have to *choose* death, in both the good and evil senses – and your anguish was because you didn't feel alive enough. And since His life comes alive in us to the extent we are truly prepared to die to our small, consoling lives, all the darkness was Light's shadow. My part in it had to be silent trust in Light, in silent surrender to the painful mystery of my own vocation, so as to offer you more wholly to yours. When you come to say 'No' to Jesus – a day I trust Him never to let happen – then there will be a deadly death and I'll write soon enough. But you are enduring the bitter death of your *secret* 'no's' and that only leads to Life. But I hope you can come here one of these days and talk and rest your weariness ...

Do you like this John and Peter?[1] The contemplative folding his hands in wonder; the active opening his out in praise; both wholly engrossed in Jesus. Peter unaware that he is old and bearded; John unaware that he is lovely and innocent. The one preoccupation of their beings is the mystery of Life-made-visible before them. A terrible sight which leaves them no room for even joy, no room to realize what the vocation costs or whether they would have chosen it for themselves: they have only to look and let Him overwhelm them. O dearest Ann, what a paradigm of your own course, and how pointless to advert, willingly, to the trivialities of life, such as how we feel, etc. (But I don't feel too bad, truly. And, symbolically, the pain is inside where no cushion has a writ to run!![2] The ulcer must heal before he[3] decides what to do, and maybe the fissure will heal with it. Fiat either way.) Hope this isn't too disappointing a letter.

1   A picture of the apostles John and Peter, no longer preserved.
2   Ann had sent Wendy a cushion to ease the discomfort of her ulcer.
3   The hospital consultant.

13 May 1977

Please, love, don't be anxious about my minor ailments. Remove me from the streets of Manchester[1] and set me again in my own green copse, and you'll see it is all part of the vocation, and a *joy*. Not that I look forward to the hospital with anything but dread, but since it is His choice for me, I only know my dread in Him. Other people's sufferings can seem worse to us than our own, since it's only in the real, the present-moment pain that Jesus is active, and we can only know that through entering into it. Not put clearly, but I trust your understanding. I don't know when the operation will be. I have to see the surgeon again on June 24 … But you know what months one has to wait. Probably it will be near the end of the year. And after that your cushion will be such a Godsent gift – only after, though; don't need it now. I've plenty of soap, dearest, and plenty of peace and no pain that Jesus doesn't bear within me. Please believe this.

If I were asked to say what you most need, it would be a deeper sense of your vocation. There is a whole area of mystery unexplored yet in your life. You have come so far along the path of love, but still too much *in propria persona* – if you follow me? You are accepting the pain of religious life, and struggling to give God its sacrifices, but you don't fully see the 'abundance' side. (I am sorry: so few chances to write and here I have a silly, sick head and can't find words ...) What I'm trying to say is that to belong to a Religious Order has a sacramental efficacy. Something of your Foundress' passionate concern for Jesus, for little ones to know and love Him, for His sweetness and sheer goodness to be bread and drink for us all: something of this is yours by right of membership – a vine-and-branch mystery, if you let it be so.[2] But you haven't fully surrendered here. Not a thing Jesus blames you for, dear one, but a real area where He is waiting to give Himself *through the Order* and never 'in spite of', which is what you are sometimes tempted to think!!

How I love the *Polish Rider*: in this world yet living in another, like the Risen Jesus. And the *Jewish Bride*, and the *Prodigal Son*, and *Jacob's Blessing*: such a treasure of a book ...[3] The Blake of *Michael Binding Satan* will be up for the Ascension here: my heart is full of its symbols[4]. Oh, how blessed we are to know He is Lord, and to abandon ourselves for His wounded Hands to bind our dragon. We cannot, we dare not approach the world's evil, but Jesus 'has overcome the world'.[5]

1   She was due to be hospitalized in Manchester.
2   An allusion to Jn 15.5.
3   These are all paintings by Rembrandt van Rijn, *see n. 7, February 1977.* Ann had sent Wendy an illustrated book about the artist.
4   *Michael Binding Satan*, a watercolour painting by the English artist and poet, William Blake (1757–1827).
5   Jn 16.33.

Ascension 1977[1]

Today is one of my favourite feasts – the day when Jesus visibly declares to us that our homeland is in heaven[2] and that we have not here a lasting city.[3] (And all these Ascension-Whit days[4] are personal celebrations for me; anniversaries of my coming to Quidenham.) So this day of heavenly detachment, of 'Love alone matters' and 'nothing else worldly counts', was a fitting day to receive your lovely letter and radiant cards.

Dearest, you know why Jesus could call Himself Lamb: He accepted to be helpless, to submit in innocence and without protection to the great ones of your world who exercise authority, accepting all that they would do in the knowledge that people are mostly motivated by ignorance and fear, not malice … I can only rejoice at the depth of your vocation. He has drawn you in a mysterious fashion into the very heart of His surrender and yet He does not hide you away in obscurity – no, He has seen to it that you will speak about Him at the Assembly, not to mention all the other work that comes along. Perhaps to reveal Him purely you have to remain extended in faith like this, with no safe ego-hold on which to stand, and no safe status role, either. The book would spring very truly from such ego-impoverishment, dearest Ann, and I very much look forward to hearing of its progress.

Thank you so much for the Gillian Ayres[5]. I have it mounted and displayed in my caravan, and often contemplate its free and powerful beauty. It is like looking into the cave of natural creation, 'the very heart of things', where God is present in the only way He can be, in mystery. You have evidently discovered some card source, because you've sent me a series of magnificent images. The big Klee[6] is lovely, isn't it? I wonder if the title, *Hermitage* and the date, 1918, are connected? He may well have felt a need to hide himself after the war pressures, and longed to believe that nature was all softness and peace. But I don't think he really believed that – there's an histrionic panache in the picture. Brave man that he was, Klee accepted pain and combat as a doorway into life.

1   Ascension Day fell on 19 May that year.
2   Phil. 3.20.
3   Heb. 13.14.
4   'Whitsun' was formerly the popular English name for Pentecost Sunday.
5   Gillian Ayres (b. 1930), an English artist.
6   Paul Klee, Swiss artist, *see n. 3, 9 September 1976.*

14 June 1977

You are already so weary, will it not be far too much for you to drive here and back within three days? I said to Janet that this seemed to me an insuperable difficulty, but she said oh no, that she would do the same – it would be worth it. So, dearest, it is up to you, but remember, among the pros and cons, that

I may be a bit shakier than usual after the surgeon's probings.[1] This makes no difference from my side, but it could mean that you'll need even deeper faith than usual to hear Living Truth through this poor, shabby medium. He presses so close on our hearts, and nearly everyone is looking in the wrong direction. Rembrandt's little servant girl knows where He is, doesn't she?[2] It was this picture I bought for the flat when we lived in Johannesburg, but never had the ears of the community to explain its mystery to them. It took me a long time to realize that sacrifice in itself is meaningless. 'The cup which *My Father* has given me'[3]: not some bitter cup I have brewed up for myself. Jesus means that we never have to guess at 'the things that please Him'[4]. We are *told*, partly by circumstance, by what comes to hand (so, for example, Jesus never left His homeland – there was work for Him *there*; and Paul did leave it, for life forced it on him), and partly by 'knowing the mind of Christ'[5], an interior knowledge of 'love that knows'[6]. But if there are no objective validations, I should always fear deception here. Ann dearest, our feelings can 'tell' us nothing, they simply make the surrender of self harder or easier, and your sense of waste and failure and resistance only means you are being forced, by Love, to take your stand more and more absolutely on Jesus and His holiness, and not, however secretly, on your own or your desires for your own.

It will be a joy to see you, whenever you come. May you find the Heart of Jesus has become yours – as it will, when you are ready.

P.S. Spy stories: is part of their appeal symbolic? Our own human loneliness amid a deceptive world and no clarity of our own.

1   Referring to the hospital appointment mentioned previously.
2   *A Girl at a Window*, painted by Rembrandt in 1635.
3   Jn 18.11.
4   Cf. Jn 8.29.
5   '... but we have the mind of Christ': 1Cor. 2.16.
6   Cf. 1Cor. 13.12.

2 July 1977[1]

We are well stocked with C. S. Lewis[2] – superb writer, almost a minor Kenneth Clark in his sphere! My favourite is *The Great Divorce*, the most moving evocation I know of the sheer reality of God. In every other sphere, the sound of what we hear ourselves say and know ourselves think can deceive us: only with God are we absolute in our bare choice. We can have of Him exactly as much as we want – and we know what we want from what we in fact have. A terrifying demand: no wonder people fear the inescapable closeness of prayer. Yet in that deathly closeness is the only Life, Way and Truth. I don't think C. S. Lewis ever really came close to Jesus, but he did to God, that essential precondition ...

Must confess with a blush that I could never have enough Rembrandt. Is this book expensive?[3] If not, maybe for Christmas?? I looked at the Thames and Hudson *Drawings*[4] yesterday – how infinitely diverse he is, and always mirroring something of God. Here is a man who did 'see' Jesus, in his own way. Next time you come, which I hope will be before you collapse under psychic pressure, we'll talk Rembrandt. No, I didn't know Phaidon had a giant paperback Rubens. I've come late to appreciation of him, but can now see through his portly beauties to the essential Rubens: a unique celebrator of God's prodigal generosity in creation, (just as Rembrandt celebrates His compassionate love, and Leonardo His Mystery, and Michelangelo? – perhaps God's pure divinity, the power of the Holy One).

Thank you for telling me about Diana … I hope you will specifically try to see her; she will be helped by you, dearest Ann. But it will be more prudent not to let her know we occasionally write, in case she is hurt. Please ask the Lord to wring something out of me for her when she is here. I feel like 'a thing thrown away', as the psalm says,[5] and deservedly so, and am very unheroic about my trivial pains. I am happy for it all to be so, knowing that Jesus, Who so gladly emptied Himself, reigns within me in any state. His doing alone. I can't feel there is anything to lament over if I am threadbare, but it could disconcert poor Diana!

How I wish that Miriam had come here to talk her vocation over with me. I cannot feel this is what God wanted, though it is so specious in its temptation: 'change your context and it will change *you*'. But it doesn't: our context is where He waits for us, and only there, just as now is the time of His presence and the only time. Say this to your dear Claire too. He is coming fully to you both, in your respective constrictions, so don't miss Him because it all seems too material and wearisome and haphazard.

Am delightedly reading *Change Without War*.[6] I feel it has helped me fold up this troubled world into a comprehensible bundle and lay it trustfully in the outstretched Hands of the wounded Jesus. So very happy over your note, with its proof of how purely you seek for Him. The flowers, surely a symbol of your heart in flower before His Hidden Beauty.

1   This letter begins with the somewhat mysterious super-scription: '2nd day of the 7th year, 77'. It has here been interpreted as the 2 July 1977, assuming that the word 'year' was written erroneously instead of 'month'.
2   Clive Staples Lewis (1898–1963), literary critic, popular novelist and Christian apologist. His fictional works, of which *The Great Divorce* is his masterpiece, generally contain a substratum of allegorical, Christian meaning.
3   Ann was proposing to buy a newly published book about Rembrandt as a gift.
4   Haak, Bob, *Rembrandt: Drawings*, Thames and Hudson 1976.
5   Ps. 31.13.
6   Buchan, Alastair, *Change without War*, Chatto & Windus 1974.

July 1977

Happy birthday, dearest! The card is appealing, isn't it? Poor little Jesus, looking out with such round-eyed apprehension at a menacing world. I hope you don't begin a new year of life with apprehension, love, but if you do, remember that Jesus has been through the whole gamut: dread, and then dreadful reality, right under the bitter waters. But He came out the other side, crying 'Consummatum',[1] and my birthday prayer is for Him to cry that out in you. He has triumphed *for* you, now let Him triumph *in* you – and oh, what joy when He can triumph *through* you! The poor world – specially here and now – waits, unaware, for that triumph.

So much love, my constant prayer, and my deep hope for you.

1 'Consummatum est' ('It is finished'): the last words of Jesus on the Cross in the Fourth Gospel.

7 September 1977

Oh, what beautiful books – beautiful everything! I am seated in the caravan amidst your bounty, in a daze of pleasure. No more brandy needed for ages – I am parsimonious with it and still have 3/4 of the last. But I'll toast our dear Lady with you tomorrow[1] and keep the other for your Vow day.[2] Let us thank God together for making you more wholly His own. Whatever life may feel like, this is, in literal truth, its purpose: He can only come to us in time and through our actual unidealized circumstances ... all 'corruptible things'[3] though they are. I'm sure Jesus felt this acutely, while having 'no sin'[4] within His pure heart to echo it back. I wonder if His being lost in the Temple was part of a child's desire to flee from the world[5] – whether He saw even then, poor Jesus, that we had made even His Father's house a den of thieves.[6] And then He accepted the grubbiness of life, just as it is, and immersed Himself in it ('was made sin' says Paul)[7], so that in the pain of knowing and seeing, he could give us His purity. So I think it's a grace when you see your corruption, both the inescapable without and the somehow secretly, though unwillingly, willed within. Dearest Ann, so much for you hangs upon your letting Jesus come to you *as He chooses*, and your responding to Him in this painful and demanding reality. I was struck (thinking of your retreat) how His parables and sayings about going out in love always put the initiative on *us* ... not with respect to God but with respect to others. The hungry, the thirsty, the lost sheep, the man robbed and wounded: none *ask* their neighbour for help. Jesus was always on the watch for what people needed – He takes the first step. And so must we. You treat me with such delicate love, you see Jesus in this poor creature. You are always holding out your generous hands to me. Something of that, in measure, is what Love urges us to do for anyone who comes within our orbit. We are to be ever running forward to greet them with respect and affection, asking Jesus to show us what their wounds are and how we may bind them ... I'm putting this so badly, love, but your holiness, I know, is going to come through a completely Jesus-centred charity. He loved us and *gave Himself for us*.[8] Let Him do this through you. Anyway, I'll pray so specially, I always do, but this retreat could be a crucial one ... As for health, truly, not worth comment. All of me is taken up by Him, and the few buffetings of the body are genuinely unimportant ... All of me is Praise, so thank Him with me.

1   September 8 is the feast of the Nativity of the Virgin Mary in the Church's calendar.
2   That is, the anniversary day of Sister Ann's religious profession.
3   1Pet. 1.18.
4   Heb. 4.15.
5   Lk. 2.41–53.
6   Lk. 19.46.
7   2Cor. 5.21.
8   Gal. 2.20.

20 September 1977

I've been looking out for your letter, knowing from within how hard pressed you are. (I won't say 'suffering' – it sounds too positive – and yet your sense of being whirled hopelessly and helplessly along in a huge machine you can't control is very real suffering.) I so hope the retreat will help. But dearest, don't 'fear' it. The Lord never 'makes demands',[1] never, never. All He says is: Let me bear it, let me take the pressure. Or rather, He tells us He *has* taken the pressure – and let it kill Him, and it was that death that gave Him wholly to His Father, and us in Him. All the anxious side of things is over, Ann love. We have conquered, in Jesus. So bear the humiliation and pain of life's bewilderments gladly, in His gladness: 'Now is the Father glorified' ...[2]

I so look forward to those lovely books. It's Janet's feast day today and my gift was, of course, some of *your* gift. I shall have the last lot to savour prayerfully.

I was distressed about those Sisters. Authority, like illness, isn't bad for us, but it shows us up for what we are. Pride, self-reliance (= insecurity) is easily hidden in lowliness: but it shows through in its ugly traits when we are in power.

Do you like the Old Warrior?[3] Battered but at peace, all his armour gone; bare headed: he waits God's verdict painfully but trustingly.

When Jesus is all to us, in the Spirit, it means in practice we have nothing tangible or sensible: death. But this is life.[4]

1   The words in inverted commas are quoting from Ann's letter.
2   A misquotation of Jn 13.31.: 'Now the Son of Man is glorified and in him God is glorified.'
3   It has not been possible to trace this picture.

4   This somewhat cryptic statement is talking about life
     in the Spirit. Insofar as it lacks tangible or sensible
     assurances it has the appearance of 'death'. But, to the
     contrary, this 'death' is 'life' for us.

11 November 1977

It is late at night – or at least late for me, feeble
woman, [who sinks exhausted after the intense Love
of the day].[1] O Ann, how fortunate I am, and how
strange that it should be an oddity like me.[2] But it
isn't 'for me', as you know – it is for all who *want*
it, and of whom is that more true than of you? I am
so very, very grateful for your many kindnesses, and
know well that it is to Jesus you offer them, and He
who must repay you …

Dearest Ann, let your sense of your poverty be a feast
for Jesus. As you say, you can only see the ugliness
because He is gleaming on you. How we hate to
see it – and yet how can we be translucified in Him
if we don't know we are dark?[3] He comes running
with the bounding joy of a Lover when we turn
away from ourselves and hold out suffering hearts
to Him. I would only be anxious about you if you
saw yourself pure and lovely – let Him see whatever
there is of that (I see it too, in Him), and let Ann be
humbly glad she sees the murk that calls out to be
cleansed …

The Vermeer is lovely, isn't it? The soul intent, not
looking at the light but living in it – using it to

do her duty. His constant theme (lacemaker, cook etc.).[4]

1   The last half of this sentence was crossed out in the original.
2   That is, to whom this burden of love is given.
3   'Translucified': a neologism for being 'made light'.
4   That is, Vermeer's constant theme. Some of his most famous works depict women as they occupy themselves with their household tasks: *The Lacemaker* is one of these (see Plate 3).

23 November 1977

I've been tempted to wait until nearer Christmas and pretend that this is a present, poor shabby thing, but it would only be cheating. No one would ever want to read it, though you might like the preface. Will you show Kathleen and then dispose of it?? ...[1] My typewriter is out of sorts, so this carbon I took for you isn't very clear. I was taken aback and rather distressed to be asked to write of prayer for the *Clergy Review* – special number some time next year, so you can get a decent copy if you want it and if they print it!! I feel it is a feeble effort, but the actual matter I am certain of ... Let me know if you think it gets anything across.

Please tell Sister Judith. how very, very much I appreciate the shawl. My head is warm at night for the first time. It's too beautiful for me, really, but when she gets to heaven, the Lord will meet her wearing it ...

I understand your anxiety (no, not neurotic, though it could be too much *your* anxiety as opposed to *his*) but I am sure the norms must arise from below, from actual demands, and not be imposed from above.[2] Principles are the great need: when we see that a stricter life-pattern is needed if we are to be free to give ourselves, then we will start to seek it. Too many of us are drifting, rather uneasily at times, not aware of what the components of our day are meant to add up to. I keep telling Janet that people must know *what* they are doing ... then they can be as 'free' as they please. But if they don't know, there is no criterion to make their choices by. But we only come to this understanding through prayer and discussion, through the very kind of sharing that our life is meant to provide ... You must love with the heart of Jesus in everything, utterly unconcerned for anything but the Kingdom, ready to see that He sees another side. Don't become more tense and divided and divisive than humanly possible. I *know* you are trying; I *know* you want to do God's will only, but it needs His own intervention through the means of a loving, gentle heart, non-critical, non-suspecting, non-judgemental: just loving, humble and pure. That's what I ask Him to do in you, and that's what He *will* do ...

P.S. I feel my letters are getting progressively more stupid. You must no longer have need of me or He would do something about it!!

1   Sister Wendy had been commissioned to write an article on prayer for a Catholic journal, the *Clergy Review*. She enclosed a typed copy for Sister Ann with this letter. It

was subsequently printed in leaflet form and distributed by the Quidenham Carmelites under the title *Simple Prayer*.

2   Sister Ann was engaged in a rather delicate administrative task in her community at the time.

15 December 1977

What a happy chance that you should have given me in large the very card I was saving for you! I am told you have my translation of Revelations 3; here are other parts of the Christmas liturgy (mine too).[1] Dear Ann, so much to thank you for, (and please thank the ingenious contriver of that admirable balaclava!!). This is just a hasty word on one or two points you raised:

(a) Never, never think that apostolic Orders demand less than Carmel or other contemplative Orders. God has chosen for each precisely the vocation that will demand all – and 'all' for you must include little prospect of romanticizing the grandeurs and austerities of your life. To love Him in your sisters, to be wholly given to His children, to surrender in a prayer that is always patchy and inadequate: [this is] part of your all. He will take the all as long as you eagerly, lovingly look for Him always.

(b) Relationships die, but since the people remain, a new one immediately comes to birth. We must have to strive to make it as loving as the other, the happy one. When Jesus knew he could expect nothing now from Judas except betrayal, he still called him 'friend'[2] – and meant it. You are too passive in your relationships, love. If you are not offered affection you don't go out in search of it. But we must search, actively offering vulnerable love, whatever the risks. Jesus pursues us with His tenderness; do you pursue those who repulse you?[3] Let Him use you to prove the utter selflessness of love …

Could that illegible word be 'niggardly'??[4] I never remember what I write. They are using a poem of mine at tonight's Carol Service, and I'd forgotten every word of it!

This Advent has been a specially loving one for me, largely dominated by what I see of total longing in your Mary card.[5] Cold or physical pain – in fact, all that is – can only deepen the capacity for Jesus, and so I welcome them, dearest Ann, while being sensible of my weakness. (One has only to look at Him to know what He wants done).

May it be an utterly selfless Christmas.

P.S. This will probably go off before your present arrives, but you know already what joy those little gay parcels give me – and the books … *What* a thoughtful friend you are – my dear mother can't imagine why!!

1   At this time the Carmelite community at Quidenham
    was engaged in re-writing its music for the Divine Office
    and Mass. Sister Wendy had been assisting them and had
    translated a number of texts for their use.
2   Cf. Mt. 26.50.
3   That is to say, those who seem to resist the offered
    friendship.
4   Sister Wendy's handwriting was notoriously difficult to
    decipher. Ann must have asked her to identify a word in
    a previous letter.
5   A picture of the Annunciation.

December 1977

(In haste). Mary will tell you of the true delight I
took in my parcels and the love that they lavished on
me. – But O, my Ann, do you really think I would
urge you to 'insincere relationships'?[1] No, love: any
loving word you write will indeed be resented if your
life does not back it up. I wasn't calling on you for an
easy gesture or two, but for a profound, humiliating
'conversion' to the Crucified Love who starts His
Royal course this week.[2] Until you have dug down
into your heart for the truth of these relationships,
and actively held them out to Jesus to be healed, you
can't give all. We *die* of giving all – and then Jesus is
born. Mary only really bore Him, fully, totally, when
she stood at the cross. Love, I know you are very
weary and under many stresses, so will not let myself
feel grief. I see through all the fear to the deepest
Ann, which so longs to be all His. Do write again
when you are free, poor darling. Yours with infinite
love and gratitude.

1   Ann has misunderstood the remarks about friendship in the previous letter.

2   The 'Royal course' mentioned here makes an indirect allusion to one of the Psalms used in the Christmas liturgy. The Psalm, which in the Hebrew original describes the sun following its course across the sky, was taken up by early Christian exegetes as a symbol of the course of Christ's life from birth to death (see Ps. 19.6).

1978

I haven't got a picture of a recalcitrant donkey, and wouldn't send it if I had![1] This is the true picture[2]: sheep content amid the snow and the incoming dark because, almost invisible materially, the shepherd's presence is their all-embracing reality. And, oh Ann, how profound that Jesus is both shepherd and sheep: 'Lamb, standing as it were slain!'[3] *All* salvation comes from that gentle surrendered victory ... You know this and live it.

Can't find words to express my delight in the cards and flower book and the beautiful backed Klee's.[4] To have the Ghost pictures[5] backed will be a ravishing gift, especially some of the later ones, which are almost overwhelming in their Beauty.

1   Evidently Ann had referred to herself in these terms.
2   *When the West with Evening Glows*, a snow scene by Joseph Farquharson (1846–1935).
3   Rev. 5.6.
4   Sister Wendy was constantly collecting pictures, many of them cut out from journals and similar sources. These would then be pasted onto card for her, hence the reference to 'backed Klee's'.
5   Klee [*see n. 3, 9 September 1976*] painted several studies of 'Ghosts' during the 1920s. The handwriting is unclear at this point but 'Ghost' is the most likely interpretation in the context.

9 March 1978

'Though He slay me, yet will I trust in Him …'[1]
My poor love, everything he does must be lovely to
us, and especially when we do not see it as lovely.
Here is your great opportunity to live out your real
trust, sinking back into the loving, pierced hands
of Jesus and letting Him offer you with Him to
the Father. Not to understand, not to desire, not
to feel resigned or happy or anything but outraged
and somehow betrayed: what scope for love at last
to take over! Please don't think I feel anything but
the deepest compassion for you, but I do know that
much will depend for you on how total your generosity is in responding. I have tried as you know, and
tried in vain, to put into words my anxieties about
the relationship between you two. I don't think it
can be defined – far too many strands that go to its
weaving, far too many minglings of the psychological
and the historical, the good and the bad. But the
main point I had wanted to make, and don't think
succeeded, has always been that my 'opinion' had
nothing at all to do with what I thought of Nora
herself. On her I pass no verdict. My verdict – I
believe the verdict of Jesus – is only on you, it is you
that is somehow being 'damaged' by a lack of love
here. What is love asking of you? I don't know, but
something He is not getting. Remember, my dearest,
that only Jesus sees us as we are. So only when we
are wholly in Jesus, seeing through His eyes, loving
with His heart, judging with His mind, can we see

another truly. (Like a modern historian, for instance, who tries to sum up his own age. He can't; can't see it or distance himself from it, since he is part of the age, modifying and modified.) No person exists for us 'out there'- only 'in here', and if my inner heart fears or repels them, then distortedly. But the Heart of Jesus accepts them wholly as they are ...

If you can base yourself on this, Ann, that only Jesus really 'sees' her, and if you unite yourself to that unseen sight of His and pray Him to make you live by it, seen or unseen, then I can only see grace ahead. I must confess that, though my compassion is very genuine, and though I hoped, in my folly, that this wouldn't happen, I feel it is a far better thing for you. If you could have moved away from her and kept in peace because she wasn't in your orbit now, nothing would have been healed for you, merely hidden. I would give anything for Stella to come back and abandon herself to the encounter. You don't seem to have an option, but if one comes, don't take it. I know for certain that God wants this whole thing worked through, entered into, transformed and not transcended.

I am writing quickly to catch the post, so forgive me if I have put it all clumsily and seemed insensitive to the tremendous shock this has been to you, and the sense you still have of somehow being vanquished. I know it, poor sensitive Ann, but this is where Love waits for you. This is the hour of Jesus: 'knowing that his hour had come and that he went to the Father'[2] ... It's the second clause that is so vital. Show Him that you know, too, that this is all the active work of His Father, not to be endured but to be used and lived into. 'He *went* to the Father': Oh Ann, love, how I am praying for you – and have been since the delay made me suspect that this would be the outcome ...

The card is for Easter,[3] and because I know most surely He has lit something within you, let His flame consume all that is mere Ann, and be only purely Jesus-Ann. He lit His own candle in the Passion.

1 Job 13.15. The circumstances behind this letter are not known. It would seem that Ann had been hurt and felt betrayed in a relationship.
2 Jn 13.1.
3 Probably a picture of a candle.

14 March 1978

Your beautiful, generous letter is pure balm to the aching desire of Jesus. You make it possible for Him to give you to the Father in Himself. What has happened is a paradigm of Love's action, isn't it? Our fears come true, and we hold out our welcoming arms to them, 'because we know the Father!'[1]

I thought that article was a 'hard saying and who can hear it?'[2], so the chorus of mild praise is rather disconcerting.

Pat has had her operation. Only six days in hospital, stitches out two days later at the surgery, and off she prances home. Very intimidating. I feel a gloomy certainty my small op. will leave me without a prance to my name ...

The three great Rembrandts: *Man with a Helmet*, *Jewish Bride*, and [?][3]. I feel one – perhaps *Jewish Bride*? – for the community. Would it be too much to give each novice a postcard of it? How generous you are to me ... My mother can't get over my luck!!

I, too, have an optimistic heart in general, but feel we must base our giving on *darkness*. I surrender, fully aware it may be *worse* than I think, but knowing, if so, that is where Jesus is ... I shall be holding you steadily in Him.

I need to brace my poor soul for Holy Week. Sorry for such a poor letter.

1   1Jn 2.13; cf. Jn 16.3.
2   Cf. Jn 6.60. The article in question had been commissioned by the *Clergy Review* the previous November.
3   Illegible.

Holy Thursday, 1978[1]

Parcel One has just come, with its beauties.[2] (I am *so* grateful – no wonder my mother exclaims in stupefaction over my good fortune in my friends!!) and its sad little note. I understand about the not writing – I know what is in your poor, suffering heart anyhow – but wish you could have a safe outlet to let off the steam of those fears.

Dear, I was careful to qualify my optimism by adding 'in general'. In this case I do not, in fact, feel much optimism, but that is an irrelevance. Jesus felt no optimism at all: 'His chalice'[3] was how He saw it from the first, but having seen that it was indeed His Father's will, He stopped all reflection of His own hopeless misery. He simply held out both hands – pierced hands – and took the chalice with steadfast love. I can't overemphasize how much I think this matters for you, my darling. Not only because we chip away at our own 'Yes' if we let ourselves think of the horror of it all, but also because 'we' can't do it. Only Jesus can do it, and for this He must have our total trust. It all becomes stiff and martyred if we can't smile in our will and believe He is all Love … It could be that, if calamity were to come, it would have been because Ann did not trust His Love. But I *cannot* believe in that – cannot think this will lead to anything but an Easter.

These exquisite, Gozzoli angels[4] see Him; we do not. Yet, as Hebrews says, it is man He has chosen, not angels[5]: poor, filthy man, for whom Jesus pours out His heart in love. Think only of Him, dear Ann, and His Love. Bind yourself to it. Promise Him only loving thoughts: His thoughts. Keep all other insights in reserve until His Love can show you from within what in these is true or false. This is a very costly surrender, but now you must jettison all confidence in your own wisdom and cling, naked, to the Crucified and Risen Jesus. All yours if you want Him ...

(P.S. Mild flu: hope it's legible! A chance to love Him through a bodily haze ...)

1   22 March 1978. This is written on a notecard bearing the text: 'Out of sorrow, joy is born'; clearly a reference both to the contents of the letter and to the liturgical season.
2   Probably the Rembrandt postcards she had asked Ann to buy for her in the previous letter.
3   Lk. 22.42.
4   Benozzo Gozzoli, (1420–97), *Angels Worshipping*. Sister Wendy had included a reproduction of one of the side-panels of Gozzoli's extended altarpiece of the Nativity in the Medici chapel, Florence.
5   Heb. 2. 5–9.

26 May 1978[1]

I am just home and cannot bear not to write, though you won't get this till Tuesday. It was heart-rending to see you go, after the sad delay had worn away your hard-won ease, yet what was lost was only physical and emotional. You stumbled away into the car and onto those lonely miles in a visible cloud of the joy of Jesus. Though I would have given anything to make you well, to send you home early, to refresh and reinvigorate you, I could see so well that this sacrificial ending was a gracious climax to our happiness. Bliss it is to dwell on the mountains, but it is fir-tipped on only the lower slopes: the steep heights are *pure* joy, and that often comes as pain, not the noble pain of great suffering, but the unnecessary small pains, the 'weariness, the fever and the fret', says Keats.[2] My poor weary Ann, my sweet, I know for certain that you sealed His joy upon your sad heart when you wept and went, *believing* in joy. The wild geese on your lovely card[3] fly into mystery, calling aloud for happiness. And their wings are at fullest span, to say: 'Yes! Yes!', and the very movement is a yearning. (Ecstasy of action ...)

I am feeling quite good, love.[4] The pain has died down and I hope to take up my beautiful pattern of life tomorrow. If all goes well, I shall have phoned you before this comes and will know how you are. I entrust you with great love and gratitude to Jesus, who must thank you Himself for your goodness to me.

1   Between this and the previous letter, Sister Wendy had undergone a difficult and painful operation. Ann had taken her to the convent of which she was superior, for a fortnight's convalescence and had then brought her part of the way back. They were met midway by a car from the monastery at Quidenham after what seems to have been an unexpected delay. Full of compassion for Ann after the emotional stress of the long and tiring wait, Sister Wendy took up her pen immediately on arriving back home.
2   John Keats (1795–1821): *Ode to a Nightingale*.

3 *Wild Geese Flying*: a Japanese silkscreen painting from the Edo period.
4 This is almost certainly an overstatement!

31 May 1978

You have never sent me a lovelier card: all urgency, as you say, yet what freedom and space and beauty, (a superb reproduction, too, which is in itself a symbol). The only snag is that my heart is wrenched by your words inside it. However, it is a holy wrench, because I know it is not so much me as 'me' you are missing; it is heaven. For His own mysterious reason, God has made me a test case – in fact, a show case, of His love. Through pure gift, He makes me heaven, in that He is heaven and He is the only reality I have: and when we are together, you feel in your own land. My sweet, you are *always* there – I just make it evident to you. Whatever He did in those weeks,[1] that at least I can see as His prime object: to make His Ann heaven at an even greater depth. And somehow that is bound up with being a lamb: a small defenceless creature that goes meekly and innocently to the slaughter of life.[2] Not any lamb, though: Lamb of God, who bears the weight of the world's sin.[3] Not feeling the joy of Jesus is part, for you, here and now, of that bearing. It makes no difference, as long as you *live* in the joy as the lamb does in the sun and springtime grass. I hope the mountain picture, so strong, so confident, so immediate, bright and exultant, can say to you what my poor stumbling words cannot.[4] You *have* the joy, the mountain, the flowing torrent, because it is Jesus, and he is the centre, not Ann.

I agree about the link, not least because these weeks with you at the convent *truly* made a link that was rather frail before. Not frail in desire, but it could compass so little. Being taken to your heart *within* the convent, within the community too, to some extent had a mystical significance. I see now why it was necessary so to suffer at Mass. The whole thing has been such a grace, love, and June 1st tomorrow has a completely new resonance for me ...

Nice letter from Vera. Will you tell her (when you write) that feeling 'not near Him' is simply the pain of His presence. Whether He comes in joy or pain, we welcome only Him. Will be thinking of you with loving solicitude on the 7th, my weary Ann.

1   While Sister Wendy was convalescing.
2   Cf. Is. 53.7. Sister Wendy often used the endearment 'lamb' when writing to Ann and it became a shared name for her.
3   Jn 1.29.
4   This picture has not survived.

June 1978[1]

Ever since Janet told me your news, I've been held in a vise of prayer, seeking to discern what Jesus wants. He wants *you*, that is all I can see, and if this job is the means that best surrenders you to Him, then I can't but urge you on to the total 'Yes' that is His own. You offered Him a blank-cheque, a gesture of love: He has filled it in and made the gesture 'real'. Dearest lamb, whether you like it or want it doesn't matter, does it? What does Jesus want? Clearly this, because if there were some other way of leading you deeper into joy, He would have chosen it. So that's my first reaction: with an ache in my heart I give you wholly to all that this job means, because this is pure Love and we trust Him. But apart from it being His way of taking possession of you, of becoming ever more your joy, I truly believe He wants something for others, directly. Despite all that has been said, I'm sure you *could* do much in the new house to show what it means to love God. Clearly the Archbishop was only concerned with one essential, a good religious for Principal. Technically Audrey was a far better choice. In fact, humanly speaking, the likelihood of you was, I still feel, 10% !! But *spiritually*, I see well why you were chosen and what the Archbishop hopes. I've every trust, my sweet, that you will be a living presence of Jesus' joy in that arid institution. My one fear, as Janet will have told you on the phone, is that you simply haven't the physical energy. But if a medical examination says you have, then I'd commit yourself to joy with perfect trust.

I don't suppose you want the book back but I send it anyhow. As for the mystics, why not read them for encouragement? Only remember the reality is very different – all they are saying is that He *does* become life to us, it really happens. But how is another matter.

I wish we could speak. I longed to phone, and first said I would. Then I saw that I must sacrifice that so as to be pure victim for you, and let Jesus be word and life for me. How significant the silent pair on my window: monolithic sheep, protectively silent, beside her vulnerable lamb.[2] It speaks to me at great depth as you realized. Sorry, I've still no typewriter, but I send this poor scrawl with deepest love.

P.S. Am ashamed to have said 'victim' when my life is pure joy, but you know what I mean: that it must be all 'given' – and received.

1   This letter responds to the news that Sister Ann had unexpectedly been appointed Principal to one of the colleges run by her Order.
2   A small, ornamental piece sent to her by Ann. For 'window' read 'windowsill'.

June, 1978[1]

Despite uninspired 'art' and verse, I am happy to have this to send on your birthday – both picture and doggerel are absolutely *true*. (Notice the dear lamb!)

You are going to your new community, not for yourself but for others, to be the Lord's joy there, and this is obviously something Jesus can effect. So you go in all poverty of Love, knowing for certain His joy is greater than your grasp and is *poured out*. Deep and tender love.

1   Written on a card that shows a rather insipid-looking Saint Francis of Assisi, seated on a log in a woodland glade, surrounded by small creatures (a rabbit, a lamb, a squirrel etc.). The verse inside reads: 'May your birthday / and the coming year / Be blessed by God above / And may you always know the joy / Of His unfailing love.'

Undated[1]

The breeding grounds, where coming last and falling flat is wholly unimportant. All that matters is to be there, living in Jesus and not in self, living in His joy and so joy to Him.

Don't you think that, when Jesus is the only Reality to us, then everything else at last begins to become real? Because all that happens, everyone we meet, all that surrounds us, all comes from Him as revelation of His Heart. 'You did it unto me.'[2] And since He is pure Love, life is the radiance of that love, and our mission to reveal it to others. He has not made you Lamb for yourself alone.[3] Or, to keep to the duckling image, we are brought to the mountain lake so that we might reveal it to others. I wish I could find the words!

1   This note is written on an undated notecard with a picture on the front of a pair of mallard ducks in a pond with their ducklings. All the ducklings are in the water

except the last, which has fallen over at the edge. The contents of the note interpret this picture with reference to Sister Ann's transfer, now effected.

2   Cf. Mt. 25.1–13.

3   The word 'Lamb' here has a sacrificial resonance.

15 June 1978

My mother's rabbit will shortly greet you, removed by Sister Michael, who came here yesterday.[1] It's not quite what I had in mind, and my mother sends a message: if it's not right (too young??) let me give it to the baby instead, (2 1/2 yr. old Rosie is due for a present anyway) and she will send us money to buy something we really like. So please be quite truthful, love. The whole idea is to give her pleasure and only you can judge of that.

I do so hope you can find a way to have a real holiday. Abroad!! Venice? Florence? A nature rather than an art [holiday] and a peaceful rest in some beautiful place in the country? God has so wonderfully put his Holy Finger on you for Him that I am still held in awe. No, love, I don't see this as the 'leap' – it is rather an event that reveals, by your reaction, that you have already taken the leap and are well under way.[2] Did you notice that this Emperor card,[3] clearly, as you suggest, bringing him nearer the breeding grounds, is not as clearly printed as the other? The lack of clarity is symbolic, I think: as one gets nearer, details *do* blur. Only Jesus and His joy become wholly real ...

My next assignment for the Cistercians is to translate St. Bernard himself,[4] which will demand great skill – his is an involved, highly polished Latin. Have not discussed it with Janet yet or come to any decision, but it *might* be necessary to procure, at last, a really good Medieval Latin dictionary ...??? Might be quite impossible but I do have it vaguely in mind to discuss with you.[5] ...

Have taken courage and used your magic putty.[6] Rembrandt's *Flight into Egypt* is up at present. Oh the mystery: the moonlit darkness of the strange country, and Jesus a warm bright Fire at its heart.

I am still in pain, bleeding occasionally, but I feel very trustful. Every detail of my life – however austere – is just right for its true function. And the little pain accompanies this in lovely harmony.

I was ashamed when Vera was here: I simply could not be wholly 'there' for her. Did she notice? The Lord had me too deep ...

1   The rabbit was a toy intended for a mentally handi-capped woman for whom Ann was responsible. The baby (Rosie) was grandchild to a couple living on the Quidenham estate, who had been immensely kind to Sister Wendy.
2   Sister Wendy is talking spiritually here, alluding to the proofs of Ann's wholehearted gift of herself to God. Ann, it seems, had questioned her about it. The following sentences continue in the same vein.

3   Possibly a picture of an Emperor penguin.
4   Bernard of Clairvaux (1090–1153), founder of the Cistercian Order and one of the most outstanding personalities of the Middle Ages. His written works include the *Treatise on the Love of God* and the *Sermons on the Song of Songs*.
5   In the event, this project did not come off. The previous year had seen Sister Wendy's completion of a massive assignment: the first-ever translation from Latin into English of the seven-volume *Commentary on the Song of Songs* by another medieval Cistercian, John of Ford (d. 1214) [ed. Hilary Costello: *John of Ford on the Song of Songs*; pub. Cistercian publications; Kalamazoo, 1977]. Her original idea had been to contribute to her financial support by undertaking translating work but, apart from the strain it placed on her, she was not happy with the rules then in force governing translation style and she decided not to pursue this further offer held out to her by the publishers.
6   Knowing her own lack of practical skill Sister Wendy could be extremely hesitant about using the labour-saving devices pressed on her by well-meaning friends. In this case the article of her caution seems to have been an inoffensive piece of Blutak.

26 June 1978

… It seems to me the happenings of the last months have carried you far on your journey – you have been given a strength and certainty that is new, and dearest Ann, at last I see you taken into joy, which is the sole desire of the heart of Jesus. You are taken, and kept: believe this, even when all 'evidence' tells you otherwise. *This* is what it means to live in Jesus and to live in faith. The whole world is different, and yet drearily the same. But now we *know*.

11 July 1978

I got this at Christmas[1] and kept it in case I got nothing better to send for your birthday – nor have I. Only a gesture of affection. I know it is pretty useless, but one of the Sisters has pasted the leaves on quite attractively. Janet is getting me a duvet quilt, so I am glad I resisted the temptation to accept your offer. But am very glad I did *not* resist the ewe and her lamb,[2] which lie on my sill and speak so profoundly of Jesus and His relationship to you and me … What tender memories I have now, all summed up in the *Jewish Bride*,[3] which Janet collected today for the community. May Jesus hold you all just so, and may each one let Him and know what she is doing.[4] How fitting that my other picture in hospital should have been Leonardo's *Virgin* – all mystery –[5] and then A's Virgin of [?][6]

1 A greeting card.
2 The ornamental piece mentioned above, *see n.2, June 1978.*
3 The postcard reproductions of Rembrandt's *Jewish Bride* requested in the letter of 14 March.
4 That is, surrender consciously to His holding.
5 Probably Leonardo da Vinci's *Virgin of the Rocks.*
6 Illegible.

21 July 1978

Just to tell you that I am holding you firm in the joy of Jesus throughout these painful weeks. Never mind if you weep, my lamb: His joy is not despite tears but *through* them. We can't even know what true sorrow is until we live in His joy.

I hope Claire has a happy few days with you and enters into the holy country where Jesus has set his Ann. Will you be going again to the Lake District together?

The pain has come back, but I am still hopeful. Anyway, it is not my concern but His.

Did you get my poor little birthday cards? The Piero[1] that came yesterday is a tremendous delight – his still, sure presences are so full of Mystery … You should have written on the Japanese geese – now I shall have to give them away. Am enjoying the Japanese Print book at present: how I love pattern and line – all yearning and yet simultaneously fulfilled. My mother has given me lots of Iris Murdoch, hurrah, hurrah. Have just finished *The Dolphin*, which at first I didn't like but then found deeply moving …

I have no fear for you, dear lamb. Just let Jesus be Love in you for *everyone*.

1   Piero della Francesca, *see n. 7, February 1977*

Undated note

Your letters are a joy to me … I see so clearly how the joy of Jesus, (and it is His joy I mean when I talk of my own), is sinking deeper and deeper into the texture of your being. Let it soak in utterly, dearest – and recognize that *all* that comes to you is the pressure of that joy. I hope that, when these tentative months are over you will find you can delegate much of the committee work and leave yourself free and fresh for the work that only you can do: you, providing the presence and the desire, and Jesus the power. Your cards are sheer delight – I've already used many of the art ones to reveal the Lord's word,[1] but so far have happily not felt called upon to sacrifice the eastern ones. I hold you and *all you write about* in the fire of His Presence and know He will transform it all.

1   That is, by writing a spiritual commentary.

13 September 1978

No wonder you send me a picture of seven beauties[1], doubtless a symbol of the seven gifts of the Spirit – His *real* charisms, as opposed to the bubble-and-squeak variety[2] – and oh, dearest Ann, how wholly they are 'there' for you. Jesus himself has chosen this work, this place, this era, not to lead you *into* the Spirit's joy but to make it present to you. I hold you there constantly. 'Spiritual role' isn't easy to nail down, in fact, being Spirit, it can't be. It depends on a constant total surrender to what He is doing in you. But on a workaday plane, one could say this: for the first weeks you will be finding out exactly what the job *is*. (Note: not what X thinks it is, though she would be hurt to realize that you see it, perhaps, quite differently. She has sacrificed herself on an altar – bitter to discover it was not God's altar but her own.) And as well as distinguishing the true or Jesus-essence of the job, you will have to distinguish how much of this is potential and how much actual. I mean, there are three concentric rings: the inner core of what *must* be done; the outer ring of what *ought* to be done; and the furtherest one of what it would be *good* to do. Clearly one has to 'work' – this is part of being human, let alone holy – but remember what Jesus said about that sacred obligation of the Sabbath, 'made for man, not man for it'[3]. Your personal working pace, your need for rest and relaxation, your interior freedom: all these determine 'how much' you do and how strenuously. Nothing must, or in a way – (knowing you are Lamb) – *can* come between the primary work of revealing Jesus. Whatever your dismay, always cling to the knowledge that this is His great desire, and looking deep into His Heart will keep you flexibly to it. Perhaps to show the Calvinists that hard work demands a loving detachment to keep it human and creative is part of your spiritual role?[4] And also one cannot be wholly free for Jesus if one lives too comfy. All this will take time, but He will give you all the time He needs. Is this any help? Please say if not. Oh, *how* I pray for you, chosen to receive and give to others such pure joy. Also I pray for your suffering friends and hope Catriona is no longer threatening them. What an image of threatened humanity, and only God can make it bearable and fruitful. Keep well!!

1   The picture has not been preserved.
2   The Seventies saw an efflorescence of the Charismatic movement among the Christian churches in Britain. Sister Wendy's humorous characterization refers to some of its more excessive manifestations.
3   Mk 2.27.
4   Not a literal reference to Calvinists but a metaphor for those in Ann's community whom she felt to be imposing an inhuman regime of work on themselves.

22 October 1978

Just business, I'm afraid, love ..... I am so very grateful for your hospitality to my family.[1] While they were here I often recalled that exquisite Martini we saw in Liverpool,[2] with the poignant acknowledgement that Jesus too, (Jesus more than anybody) felt the pain of not being able to 'speak' to His own kin.[3]

As time goes on, you may find that it's not worthwhile enough to write weekly, and alas, get no reply. But until then, might it not be good to make these dear letters a sort of spiritual review of the week, making the writing an act of deliberate prayer, in which you try to isolate what the week has taught you, what needs it has uncovered in yourself and others, what prayer your deepest heart is making, etc.? Only if this *helps*. But it's imperative the flood doesn't cover your head, and this might provide a detachment.

... Yes, Ann lamb, of course I will come if you are dying or even seriously ill, but perhaps the Lord will summon me first? And I think the 'message' for you in Pope John Paul I's death (and his succession by so resolute a man) is that God is all. A vulnerable child or a strong presence: He can set either in the Chair of Peter and ask only for surrender. The weight is His. *Your* weight is His: let Him bear it, and all is well. To know that Jesus is all doesn't mean that the world's needs and pains can be forgotten, lost in Him. It means they achieve their full weight and anguish, but in joy, because Jesus irradiates them with Himself, dearest Ann.

P.S. 23rd Have just had interior injection, hence rather wobbly writing (alas, I suppose, really no worse than normal). Next appointment January 21st, with such reiterated asseverations that there was nothing to worry about that I feel mildly charmed! But I *don't* think it is serious, Ann lamb, just a small pain to bear with gratitude.

1   Sister Wendy's family were currently living in South Africa but had come over to Britain to visit her that summer.
2   *Christ Discovered in the Temple* by Simone Martini (c. 1280–1344), a Sienese painter (see Plate 1). This picture is in the collection of the Walker Gallery, Liverpool.
3   Cf. Lk. 2.50.

22 November 1978

I do hope you're not anxious about my little setback.[1] It's essentially trivial, you know, but causing inconvenience at present. I keep still and wait, looking to the Lord and utterly content. Won't tell you all the gory details, but only because it's not worth it! Don't you think it is significant that this whole pain-stretch of mine should coincide with your traumatic year?

Everything you say makes me more and more sure that *this* is *exactly* how the joy of Jesus, the ecstasy of action, is going to take possession of you. And I know you know this too. Of the three aspects of your present summons, Ann-lamb: efficiency, (as in the big and isolated decision-making), virtue, and loving warmth, it's the third you must hold out most often to Jesus. Under the pressures you endure, especially this first untried year, the first can loom largest, and you can feel the job is most likely this, with a stern grip on virtue. But the machinery, though essential, *has to be* alive with Jesus if it is to do its real work, and not just keep the place functioning, an end in itself. The college is only there to show Him to the world, and first to His own internal world of staff and students. You have a great capacity for warm love, my lamb, but you often don't show it – so your goodness can seem aloof and people aren't encouraged to burst out of their own fears and insecurities and *see* what it means to live surrendered. I don't say this in the least as 'rebuke'. No, I'm very happy about you: I say it as a reminder only.

1   Sister Wendy was still experiencing some unpleasant repercussions from her operation the previous May. In an undated note from about this time, she wrote: '... it's not "my" body. This is something that physical suffering does bring home to one: the glory – fearful glory – of being body and soul, the possession of God. Who suffers? Who rejoices? Is it me? Or Jesus? We are one.'

22 December 1978

Your poor suffering letter has just come, but of course I've been very aware of the weight of loneliness and misery that Jesus has laid upon you. But that's it, isn't it? Jesus lays the weight, and Jesus carries it, *never mind* whether you feel His support or no. You *know*, and you know too that He chose you very deliberately to do this holy work of His and be His joyful presence in the cold north. My heart aches for you, but my deepest heart rejoices. I know that awakening dread, and still find no better way to cope with it than I did as a child, and that is to give my day away in advance to Jesus. His day now, I specifically renounce anything for me in it. Then everything – sunlight, a smile, a hot drink – is sheer bonus, and all the hard things, being His already by gift, are free to receive His imprint. I know too that dreadful sense of not speaking the same language, but am sure this is not 'meant' by Jesus. One of His own names is Word, and if they do not speak my language then, somehow, I *must* speak theirs. This is often easier in one-to-one encounters, so I hope you can manage to meet, in pure love and reverence, the different people on these committees and let Jesus break through the communication barrier. How can they receive His joy from you unless they can become aware of it? O Ann, how I pray for this!

Love, is there nothing consoling *anywhere*?[1]

Your lovely presents have just come – how can I thank you? The two Japanese books look even lovelier than the first instalment, but the four will be my Christmas treat. ALL you send me delights me, my only fear is that you are depriving yourself, which I would grieve to hear. I was cross with myself for so blithely asking for more cards under the new dispensation,[2] but I can assure you I make good use of them. I have both the Botticelli before me – infinitely tender – how human and defenceless He is in the drawing, how radiantly the heart of the great bright world of the painting. As to 'light-on',[3] it may be different for a saint, but for me it means that the great feasts are a bliss so keen as to be almost unbearable. I am always living in the reality of Jesus, and can cope best when exterior life is monotonous and undemanding. But the feasts make the exterior repeat aloud what is happening within (O this is all wrongly put) and I have to 'look' and still keep going. I haven't explained, but my dear Ann-lamb will always forgive me my stumblings.

1   This is a plea. Ann was inclined to focus on the dark side of her difficult situation.

2 It seems that new monetary restrictions had come into force in Sister Ann's community.

3 'Light-on': an expression coined to designate a rare form of the mystical state in which, in Ruth Burrows' words: 'the person sees that she is held in God's embrace; the whole being knows it and responds, surrendering to his love'. And this union 'is not only known with certainty, it is also seen', (*Guidelines for Mystical Prayer*, 2nd edn, Burns & Oates [Continuum], 2007).

1979

22 January 1979

This is a little self-indulgent, but as you have been
at my side in every step of the way, I think I can
send a word of 'alleluia!' now that I am officially and
finally healed. Pat's card is not as lovely as yours, but
very comforting to know that Red China retains her
traditional artistic sensibilities![1] I was so glad to get
your dear brave letter – interested in the cards and
enchanted by the *Courtier with Deer in the Autumn
Sunlight*.[2] How very unlike your life! And yet, that
tranquil freedom must be at the centre of every life
in Jesus. Poor lamb, you haven't felt much of it so
far, but there is a real change in this last letter. You
are more free, more tranquil, more able to look at
Jesus and 'be' without being swamped by circumstances. Physical fatigue must have a part in this,
and getting *au fait* with the sheer newness of it all. I
haven't the least fear that the job will ride you. No,
I can see my Ann-Lamb grasping all it entails, not
within the compass of her own hands, but allowing
the wounded hands of Jesus to do it for and through
her. I'm so glad you have found a friend. I pray you
may find friends, too, on your staff, not so as to 'win'
them, but in the sense of discovering the beauty
that God sees in them and helping them to reveal
it to the world. I think you will need to have a very
living faith in them, love; not based on what you see

(which may so often disconcert) but in what you believe *Jesus* sees. People can only flower when they sense we revere and love them. I pray so often and so earnestly: a prayer that is always heard, being not mine but His.

I've still got the Hokusai and Hiroshige[3] books – such precise and lovely statements of Jesus the visible glory of the Father.

1   Presumably the card in question was of contemporary Chinese origin.
2   A classical Chinese painting. Unfortunately the postcard reproduction of this image has not survived.
3   Hokusai (1760–1849) and Hiroshige (1797–1858) were famous Japanese artists and print-makers, Masters of the ukiyo-e ('pictures of the floating world') school.

27 February 1979

(Have just read in Kierkegaard: 'the model is called a lamb – that alone is a scandal to the natural man, no one has any desire to be a lamb'[1] but my Ann is gradually experiencing the full quality of what Jesus means, and *does*, in her secret depths, truly desire it.) . . .

Janet asked me to give her some ideas for a nightly conference on the gospel reading of the next day during Lent. What I've done is poor, but I thought you might find something here to use. Haven't done further than Week 2 yet. I find this sort of thing very draining – who can look deep into the Word and not be swept away? Not me!

I know exactly what you mean about the political atmosphere being bad for your suspiciousness! But how can Jesus cleanse you unless you have the opportunity to fight your way from suspicion to a wise awareness? Knowing 'the motives' isn't suspicion: He knows 'what is in man'[2], and feels only love and compassion. I think the key is reverence: 'seeing', (or thinking we see) – can never be more than partial, since only He can *evaluate* the motive, existentially. We must see and love and lose none of our sense of the other's mystery and beauty. Do you know what I mean, dearest? I am sorry about the disappointment in Miss Samson: use it to open your eyes, in love, to expectations others may have of *you*. Anyway, I love you!! And am humbled by your goodness to me.

1   Søren Kierkegaard: *Journals and Papers*.
2   Jn 2.24–25.

11 May 1979

You are often in my mind these days. One can be so tempted – or rather, one can instinctively, without even seeing any temptation, 'cope', exert all one's energies and impose one's will. Yet the *real* work can only be done in Jesus, and all the rest is what Paul would call 'flesh', if the Spirit of Jesus is not expressed in it[1]. But how this tortures our pride and our constant need to feel on top of a situation, never mind how! So I pray very earnestly that you *are* on top, but only in Jesus, so that all that is achieved is a living achievement, not a structure that will one day be discarded. He has set you over the school to be His living joy to it, and so He will make it possible.

However, I am really writing to tell you I am having another bad bout of pain and bleeding.[2] It will pass eventually but, although trivial, I feel I owe it to my kind and loving Ann to tell her. I take a little of the brandy after Mass in my drink and find it such a help – all thanks to you. I also wanted to tell you of recent art acquisitions. Pam[3] gave me the Skira/Macmillan *Chinese Painting* and *Persian Painting*[4], plus a half-price paperback of Persian Royal Manuscripts. These are all exquisite … Then I am getting *Portrait Painting* – it's a new Phaidon series – and *Giotto* in the Time/Life series. Show you when you come, dear Ann. Meanwhile I am delighting in your latest gifts. Eastern art seems inherently 'sacred'. Dear Canaletto is a refreshment, with his spaces and elegances, but even the least Chinese sketch has infinitely more contemplative depth to it. Pam gave me this for you[5]: charming, wistful and degagé maiden in a timeless setting. That is where the real 'you' lives: unprotected and beautiful. Reveal her to all, as this girl so sweetly does!

Our letters will probably cross, but never mind. You are ending the year far happier than when you began, aren't you?

1   Cf. Rom. 8.1–13.
2   Sr Wendy still had not fully recovered from her operation the previous year; *see n. 1; 26 May 1978.*
3   The 'Pam' mentioned in the letters refers to Sister Wendy's blood sister.
4   Cahill, James: *Chinese painting* and Gray, Basil: *Persian Painting*, both Macmillan, 1977.
5   She enclosed a postcard of a Japanese design from the Edo period.

2 July 1979

Your last but one letter said you would be making your retreat at the beginning of July, so I hope this comes opportunely. I shall be praying earnestly that these days alone with Love will draw you very deeply into Him. The last thing, dearest Ann, that I would want would be for the time to pass in self-examination or reproach, but when one can tranquilly hold out to Jesus our real wounds – sometimes quite different from what we think are wounds – then He can heal us.

First, impatience – not in itself, poor overburdened lamb, but for what lies behind it. Impatience means: '*I* am superior, it is *my* convenience that counts, my servants must do *my* will.' Of course there has to be efficiency and a chain of command, but always as a 'fellow-servant'. This is how God's world is – crammed to bursting with frustrations and checks: Jesus held it to His heart and let it kill Him. If we think of other people as ipso facto greater than ourselves, and we their happy servants, then we can help them to overcome the shame of inefficiency.

The other thing is rather the same. You are at home *most* with the students. Might not this be because, hierarchical woman that you are, your 'place' with them is quite definite? Not that you are only at ease when the other is below you, no, I think you are happy with those above, too, but what about those on a level? Time was when the principal stood alone on the top tier, with staff and students beneath, but today's staff don't function like that. And it's the equals, or at least those who don't feel securely 'placed' in our regard, who can threaten, who have to be met, not in a role that we can play graciously, but in our bare selves. I feel strongly that one of the great ways you are called to be the joy of Jesus in the school is in this loving, accepting relationship with the staff. And Jesus cannot wholly get at you until this terrible effort is made, my dear lamb. The cards are meant to say this, too: Hubert on his knees, off his horse, and worshipping the Lord in this stag.[1] He has to *look* for Jesus, to hunt Him, and even an animal reveals Him ... Kneel before all your sisters like he does, love, with defenceless hands and sword sheathed. The other picture says that this exquisite black-and-white clarity belongs to art, not to life.[2] We can never see like this. And if we are ever tempted to think we do, we must will not to believe our judgements. Other people are mysteries and we must enter into their cloud, not hope, or presume, to drag them into pitiless brightness. Not until we are wholly lost in ecstasy of action, and even then, the vision may be too overwhelming to take clear back to the world with us.

1   There are many representations of Saint Hubert but it is not known which one Sister Wendy is referring to here. The most famous is probably that of Jan van Brueghel. According to legend, Hubert, a courtier at the court of King Pepin of France, was out hunting when he saw a vision of a crucifix, suspended between the horns of a stag.
2   The second picture has not survived.

July 1979

I deliberately send this [birthday card][1] because – don't laugh! – *because* this little Mary is not 'spiritual', not 'The Blessed Virgin' and not pretending to be. A sweet, lovely, rather dim girl, whose beauty Fillippo Lippi loves to celebrate. And in *not* being spiritual, in just being ordinary beauty, it *does* reveal the Lord. He is in all that surrounds us, the pretty face as well as the bare and jagged mountain background. 'Take me as I come', says Jesus. For my dearest Ann, holding her up just as she is to Jesus, with deep love and gratitude for so much.

1   A detail from Filippo Lippi: *Madonna with the Child and Two Angels*, 1465.

10 September 1979

Can you bear my writing for the sake of the card?[1] Two little wrens delighting in the Lord of the honeysuckle. Not as joyous and free as the Japanese paintings, but the same message. It made me very happy to see you and happier still to see in you that Jesus is preparing His bride. The King's treasures are poured richly out when hands are humble enough to receive and share them.[2] You don't need me to say how earnestly I'll be holding you up to Him this crucial year. Humble love, which is what relationship really means, can't be learnt except in the sweat of actuality. Your sweet, generous resolve to let Him serve the College and the world through you *can't* but bear fruit, love. But the depths and delicacies of His love, which is joy – or rapture of action – are infinite, and I hope much life is left you to plunge ever deeper into the total surrender of Jesus ... I hold you in the Lord's love, dearest Ann, and ask Him to irradiate you with His joy.

1   Sister Wendy's handwriting was notoriously difficult to read. At this period she usually tried to type her letters but was anxious not to spoil the picture on the card here by putting it through the typewriter.
2   Cf. Mt. 2.11; Ps. 72.10–11.

27 September 1979

Aren't the National Trust prints lovely?[1] Poor lamb, their clarity, harmony and certainty must seem the very qualities absent from your confused and hasty world. But, dearest, it is only so *outwardly*. The real you, hidden in Jesus at a depth and in a close embrace that you cannot either see or touch or even know (but through faith), is absolutely sure and tranquil, like these lovely landscapes. You *do* know, even though your 'mind' doesn't. We can't even imprison in words what it is that you know – all words are too weak and wavery – but that Jesus supremely is and that you want to be all His and fulfill for Him the work that burnt up your Foundress' heart with its urgency, this He has made the bedrock of your existence.

I can well imagine that the second year, uncheered by the excitement of all beginnings and with no possibility of pleasant surprises, must be even harder than the first, (especially for a romantic!). Your letter touched me, and how deeply it must touch the Lord. You are just where He chooses, dear Ann, and neither you nor I would wish you otherwhere ... Very glad you are chewing the cud of *Hidden Face*.[2] Thinking at depth about these mysteries is the greatest part of 'our part' in prayer. I mean, as preparation for prayer, so that we have open eyes to see Him when He appears. Most of Küng's *On Being a Christian*,[3] from 'B' on, is good, too, though wordy. At present, my after-Lauds[4] book is the *Chinese Watercolours*[5] – fine text and enchanting pictures ... I hold you up before Him with confident love.

1   This picture no longer survives.
2   Göres, Ida, *The Hidden Face*, Burns & Oates, 1959; a study of Saint Thérèse of Lisieux.
3   Küng, Hans, *On Being a Christian*, Collins, 1977.

4   At this period, Sister Wendy used to go to the monastery guest chapel in order to join the Carmelite Sisters for the Morning Office of Lauds.

5   Hejzlar, Josef, *Chinese Watercolours*, Cathay press, 1978.

October 1979

Not great art, but 4 magical little pictures[1]: the 4 elements that make up our world. *Our* world is Jesus – and the 4 elements are:

His earth: His unshakeable trust in His Father, the most 'fundamental' trait of Jesus, this.

His air: the limitless freedom of being a Son: open to all God's breathings through the Spirit.

His fire: all-consuming and light-giving Love.

His water: utter surrender, taking no shape, having no movement, except in *response* to the Spirit …

Notice that earth is the element on which all others depend …

Jesus *is* our world – we don't have to create Him so – He was given to us by the Father so that we too might be His universe of joy. (Worth taking a week at a time to contemplate what each element means … to open our hearts to receive Him thus …)

1   These pictures no longer survive.

20 November 1979

Books arrived today; spiritual manna. But the Mary card [arrived] on the Day, urging me to earnest prayer. Special intentions ... for you to enter fully into the truth of your life, (truth as opposed to *fact*). Like this enchanted Palmer landscape[1], God sees the desert of our inadequacy as blossoming, if He calls us into it. Probably it was a rather bungled Flight: they didn't know the way and they left their possessions behind. But all He wanted was for them to *be* there: He did the rest. Fiat.

Note Mary and Joseph are apparently falling off the slope but are blissfully unaware!

1   Samuel Palmer, *The Rest on the Flight to Egypt.*

Christmas, 1979

You are so much in my heart throughout this toilsome second year, without even the refreshment of novelty, but not a weight on my heart – I know you are truly trying to receive Jesus in His pure fullness and let Him shine out in what seems drudgery and unsuccess. Maybe He has arranged everything about you so that you can give Him the pure love He has craved for so long. The basic is trust, love. Trust isn't the cherry on the top, it's the whole cake! We don't love Him without it, because that means that we do not know Him. From the knowledge of what God is, trust flowers of its own accord. Dear Ann, when we say: 'I can't do it, I can't live up to it – what is the "it" ?' The 'it' of our lives is to let Him love us and love others through us. That involves full attention on all the day's activities, but in themselves they don't matter. He could get all these ends fulfilled in other ways. But the receiving of His joy, the statement in a life of surrender of what Jesus is: only each individual can do that. The Order was meant by God to do nothing else – certainly your Foundress did only that, proclaiming His goodness in her being, unable not to press on all she met the sheer beauty of God, just in being herself. Your vocation, love: and it means you can't afford to have anything but Jesus. Any willed wanting of other things limits your capacity for Him – but the unwilled, that is a sign of one's failure and poverty, the sharp pain of which drives us to Him as nothing else. To me contrition and shame are the surest signs of His presence. They set us free if we use them. What precious gifts He gives my Ann, at Christmas and all the year round!

It might seem bathetic to move on to my gratitude for your gifts to me, but it isn't! They are essentially spiritual, aren't they, Ann? An expression of the generosity and tender thoughtfulness you want to lavish on your Lord and strive to lavish on Him in your sisters ... And I do pray with all my heart that He is repaying your goodness to me by taking you ever deeper into His joy in the ecstasy of action. Happy Christmas.

Christmas card 1979

This seems to me a most beautiful image of the meaning of Christmas[1]: tenderness, peace and security, (all lit by the mysterious glow of the moon). Jesus, Lamb of God, comes down to enter our sheepfold – lamb of sacrifice – and in His entering He makes all our sacrifice sacrificial, redemptive, pure as His own. We no longer stumble through life as beasts, we *live*, as lambs in Him. And as well as Lamb, He is Shepherd, enclosing us in the sweet warmth of the Father's Home, which is not only 'in heaven' but *here* because of Jesus ...

1   Samuel Palmer: Christmas, or *Folding the Last Sheep*, (etching).

1980

23 January 1980

Mostly from my sister – had more but gave them away with unedifying anguish.[1] *Please* use as you like, but any you send to me I *can't* give away, so am not being generous.

All the robins I know are loners out of timidity or else aggression – often both at different seasons.[2] The human heart must make sure that its loneliness (like every other suffering) comes not from God but from its own fear of rejection of others. You are hard-pressed, dearest Ann. Never mind, that pressure is meant to supple your soul for Love. Set your heart before the world as crumbs for their eating, and delight in the birds that come! *Lovely* waterbird stamps and crosswords.[3] (Am now well supplied.) Am rich in all ways, and in your affection.

1   A reference to some picture cards.
2   Her note is written on a piece of card with a cutout of a robin stuck onto it.
3   New editions of postage stamps often give rise to comment in her letters. Sister Wendy enjoyed receiving new stamps with attractive designs.

9 February 1980

... Books for spiritual reading: am myself rereading John Marsh *St. John* (Penguin), which never fails to shed light on Jesus.[1] There is some good stuff hidden away in Hans Küng's *On Being a Christian*,[2] but one has to read selectively to escape the bitterness and the futile bits, relatively speaking. But there are insights all the same. (His blanket condemnation is a tragic mistake – this poor, over-certain Pope needs much prayer not to become hardened away from the Spirit ...) Janet sometimes speaks of a good book she is reading, but by the time she has finished she usually forgets I am interested and so I can't give direct recommendations. Would you like me to ask her, though? De Caussade is *fine*,[3] but I think you should always make the interior book a sandwich between objective and loving studies of Jesus: if I'm clear?? But equally feeding for the soul are people like Patrick White[4] – try *Voss*, and the profound *Riders in the Chariot* – or Doris Lessing's[5] *Memoirs of a Survivor*, *Golden Notebook*, *Summer before the Dark* – or Murdoch,[6] say *Henry and Cato*, *Fairly Honourable Defeat*, *Bruno's Dream*. In a zany, poetic way, much wisdom in Saul Bellow's[7] *Henderson the Rainmaker*, *Humboldt's Gift*. All these people are earnestly concerned with serious spiritual issues, but one may have to labour more to focus them truly than with the more overtly spiritual authors. Any help?

Never say, love, that your life has become 'secular'. There *is* no secular: doesn't Jesus make that painfully clear? No compartments. 'My meat is to do the will of Him who sent me.'[8] We would probably say: my bread-and butter, my ordinary living sustenance. And He saved souls by commonplace *physical* means, by catches of slithery fish, by changing water into wine, by healing bodies, with all their smell and dirt. Your work, administrative and technical as most of it is, is *radiant* with spirituality, if you only believe. Dear lamb, nothing I say that you don't *know* – but as you comment, belief is another matter. If we choose to believe, we can ignore all the feelings and failures and fatigues, and simply cleave through thick and thin to Jesus. I sometimes marvel at your patience with me – it could sound so glib – yet I believe with all my heart that the one thing necessary is always *there*. You *have* the joy of Jesus – and what else could ever matter? And I know that you do truly want and try to share it with others.

I hope the short break at the Convent has rested you for your struggles with the Cardinal.[9] What often comes to my mind here is: 'You would have no power over me if it had not been given you from above.'[10] Jesus did His utmost to evade capture and their condemnation but *essentially* He knew it didn't matter! No human authority can thwart God, though they may change the outward forms of His will. And equally, your sacred responsibility for the Community is derivative – you yourself do not bear the real weight. Let Jesus bear it then, the Holy Lamb, and be free and peaceful in your strivings. But you can't *feel* this, I'm sure. Never mind: all the more gift to God, dearest Ann.

1 Marsh, John, *Saint John*, Pelican 1968.
2 Küng, Hans, *On Being a Christian*, Collins 1977.
3 Jean-Pierre de Caussade, *see n. 3, 30/12/75.*
4 Patrick White (1912–90), Australian novelist and playwright.
5 Doris Lessing (b. 1919), Zimbabwean-British novelist, poet and playwright.
6 Iris Murdoch (1919–99), Irish-born author and philosopher.
7 Saul Bellow (1915–2005), Canadian-born, American author.
8 Jn 4.34.
9 Cardinal Basil Hume, the Archbishop of Westminster. There was some difference of opinion between them regarding the future of the Order's school.
10 Jn 19.11.

26 February 1980

What lovely things you give me – and the loveliest is the assurance that you are striving with all your heart to receive and to *be* the joy of Jesus, above all now as Holy Week approaches, and your own difficulties throng painfully dense. It sounded to me, though, that last week's encounters were more encouraging than you had feared? ...

Am keeping that enchanting book for Easter: *very* thrilled to receive it *and* on the day of the Great Yes, as you say.[1] I hope you like this happy, sturdy little Jesus, with His unromantic, Hausfrau Mother and the two ugly little angels defying gravity in their joy.

May you, too, stand on your head, suspended in the clear air of Love, aware only of Jesus. How free His Love made Him. Even death became another way of loving. Till Paschaltide.

1 This may be a reference to one of Sister Wendy's anniversaries, of which two fell in February.

15 March 1980

Have just received your note, and books, to which I eagerly look forward, and am now writing in haste to catch the post. I really only want to say that I am enfolding you in Jesus, wrapping you round tight in His strength and sweetness, protected against all evil that is in our own hearts and those of all people. You are a brave woman, my lamb, and I feel proud of your courage. Perhaps it was for this, and the clear-sightedness of a newcomer on the inbred Scottish scene, that the Lord chose you. The only danger would be if the effort to dig in and hold firm in any way harden your heart. This seems to me precisely the difference between natural courage and the fortitude of Jesus. In Him we are both bold and gentle, firm in opinion and humble in discussion, adamant for the truth and always searching for deeper insight. The other may be wholly or partly innocent in seeing it all differently: embrace them (in spirit!) and leave the judgement to Him ... Of course, love, the very drama makes your situation less radiant, in a way, than the normal, humdrum fidelity.

Yet I know how much it all costs you. He can pay the cost only *because* of the humdrum fidelity in you. So I feel only praise and intercession for my Ann-lamb, praise at what He has done in her, intercession that He will do it more, and more in love (as you long yourself).

Undated[1]

The suffering of a wholly surrendered heart: Mary is quite unaware that she resembles the Crucified and that she redeems the world in this love of hers. Everyone in this group is in anguish, touching bottom, yet what strength and peace: because none is thinking of self, each is believing in will …

1   This short note is written on the back of a detail from a painting of the *Crucifixion* by Fra Angelico. The detail shows the Virgin Mary at the foot of the Cross, supported on either side by Saint John the Evangelist and one of the Holy Women, so that she seems to fall back against them in the form of a cross. Saint Mary Magdalen, seen from the back, is embracing the Blessed Virgin with both arms around her waist. Sister Wendy's commentary on this scene is meant to be read with reference to Ann's current, difficult situation.

22 April 1980

No wonder you succumbed in London, the tensions and pressures are great.[1] But they are pressing and bending you into the joy of Jesus, that radiant and gentle form that alone reveals Him to men. I am only sorry that your stay there was short and, in another way, also a pressure. Lovely cards: lovely prospects of more. How can I thank you adequately? ... As for your present situation, you are called above all to be true to the compassionate love of Jesus. As long as you see deviousness, obstinacy and blindness as *wounds*, to be recognized and guarded against but only in the love of a fellow-sufferer, then all will be well. Had meant to make this point more explicitly but concluded it wasn't 'necessary'.

Yes, love, keep *God and His Image*[2] until Janet asks for it back. You also asked what manuscripts you hadn't given me: only three – Celtic and Anglo-Saxon; Late Antique and Early Christian; Hebrew ...[3] All these for years to come; 1980 is bumper already! ...

Look after yourself, my love. Let *Jesus* determine when the lamb is to be slain!

1   Ann had sought out some relaxation by visiting a museum.
2   Barthélemy, Dominique: *God and His Image*; Geoffrey Chapman, 1966.
3   A series of British Museum publications on early manuscripts.

21 May 1980[1]

The 'tears' of the job (metaphorical I hope!) are already dissolving into 'life-giving rain': life-giving for others and for you, because the Life who is Jesus can only come to us through the actuality of our own life. And all in that life is chosen by Him – or used by Him – to communicate Himself. However, this is really only a note to … thank you, dear generous Ann, for so much – cards, stamps, Love in itself and in its manifestations. *Very* grateful for Vermeer,[2] though I am afraid my talk, noteless alas, wasn't really quite on their wavelength. I was essentially trying to show that Vermeer – like Cézanne,[3] Piero,[4] Rembrandt[5] – was a mystical painter (the very opposite of poor melodramatic El Greco)[6] and his special grace was to appreciate and make visible what Light is. All light touches is shown at once as beautiful – and only in the Light can we see this beauty, which is sharing truth, irrespective of qualities. Will expound when next we meet if you like!! …

May your Pentecost be profoundly receptive, dear Lamb. I think St. John's account of it is more true to experience. 'He breathed on them.' Said: 'Receive the Holy Spirit.'[7] But St. Luke's externalizing does make His will clear: overwhelming power; words that are not ours; Love that burns.[8]

1   Written on a green-coloured card bearing the text: 'I long for your tears to dissolve into life-giving rain'.
2   In a short note written previously Sister Wendy had enquired whether the National Gallery of Scotland could supply her with a large-sized print of *Christ in the House of Martha and Mary*, an early painting by Vermeer in its possession. She had been invited to give a talk to

the Carmelite novices at Quidenham and intended to base her remarks on this picture. It seems that Ann had responded by having the print sent her as a gift.

3 Paul Cézanne (1839–1906), Post-Impressionist painter whose technique effected the transition between Impressionism and Cubism.

4 Piero della Francesca, (*see n. 8, February 1977*).

5 Rembrandt van Rijn, (*see n. 7, February 1977*).

6 'El Greco': the appellation given to the Greek painter, sculptor and architect, Doménikos Theotokópoulos, who became a foremost artist of the Spanish Renaissance. Although often referred to as a 'mystical painter', Sister Wendy found his exaggerated, Mannerist style too melodramatic to meet her criteria of the spiritual in art. However, she would subsequently grow in appreciation of his work.

6 June 1980

No, love, I couldn't possibly write out how I see these great mysteries of faith, and still less in the compass of a letter![1] But the essential answer would be that the truth can *never* impede or stifle us – it can only lead us into the full flowering of our human potential, which at its deepest is the potential for God. So anything the Church teaches that seems inhibiting: [either] I am not understanding what is taught or the Church herself has still not fathomed the inner mystery of what she is teaching. We have to say always: what truth of God is this dogma trying to enshrine? That we are a family of whom God is the utterly faithful Father (infallibility); that Jesus, the revelation to us of God, is total Life (resurrection); that Jesus is the unique and mysterious gift of the hidden God (virgin birth), etc. I see that I have already used 'mysterious' three times, and that is fitting: the faith is not at all a matter of bowing down – even if we want to, – to 'Authority', still less of 'assenting with all our heart to what we know not to be true!' It is accepting that we are made to see and love God, not just on our own (though this is profoundly personal and individual), but serving and being served by others. '*Our* Father!' says Jesus. If she believes this, she can search fearlessly. The card of the word 'alpargates' that is on the way is for her,[2] the leaves for V., and the peaceful silence that comprises and indwells multiplicity, for my dear Ann-Lamb.

If you intend to come in the summer, better let me know quickly as the Guest House is fast filling up its bookings. Thank you for reviews, though almost nothing appealing – just as well! ... Have just spent almost my last penny on the big paperback life of Robert Kennedy; very well worth it. We share a fascination, in the abstract, of politics!

O the lovely cards – my dearest up to now is the Japanese nude, so pure and tranquil, but all are lovely.

1 Ann had asked Sister Wendy's help in explaining certain points of Catholic faith to an enquirer.
2 'Alpargatas', a Spanish word still used today to refer to the rope sandals prescribed by Saint Teresa of Avila for Discalced [i.e. unshod] Carmelite nuns. The card in question here used the shape of one of these sandals as part of its design.

1. Christ Discovered in the Temple, Simone Martini
(1284–1344)

2. The Polish Rider, c. 1655, Rembrandt Harmensz (1606–69)

3. The Lacemaker, 1669–70, Jan Vermeer (1632–75)

4. The Sleeping Shepherd, 1834, Samuel Palmer (1805–81)

5. The Egyptian Curtain, 1948, Henri Matisse
(1869–1954)

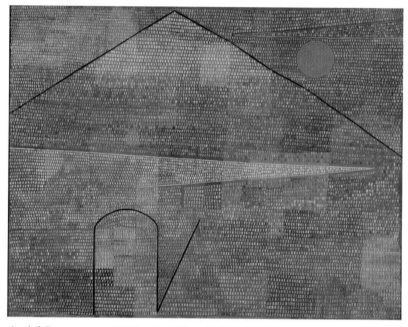

6. Ad Parnassum, 1932, Paul Klee (1879–1940)

7. The Figure 5 in Gold, 1928, Charles Demuth
(1883–1935)

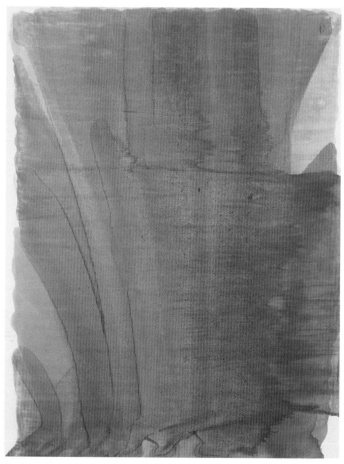

8. Breaking Hue, 1954, Morris Louis (1912–1962)

24 June 1980

I wrote last week but am writing again because of the
offer. In the abstract, to teach in the catechism course
has always seemed to me the ideal use of what God
has blessed you with – and the course itself would
benefit so much. But I'm not sure how you would
feel about 'exile' and 'aloneness', the living out in
actuality of our human condition. We need to talk
about all this. However, can you let it go till later?
Will there be a place in the course if you wait? …
An MA as a necessary step to a definite job is quite
different from just vague 'higher studies' …

The card says of all this: 'Ask and you will receive',[1]
but the hands are surrendering rather than asking, or
better: what we ask is to surrender, what we receive
we desire to be purely Him, and we trust Him to
make us His Possession in whatever way He chooses
…

Oh Ann, what a sacred year this has been for you,
exposing you to the full force of His holy Love! Will
you let me know when exactly you go to Japan, etc.?

Will be writing soon for your birthday.

What lovely cards and cuttings (Georgia O'Keefe)[2]
and quotations you've sent. I very much like that
definition of prayer from the National Geographic
article.

1   This card no longer survives.
2   Georgia O'Keefe (1887–1986), American Modernist painter.

1 July 1980

One of the novices produced this meditation on Elijah – from the Carmelite angle but it is all deeply applicable for you, and I wondered if it would be of any use for your retreat?[1] The Elijah stories fall naturally into separate episodes, and might make a useful framework for your prayer?? But this is purely your decision, love. Anyhow, I enclose a picture of the prophet – both wayfarer, with his staff, and man-at-rest, in his cave: bearing the light of God on his brow, but for *others*, content himself to look longingly into the distance, and await God's revealing … ready to move off at a summons, or to stay, (notice he has brought his cushion with him, very sensible, in case it's life for ever in the cave); and see how the rock and outer cloak and inner cloak enclose him … ('put ye on the Lord Christ' …[2]). Meanwhile I pray with all my heart that these days are still and restful for you – much as the weary Elijah rests here, tranquilly renewing his energies for the work of God, and in the resting, surrendering his soul and all his own plans in love. I shall be sending you a card for your birthday … and praying specially too for you on the 14th, when ten years ago you welcomed me into the antechamber, as it turned out, of heaven.[3]

… To face our mortality means to recognize reality, doesn't it, and all truth is Jesus. Whatever it feels like, there's no other happiness.

1   The Old Testament prophet, Elijah, was considered to be the paradigm of the hermit in the early days of Christian monasticism. This was a tradition that the first Carmelites, founded in about 1206 during the period of the Fourth Crusade, made particularly their own, even going so far as to canonize him as their 'Founder'. The Elijah cycle forms a distinct unit of stories in the biblical narrative. (*See* 1Kings 17–2Kings 2).
2   Rom. 13.14.
3   The 'antechamber' refers to Sister Wendy's first attempt to embrace a contemplative form of life when, in July 1970, she left her teaching Order in South Africa to try her vocation as a Carmelite nun in England. Ann had welcomed and supported her at that time and, when the experiment failed, accompanied her along the way that led to her living as a solitary at Quidenham – here, by implication,'Heaven' itself.

8 July 1980

I have just been reading a little life of de la Salle,[1] written for boys and repulsively illustrated, but I found it moving. A wealthy and aristocratic young canon, without the least interest in schools or the lower classes, and clearly with a natural distaste for power and control that made the role of founder and general supremely unappealing – he wasn't even drawn to the religious life: yet step by step, through coincidence and chance, he found himself involved. At each step he was faced with a choice, and the answer 'No' would have impeded the work of God, not gravely, but, at the moment at least, unmistakeably. His great natural quality was prudence – and his great spiritual gift was a wholly committed faith. Never once did he apparently feel enthusiastic for his vocation, and never once did he shirk its full demands, and the effect was that an idealistic, devout youth was unselfed into a true saint who revealed Jesus wherever he went. You are of course specially in my mind at the present as our tiny jubilee draws near and your birthday feast[2] – and the parallels struck me very forcibly. You are in some ways not unlike John-Baptist de la Salle, not least in that everything in your actual here-and-now seems to me God's delicate fashion of unselfing you and leading you where you would not have gone 'on your own',[3] even your most spiritual and consoling 'own'! And a profound understanding of what Jesus is, and that He has deliberately chosen you, through seemingly ordinary means, is the answer: total faith which irradiates you and 'gives light to all in the house'[4] – and who knows the size of that house?

1   Jean-Baptiste de la Salle (1651–1719), priest and founder of the Institute of the Brothers of the Christian Schools, popularly known as the De la Salle Brothers, a teaching Order. He proved to be an innovative reformer in the field of education.
2   *See n. 3 above.*
3   Cf. Jn 21.18.
4   Mt. 5.15; Lk. 11.36.

10 September 1980[1]

Soon – perhaps already – Vera will be in the land where Klee's bright enchantments are reality, and where ignorant youths and clumsy bureaucrats drink deep of Love and Light.[2] The true home of our hearts is God's mystery: I know you live there already, whatever you may feel. So much love and gratitude always.

1   Sister Wendy appears to have thought she was writing this message on the back of a reproduction from Klee. A postscript expresses her reaction when she turned the card over: 'Charming Japanese card, but ah – the Klee!!' In fact, she was mistaken once again: the picture on the card was taken from a photograph of a lake near Quidenham.
2   Vera was Sister Wendy's cousin. Her death had been anticipated for some time.

1 October 1980

I am quite ravished by the Klee, and interested by the challenging Pre-Raphaelites,[1] (whom I have dismissed too scornfully in the past – et tu quoque!) ...

Dearest, the point of suffering, which includes (perhaps inevitably) feelings of faithlessness, is that it comes to us as something brutal and meaningless. If we could 'see' that it is redemptive, there would always be a part that was *not* suffering. Jesus didn't 'see' and that *was* the suffering. But oh, dearest, how beautiful the trust, the complete surrender to the Father that cried out in the suffering of Jesus. It is real trust, a living surrender, such as is only affirmable through suffering. It means so little to accept the weight of all we do because of Jesus, when we can see for ourselves that all is well, etc. You give Him the sweetest wine of love when you accept that Jesus takes your life into His and redeems mankind through it ...

1   The Pre-Raphaelite Brotherhood presented itself as a Reform movement in British art and literature of the late Victorian era. Its members made a conscious effort to restore something of the style and technique of the Italian Quattrocento (that is to say 'pre-Raphael') to contemporary painting. The reference here arises from a gift of books from Sister Ann to Sister Wendy.

7 October 1980

I have had this ready for 'the Day' when Vera's long struggle ended in the triumph of Jesus.[1] 'Day of Joyous Encounter' indeed – because that's what the descent was surely, His coming down into the agony of our death to take us up to the Father with Him. First Jesus had to go down into the pit of His own, lonely death, the only true death ever died, because we have Jesus saving us in and through our deaths, and so, for us, 'death' means Life, means Jesus. Your constant thought of it over the years is meant to be a great source of hope: it tells you this life isn't your *patria*, that Jesus is, if you choose to 'follow Him'.[2]

So very happy that you are now seeing what is asserted in *Before the Living God*.[3] To accept trustingly to have no virtue, no life even, that is one's own, and equally profoundly to yearn after Jesus unfeelingly in the bits and pieces of daily life: that is ultimate surrender, and Janet is the only one I've ever known who makes it. And my dearest Ann moves steadily towards it – a shattering joy to me ...

1   Sister Wendy had been informed beforehand that her cousin was dying. *See n. 2, 10 September above.*
2   Cf. Mk 6.1.
3   *See n. 1, 10 June 1976.*

28 October 1980

... The sort of devoted love, that unhesitatingly puts the other first always, is rare – yet isn't that the very love Jesus so supremely enfolds us within? All loving friends – as you are to me – are lovely images of that overwhelming Reality ... Life is too rich to be fully used, only Jesus made everything 'work' on Him as the Father intended, but it becomes progressively His revelation as we turn away from self and surrender to Jesus as He comes to us. How feebly I put all this. I feel ashamed ...

I'm perfectly content with what you've given me. A bumper year for art books – and somehow, mysteriously, a bumper year for you. How sweetly and powerfully He supples your stiff fearful heart and widens it out to receive all mankind. Dearest Ann, to see what Jesus does in you is the profoundest joy for me. Always many things I'd love to say, but they must be sacrificed. Won't we 'share' radiantly in heaven …

11 November 1980

I was so pleased to get your letter today. This is a precious gift He has given me, and it matters so much that all of us should be one in the 'Suscipe Pater' of Jesus.[1] Whatever the eventual outcome, it can only be love, a fresh and deeper way of receiving His joy … It is always springing up from the wounded Heart of our Loved One, and if our own wounds unite us to that, what grace, what salvation for all our 'family'. I knew that, after the first death-images, Sister Janet would be optimistic. And I thought you would be pessimistic![2] As for me, like the doctor, I simply don't know. But we shall know soon. I am going in on Thursday and starting tests on Friday. The doctor is a noted cardiologist so I am in excellent hands.

Nothing could be less magical than Heath Robinson,[3] but I must say their witty clarity is charming. What lovely cards you send me! This Van Gogh is very apt, I feel: the springing tree of hope, yet, typically it is tortured[4] … I haven't used it in case you ever want to send it, some distant day. The Pre-Raphaelite book is highly entertaining …[5]

I hope you get confirmation soon about Maureen – and yet, isn't it true that these times of helpless waiting, when we have done all we can and are held up by events and others, are the times of greatest surrender when the action that went before and will follow after is taken most fully into Jesus and made His? I see this so clearly, watching Janet struggling with the intractable difficulties of the Foundations.[6] (For her, poor dear, my little illness is sadly mistimed.) I often think of you at college, too, set free for Joy precisely in these times of frustration ...

Still have to write home and am growing a little feeble, so shall only commit you totally to Joy as I ever do, and try to repay you for your constant generosity to me.

1 'Suscipe sancte Pater': the first words of the prayer spoken by the priest as he makes the Offering of the host to be consecrated during the Latin rite of the Mass. Sister Wendy here identifies with this act of offering to the Father as she prepares to go into hospital for cardiological tests. In a short note, written some years earlier, she had expressed something very similar in another context: 'Once we have said Yes to Love however feebly or fearfully, He will say the words of Consecration over the bread He Himself has ground and baked and set on His altar. And then the people of God eat the bread. If we let Him, they will eat us and receive Him ... He is not content that you should just love Him. He asks to take you and give Himself to others in you – and not in any way that pleases or glorifies. Never fear it, please, or better let your fear rivet you to the Father, as Jesus' own fear did. It *is* His fear in you really, and that too, is the Father making you pure Jesus-Bread.'
2 She is referring to their automatic fear, when they heard the news, that she might be gravely ill.

3 William Heath Robinson (1872–1944), an English cartoonist, best known for his drawings of absurd and improbable machines.
4 This card has not survived but, from the description, would seem to have been Vincent van Gogh's *Peach Tree in Blossom*.
5 *See n. 1, 1 October 1980 above.*
6 Sister Janet was at that time negotiating the purchase of a property in which to found a new community.

11 November 1980

Dull business letter! The great thing is that there is no disease – only impairment, (possibly connected with a silent coronary) and hence pain and weakness. But they are best ignored as they can't be helped and 'mean' nothing, essentially. Blood pressure 'odd', but natural to me, and ditto the weight. All in all, I live as sensibly as I can (= much as before), and bear the cost of my special and blessed vocation ... The whole consultant business was liberating, DG. (And he is a blend of Fra Angelico and El Greco!!)[1] ...

Janet asked me to plan something for the community for Advent:

Week 1 – 'The creation waits in eager longing.'[2] The unredeemed world – the unredeemed areas in us – can't see – can't stand true – how eager our longing?

Week 2 – 'I tell you that Elijah has already come and they did not know him.'[3] The redeemed world – the Church – set at the heart of chaos to be 'Jesus' – are we using our redemption? Do we 'know' Him? Mass, sacraments: how radiant with Jesus for us?

Week 3 – 'Herod had long desired to see Jesus'[4]: What do we desire? And *why?* The real reasons for wanting to see Jesus – do we hide behind false ones?

Week 4 – 'I have come to cast fire,'[5] etc.: Turn away from ourselves to *His* desire – how He longs to come to us and inflame us – the rapture of Christmas for Jesus ...

Thank you for all you do and are for me.

1   It is not clear what she meant by this remark.
2   Rom. 8.19.
3   Mk 9.13; Mt 17.12.
4   Lk. 23.8.
5   'I have come to set fire to the earth, and how I wish it were already blazing,' Lk. 12.49.

27 November 1980

I am living very slowly, sensibly and happily, so do not fret.[1] Accepting all *as it is* unless He shows He wants a change. Your cards give me such joy – often what they reveal of your growing surrender is the most beautiful part of them!

I have asked Janet to urge the Sisters to pray very specially for Claire. These 'little ones' have a function of great spiritual dignity[2] and I hope with all my heart you will find the right nest for her. What with you searching for a refuge for C. and Janet searching for a property, and both these searchings a symbol of humanity's striving to find Jesus, and much more, Jesus' wearing Himself out to find and harbour humanity, I am kept at a stretch.

Thank you for welcome stamps and, ah, most delightful books. Such a joy always. Now we have all we want of the Pre-Raphaelites, (except, if Mary is ever in Manchester Art Gallery, a postcard of the Rossetti *Astarte* which is said to be the *one* great picture they produced. None seem great to me, but charming when seen aright).

Am speaking to the novitiate[3] on Chinese art next week, by way of a 'test', to see if I can. So much mysterious beauty on all sides – it is hard not to be swept away by His overwhelming presence. But swept or unswept, as long as He possesses us wholly. What passionate longing in Advent ...

1   Ann was still concerned about Sister Wendy's health following the episode mentioned in her letter of 11 November.
2   Claire was mentally handicapped.
3   The Carmelite novices at Quidenham.

December 1980
Happy Christmas, dear lamb! May the radiant Child sweep you up into His joy and share with you the

Father's mystery. I am starting this before I hear
from you, but I can safely say 'thank you' in advance
– always so much to thank you for! I was just thinking
that this year you have given me a superlative
set of books: at the moment I am contemplating
Spencer with immense delight,[1] with Rose windows
in reserve[2] ... Do you like these cards? They seem to
be very, very nice – not rapturously beautiful – like
some of those Chinese landscapes – but then my
heart can barely cope with the Lord without adding
extra intensities ... I am always least able to speak
of Jesus at times like this when His pressure is more
overwhelming. How I hope, tired and ill as you are,
that the fresh sweetness of His nearness will flow like
healing oil over your fatigue – whether you feel it
or not. But I know you live in the certainty of these
things.

1   Probably: Robinson, Duncan, *Stanley Spencer: Visions
    from a Berkshire Village*, Phaidon 1979. Stanley Spencer
    (1891–1959) was an English painter with a visionary
    perception of British village life, into whose common
    daily round he read the personalities and events of the
    Gospel.
2   Cowen, Painton: *Rose Windows*, Thames & Hudson,
    1979.

1981

12 January 1981

I was comforted to get your letter today, (slow post isn't it?), because your last letter sounded so threadbare and weary. How strange, and how beautiful, that I spent Monday morning praying for you, and you were the same day urged to make a day of recollection. So you see how closely the Lord keeps us united. I hope you will now be able to feel more secure about Claire's future – one problem at least on the way to a solution – and as for the rest, maybe you are coming to the time when one has to say: 'It's a mistake, it won't work, I've done all I can to prevent it, but I've been overruled and now I open my heart to Jesus *in* the mistake and do all I can to make the best of it …' Only you can know when further opposition is productive. Certainly the tension of opposition becomes too harsh after a period, and tends to swamp our capacity for deeper things. Poor darling, you have fought bravely, and if this is defeat, it can only be on one level. The essential level is one of such loving surrender, such trust in God's power to raise us from the dead, that there you are always victorious – because Jesus is.

Come any time for your retreat, love. Tell me when it would suit and I'll ask if there is room. On a bodily estimate, you need some time at rest in Him, but I don't fear for you spiritually. My body: well, heart a little painful at times, but the main difference is inability to do much. I never do do much, so it's quite unimportant.

Your letter made me think with pleasure on my stupid rejection of Klee, that luminous painter. Not pleasure, of course, in my limitation, but in the hope that at last there may be some sign of improvement. I see everybody else growing, but not me! As well as those Athena cards, Pam[1] sent me an Athena print of Klee's, one of the final paintings when he knew he was dying, and there is that deep, tragic, wholly living joy you spoke of in Beethoven. I feel a bit mean, because this is one of those rare gifts I can't share with the community, much as I'd like to.[2] Klee seems to move through the world of pain quite untouched and yet most sensitively responsive. In an earthly fashion, an image of Jesus, who shares it all and agonizes, yet holds in Himself the 'answer' – as we do, too, through His gracious gift.

Both your new books sound so lovely, and I look forward so much to showing you the beauties of the Christmas acquisitions … Books from all friends are a delight, but yours are special, partly in themselves and partly in the motive of the gift and what it represents of desire for God.

1   Sister Wendy's blood sister.

2   Sister Wendy's generosity was boundless and many of
the gifts she received would eventually find their way
either to the Carmelite nuns at Quidenham or to some
other friend. In this case she is saying that the gift is so
precious to her that she will be keeping it for herself.

29 January 1981

That's one of the loveliest cards you have given me!
It lights up the cold caravan with its visual alleluia!
I wish Rosenquist[1] had developed this lyric vein
instead of his massive disorientated line! ...

I am so glad the apostolate of revealing Jesus as
our true and only Healer is building up. It will
spread by word of mouth, I imagine, as various
Sisters share their appreciation with others. Have just
read a catalogue by the artist-photographer, Duane
Nichols, ex-Catholic because the image of God he
was given was so punitive and unjust. 'I'm nicer
than God,' he says. These false images are so deep
in the subconscious that most would repudiate them
– would not dare to confess (as he does) that this is
how they see God. It wrings the heart to see Jesus
so misrepresented by His Friends and His Church.
But we see what we *want* to see. May you find many
who desire the pain of truth and its disturbance. You
won't neglect to write, will you? Make a start!

You may like *Mirage*. Notice that the illusory is far
brighter and sweeter and more understandable than
the shadowed wastelands of reality all around.

Are you well? Hope you can get to the John Moores Exhibition[2].

1   James Rosenquist (b. 1933), American artist and one of the protagonists of the Pop Art movement. It is not known to which of his works Sister Wendy is referring here.

2   An exhibition of contemporary British art held biennially at the Walker Art Gallery in Liverpool.

Feast of Light '81[1]

My garden is glimmering with snowdrops – can't bear to pick them, but I send you the thought of them, gleaming and singing and praising God. I am agleam too, with joy over your enchanting present. How very good you are to me, dearest. Nothing could have given me more pleasure than this Klee, which somehow, at present, speaks to me so profoundly of the holy mystery, the light-hearted surrender to the essentially hidden God that only total faith can open its heart to …

The 'meaning' of Klee is always beyond itself, offstage and yet central. The more Jesus fills our life, the more this pattern becomes true for us as it was for Him: in no way is He His own 'meaning'. The very beauty and strength that He is all comes from that 'not of myself' which must have been both utter joy and confidence and (as the temptations show) hauntingly, frighteningly painful.[2] You are called to enter deep into this 'My Father's will, not my own' attitude, as you work out the future for your community. It *could* be that this future is the folly of the Cross: He will show your attentive heart through circumstances. He only asks you to listen, and to love, without judgement, those who 'do not know what they are doing'[3] ...; you know that love looks beyond to the face of Jesus, and only longs truly to do what He would do. So I wrap you in my tender prayer and feel no anxiety.

Hebrews: Spicq, in French, is the best commentator.[4] What a mystical epistle it is; my favourite, too ... Would love to write more but must be sacrificial.

1 2 February the Feast of the Purification of the Blessed Virgin Mary or 'Candlemass', according to the old rite. It is now called the Feast of the Presentation. The morning liturgy begins with a candlelit procession in commemoration of the day when Mary and Joseph presented the infant Jesus in the Temple at Jerusalem. (See Lk. 2.22–28).
2 Cf. Mt. 26.39; Mk 14.36.
3 Lk. 23.34.
4 Ceslaus Spicq OP, an important French biblical scholar and author of several New Testament commentaries, notably on the *Epistle to the Hebrews*. Sister Wendy did not read French, nor was this commentary translated into English at the time, so she must presumably be recommending this book from hearsay.

Undated

Just to reiterate that I am holding you steadfast in the radiant joy of Jesus, letting Him suffuse you with Himself. *Now* you see why He chose you for this work. In these dark, distressful (and stressful) days, the mystery of whatever He wants to accomplish demands a very selfless servant. Here is the occasion above all for the 'ecstasy of action'. However much of a failure you feel, and all the more because you feel it, I know you cling to Jesus and beg Him to do the Father's will ... Like these great glowing apples[1]: their beauty comes from total acceptance of reality, that very active virtue of surrender. With Jesus as your inner sap, you will fill out the full dimensions of the Spirit's desire for the whole Order.

1   This note is written on a notecard with a picture of two ripe apples hanging on the end of a branch.

1 April 1981

I look forward to our meeting. Maybe it will include your birthday? I enjoyed the charms of Kenneth Clark's insights on Our Lady's day[1] – it was a lovely treat – and am keeping Modigliani[2] and my second reading (far too flat a word for this experience!) of Klee for Easter.

We've been given the Picasso restrospective volume, very similar in format to that magnificent Spencer,[3] and I believe there are one or two other presents expected for the forthcoming Profession.[4] Will tell you if I think any may clash, but you have already this year brimmed my cup with light. So many of the books you have given me are like great stars hung above me, bright with the glory of the unseen Sun that is their life and ours. And your cards, too – the last two paradisal Indian scenes are very moving: not only our true *patria*, but the land where we do actually live already, if we look deep into Jesus.[5] 'The kingdom of heaven is come upon you.'[6] The alpine flowers, so hopeful, so thriving in their dead context, say the same. And perhaps this is the fundamental reason for your being where you are, to proclaim by your joy amidst so much that is not Kingdom, that it's precisely in these harsh, practical conditions that Jesus takes possession of us. What could have been more worldly than His own 'baptism'[7] – and He longed for it, (when shrinking) because it would set Him free for the Father's love to come to us.

More and more the Passion seems to me victory so intense that Jesus Himself could not have said whether it was suffering or rapture – or rather, it was (and is) *both*, and what we 'experience' is only the envelope for the other. The whole setup of your life is beautifully disposed to share His selflessness of love with you, not so? Have prayed so much for the last meeting (25th) and will do so for tomorrow.[8]

Are you buying, or have you bought, the Penguin 'Playing Politics'[9] – a *game*, I think!! Should fascinate us both. Wish I could spend time talking of these charming things!!

1   'Lady Day': the feast of the Annunciation on 25 March.
2   Amedeo Modigliani (1884–1920), an Italian painter who worked primarily in France. Ann had given Sister Wendy another volume in the 'World of Art' series: Mann, Carol, *Modigliani*, Thames & Hudson, 1980.
3   *See n. 1, Christmas 1980.*
4   One of the Carmelite novices was due to make her profession of Vows.
5   That is, Paradise is not just to do with our homeland in heaven but is where, in Jesus, we already live now.
6   Cf. Mt. 12.28: 'But if it is by the Spirit of God that I cast out demons, then the kingdom of God has come to you.'
7   Jesus' death. Cf. Lk. 12.50: 'I have a baptism with which to be baptized, and what stress I am under until it is completed'.
8   Sister Ann was still heavily engaged in meetings regarding the future direction of the school run by her Order. Ultimately she would lose the battle. Sister Wendy, with her usual sensitivity and compassion, wrote when all was over: 'A chance ... to say how sorry I am about the merger and all it has cost and will cost. But at least the struggle is a "clean" one now, having entered the realm of "did you not know that the Christ *had to* suffer?" (Lk. 24.26) Perhaps, in this straightjacket, the Lord's work – your Foundress' work – begins anew in an entirely new dimension? And He chooses you, not to carry on in the dimension of the past, but to launch into the unknown waters of His Mystery? ...'
9   Conjectural; the writing is not clear.

26 April 1981

Did you get my letter of the 1st, love? I ask because the Guest House is filling up its summer bookings, so you should move quickly. This is really my sole reason for writing, but what a joy to be able to thank you for the Paschal splendours you provided: rich spices and ointments for Him as He lay in the garden, dead and risen.[1] Will you allow me to keep the casket – one of those 'see-Naples-and-die' kind of experiences!! – in the deep freeze until June 1st? That's my 10th anniversary of coming here, and so magnificent a gift, if I ever dare to eat it, would fittingly signalize the day? Am presuming your permission meanwhile. And, oh, the lovely books, Mucha[2] and Whistler[3] all charm, and the cave artists all worshipful and observant.[4] You delight me so, and the other books are all very much to my taste. (Why do you and I love spies? The dark and dangerous underworld where evil is kept in check: could this image forth to us Christian life??).[5]

I was sad about poor little Claire's unhappiness: may it 'endure a night'[6] and then be forever forgotten. But am anxious about your journeyings in the snow, and hope your next letter has comforting tidings … Looking at that most enchanting Klee card, I thought of how these little ones are hidden from us in the sea of their deprivations, yet beneath its opaque waters, they are like bright shining fish for the Lord, free sometimes as land dwellers in the sun can never be.[7] What goes on between Jesus and His little ones in that hiddenness? In our prayer we are all beneath those waters, and perhaps for most people, their earth selves cannot know what 'happens' or how lovely is their soul's dance before Him.

Special prayer for the big meeting. Yes, my dearest, I do keep you enclosed in the joy of Jesus, ever more deeply. Breathe deep of it.

What a happy symbol that your letters always come to me enclosed in beauty and enclosing it too. Those British Museum cards are quite beautiful.

1   An allusion to the Gospel narratives of Jesus' burial, conflating the Johannine with the Lukan account (Jn 19.39–42; Lk. 24.1).
2   Alphonse Mucha (1860–1939), Moravian painter and decorative designer in the *Art Nouveau* style.
3   J. A. McNeill Whistler (1834–1903), American artist who worked in Britain for a large part of his career.
4   By the 'cave artists' Sister Wendy is referring to the prehistoric cave paintings to be found in parts of Spain and France, some of which are thought to be up to 40,000 years old. It is generally supposed that their original function was religious in nature.
5   Reading murder mysteries and spy stories was one of Sister Wendy's more unusual recreations and, as a rule, she would get through two or three a day. She claimed to take delight in pursuing the ultimate triumph of good over evil through the evolution of the story.
6   Cf. Ps. 90.4. By 'little ones' she is referring to those, like Claire, who are mentally handicapped.
7   Klee (*see n.6, Ascension 1977*) produced a series of fish paintings.

4 May 1981

What lovely cards you send me! (I've long wanted an Uglow!)[1] The magnificent Klee is all about maturity, I think. We see three 'heads': the child rudimentary in its simplicity; an adult in a sophisticated version of this simplicity (i.e. older but no deeper or wiser), and the large fragmented head of suffering maturity, all complex and painful, but making a whole in its truth to experience. Your Foundress' 'simplicity' is of this last kind:[2] infinitely complex and real but angled into a simple *direction*. It is often mistaken for the second kind, a simplicity that really involves avoidance of life's profundities: 'simple-minded' instead of (like your Foundress, who only follows Jesus here) 'simple-hearted' ...

This weakness: could it mean you need a physical check-up? Also, could it suggest you are too eager for *your* part? To be His word must mean the work is *His*. But I think mostly – whether that is so or not – you are only paying the price of the deepest apostolate. We preach Jesus only in our own poverty and weakness and He graciously shows you this.

1   Euan Uglow (1932–2000), British painter, particularly of nude and still life studies.
2   That is to say: the Foundress' spirituality of the virtue of religious simplicity corresponds to Klee's depiction of maturity.

15 May 1981

Yes, miserable penned little notes I send! Feel a shamefaced realization that they probably say a lot of what I am – or rather would be without the all-encompassing Grace of God. He holds our misery in His wounded Hands and all the pitiful, mean and broken elements cohere in His Beauty.

How lovely the way He gives you the work every month. It is 'mission' at its purest, isn't it? And the need to depend – and be up for 'judgement': how precious!

Cards enclosed: some are most beautiful – all, really. Have now supplied you and expect a line or two every so often to report 'progress',[1] i.e. what *He* is doing within His Lamb ...

Let us know after 23rd.[2] Submission is such a profound entry into the way of Jesus. As the card shows,[3] we are called to wait, empty bowls, alone in the light: the use is His affair, and He can give the bowl to *anyone* and fill it with *anything*. His affair.

Most grateful, love, for all those superb cards. Isn't G ...'s[4] *Roundabout* terrifying: the round of self that deadens?

1   She means that the cards she has sent are meant for Ann
     to write her progress on and then post back to her.
2   The meaning of this is no longer known.
3   A picture of a pottery bowl.
4   The artist's name is illegible.

6 August 1981

The book hasn't yet arrived, but am writing now in case you are hurt by what might seem supine ingratitude! (Will send a postcard when it comes.) But I am quite glad for the delay, as your Turner book is engrossing me with its intelligence and profundity and beauty![1] And then the future delights of your inspired purchases in Edinburgh. With reluctance I admit that we have AP's *Labyrinth Makers* – first class! though perhaps *Tomorrow's Ghost*, the only one we don't have, is his best.[2] All are good. And then, my sweet, those magical cards, and from mystic Glastonbury, too! How much happiness you give me. As we could expect, the Lord has chosen for me the one friend who enters into the deep heart of His love, and in that secret place helps me to surrender. (Put all wrong!)

It couldn't be a lovely holiday for you, especially with such news of Claire.[3] How can we ever doubt, love? We blunder ahead, thinking all is going wrong, yet because we have tried to do what we could, He has been free to do what He wanted – not at all what we thought, and infinitely better … His general pattern; He is always like this. So lie down in peace beside Him, dear lamb, even while, on another level, you may seem to be all taken up with work and struggle. He showed you 'presence' during your retreat, and how it is formlessly the reality of all form. (Which reminds me of how very, very much I am looking forward to the mounted Klee pictures. But please, only if you have time! Have said I'll share Klee with the novitiate, but not just yet. Janet gives me all I need, so there is nothing at all to worry about ...)

Very dull letter, but what need of words? I have enfolded you in His joy and He sings within us. Very loving and grateful ...

1   J. M. W. Turner (1775–1851), British Romantic landscape painter who transformed the depiction of light on canvas and thus paved the way for the Impressionists.
2   Price, Anthony, *The Labyrinth Makers*, is the first in a series of spy stories featuring a hero called Dr David Audley.
3   *See n. 6, 26 April above.*

14 August, Eve of the Assumption, 1981

The book has just arrived, and it is SUPERB!! It would be a wonderful book for teaching from, so perhaps you will have it before I can show it to you next visit? Nobody amongst the various authors had the courage to 'unveil' a Klee, but there is a Kandinsky[1] and Rothko[2] and a glorious Matisse,[3] which begins by saying he is the key artist of the century. (Haven't you any friends in Pennsylvania, where a wily old bird called Barnes early cottoned on to what Matisse was after, and shared a scintillating collection between Merion,[4] and Baltimore?[5])

I haven't really looked at your lovely, lovely gift, as I feel it is meant to be tomorrow's joy,[6] when we make our great affirmation that Jesus is so fully

Life that, of course, 'all who live in Him'[7] must be totally and radiantly alive for ever. 'I belong to the Lord, body and soul': that is what *Ecce Ancilla* means, isn't it? ... The picture is of freedom, joy – the instinctive soaring of the heart that He takes to Himself.

1   Wassily Kandinsky (1866–1944), Russian painter and initiator of purely abstract art.
2   Marc Rothko (1903–70), an American-Russian painter, generally categorized as an 'Abstract Expressionist'.
3   Henri Matisse (1869–1954), a French artist in a variety of media and one of those who most influenced the direction of modern art.
4   The Barnes Foundation, which possesses a large Matisse collection, is actually situated in Philadelphia.
5   The Baltimore Museum of Art, in Maryland, holds the Cone Collection: the greatest collection of works by Matisse.
6   The Assumption of the Blessed Virgin Mary, body and soul, to fullness of life in God is celebrated by the Roman Catholic Church on 15 August.
7   ... for to him [God] all are alive', Lk. 20.38.

29 October 1981

A very brief word to tell you I have held you very close to Jesus during these breathless days. He Himself, the Spirit of Jesus, has been your Breath, and only this *could* He be. So it is all overwhelming grace, as you know. Very happy to hear about Claire. A strange and beautiful link: her old home offered Janet furniture for the foundation so Claire's washstand etc. will end up in Carmel ...

Christmas 1981

I know this has been a specially hard term, and I've been swept away, time after time, into prayer for you. The joy of Jesus, that gentle freedom, draws you more profoundly in proportion to the stress of work and decision. But you know that, and you must feel perfectly happy to tell me at any time that any explicit help I can give is no longer needed. The *real* 'help', His coming to you through my prayer, goes on and always will.

Well love, the cat is a painfully homemade calendar but I hope you like it all the same! What she says is that her face may be plain, but look at her superb rear! In other words, there is always more to others than appears, and the hind-part magnificence is what the Lord sees, and we in Him. If we take it on trust that the drabbest, most off-putting person has somewhere a glory, this shows, somehow, secretly in our attitude.

I also enclose a little collection of modern masters. I'm sorry the Matisse isn't in colour, (rich, glowing, primitive reds and greens) and that this is not one of our glowing Klees, and also sorry for the accidental preponderance of nudes! ...[1]

1   The ending has been lost.

1982

2 January 1982

I wish we could meet to talk over the situation, but you don't 'need' me, Love. You have the necessary experience in administration, the essential sensitivity to the real human values at stake, which keeps expertise alive and sweet, and you also have – greatest of your endowments – a heart longing to be pure, so that you do lovingly strive to 'seek first the Kingdom'.[1] The problem, of course, is knowing where in practice the Kingdom actually is. I see that here you have to blend together several priorities. Your first concern must always be to the students, to see how best to form them – or help them form themselves – into thinking, feeling and acting educators. It all sounds so simple in theory, but I know you have to do this with the staff to hand. I suppose that the staff from the other college are, in theory, simply newcomers to your own, and how you use them depends on getting to know them? But there must be so many other considerations that tie your hands. I know for certain that all you want is to show Jesus to the students so that they may show Him to the children. Perhaps that begins by showing Him to the staff?? If the difficult ones can believe that and that you revere and love them, (again requires that you *know* them), some of their resentful demanding may fall away. So the only practical advice I can give is to dialogue and listen as profoundly as you can. What God is asking of you can only be to look at Him and try. That *is* 'success'. Who knows what His deepest purpose is for the college? The real work is often done in the ways we least expect.

Poor lamb, I hope these stammered words aren't amazingly flat. The answer seems to me to lie right at the very heart of the Jesus Mystery and in that ambience. Words simply fail ...

Today your parcel No.6 arrived, to my exhilarated delight! What treasures! The earlier parcels, especially the superb 'Matisse' and the hauntingly lovely 'Birds' and that most intelligent and beautiful 'History of Art', had already crowned 1981 as a Bumper Year, and now the New Year has begun with these delicious fireworks of affection!!

You'll have had my previous letter, but I carefully avoided college because what the Spirit is saying, His practical emphasis, can only be heard in their specifics by you. But His general call to Love and sacrifice, to warmth, compassion and reverence, are clarion clear, not so?

I sit here surrounded by your bounty ... some of which I'll be allowed to keep till February, please?[2] Your cards have all been so lovely, too. I am rousing up enough generosity (how paltry I am!!) to part with most, but feel meant to keep the radiant self-forgetfulness of that most luminous Angelico.[3] The Edo Exhibition[4] must have been marvellous. I see it all 'within' and praise Him. The butterfly card silently affirms the Mystery of God. If you like Meinrad's card, get for college her book on the 'Tree'.[5] She sent us a copy – most moving. Wish I could give it to you, dear Ann Lamb.

1   Mt. 6.33; Lk 12.31.
2   2 February, the Feast of the Presentation (*see n. 1, Feast of Light 1981*) was the anniversary of Sister Wendy's entry into religious life. She usually saved some of the contents of Ann's regular Christmas food parcels to celebrate this occasion.
3   Fra Angelico, (*see n. 1, 20 December 1974*).
4   An exhibition of Japanese paintings of the Edo period (1600–1868).
5   Meinrad Craighead, a contemporary artist. *The Sign of the Tree* (1979), a collection of prints, was produced while she was a member of a Benedictine religious community.

26 January 1982

Come soon before you are too tired to talk! I would love to use this unexpected opportunity, but since you will be coming, I must wait. The books sound most alluring!! Pam gave me some and I'm getting the new *Matisse in Russia* for my birthday, but it hasn't come yet. Will talk about all this when you come ...

How exquisite those Japanese cards are, so masterly in their grace and assurance.[2] The enclosed are just the opposite: fragmented and beleagured man held together by a central force though all conspire to wrench him apart. For us, that central force, stamping us with the great seal of individuality, is Jesus, isn't it? He is our authenticity, our truth, and not despite the pressures but through them. Something of this true nobility I see in Giacommetti, don't you?[3]

Have had some letters re: would-be hermits.[4] How to get it into their heads that the very things they want to escape – and that *you* live in – are the ways He possesses us!!

Delighted re: superior, though daunted for her, whoever she is (you??)[5] Can't say how very glad I am my Lamblike Ann is coming.

1 *See n. 4 above.*
2 Alberto Giacommetti (1901–66), Swiss sculptor, painter, draughtsman, and printmaker.
3 Sister Wendy's reputation as a hermit and woman of prayer led other would-be hermits to contact her, hoping for her support. In her view, many of them had ideas about hermit life that were misconceived.
4 Sister Ann's community had just elected a new Superior. Sister Wendy does not seem to know the result at this point but conjectures that it might be Ann herself.

2 March 1982

Your friend often comes to my mind,[1] and I feel justified in writing with two suggestions, dear Lamb.

First, will you explain to her a little, perhaps as you drive down, how the community differs from others? She will have heard misleading things elsewhere, I fear. The difference, as I see it, (and this is why there is such an influx of fine vocations), is that the life is one of great fervour. The Rule is taken in all earnestness, setting themselves to keep faithfully all that St. Teresa taught about prayer, enclosure (many weird rumours here, for some strange reasons), silence, fasting, etc. But it is an intelligent fervour, inner-directed, so there is also a great and happy freedom. The girl who is to enter in Easter week, put it as being a union of intense seriousness and genuine spontaneity, both qualities, as you will agree, being necessary. What they've done is take every element in the Rule and Customs and hold it up to the Lord, so as to decide together what its purpose is, and then, whether it is in fact fulfilling that purpose or should be differently expressed ... More of this when you come. (How nice to be able to say that! Letters are so inadequate, at least in my faltering hands – I always enjoy yours, the said and the unsaid!) ... Don't drive; keep your strength, such as it is at the end of term, to cope with me! You will be perhaps relieved to know I am fast degenerating mentally and am unable to take much profound emotion in public!

Oh Ann, such lovely birthday presents! So different, too. Mucha[2] almost too pretty to be an 'artist', but a decorator is just what one wants, at times, and strong massive Rodin.[3] I have bought the Thames and Hudson (World of Art) *History of Sculpture* and am enthralled by it. Pam gave me the Tate Gallery's paperback of Henry Moore drawings, which I've kept to show you. Their dignity and mystery are overwhelming. And I *love* his sculpture. How strange that from Michelangelo to Rodin, hardly any; then from Rodin on – surely not fortuitiously – Moore, Brancusi, Hepworth, etc.[4]

I was very taken with your Vermeer comments. I have never felt convinced, myself; the feel of the picture is too grave for so plebeian a theme . . .[5]

I've studied Modern Art diligently now, searching for another Klee, and though it fascinates me (early Sienese is the only period – well, primitive Renaissance generally – I find more rewarding), Klee stands alone. Next to him comes Matisse, that lyrical and profound Master, and Picasso is a very poor third. All power and no beauty, but he fascinates, not so?[6]

He holds you in His Fire, dearest.

1   This was a young woman who wanted to test her vocation to the religious life.
2   Adolphe Mucha (*see n. 2, 26 April 1981*).
3   Auguste Rodin (1840–1917), French sculptor.
4   Henry Moore (1898–1986), English sculptor and artist as was also Dame Barbara Hepworth (1903–85). Constantin Brancusi (1876–1957) was a Romanian-born sculptor who worked mostly in France. The gist of

Sister Wendy's remark here is that during the centuries between Michelangelo and Rodin sculptors of genius were lacking but that, after Rodin, a number of brilliant contemporary sculptors had came to the fore.

5   It is not known to which of Vermeer's works Sister Wendy refers here. Possibly *The Allegory of Faith*, a painting uncharacteristic of the artist's work in general, which has been variously interpreted by art historians.

6   With regard to Picasso, see *n. 4, 9 September 1976.*

22 April 1982

Your exquisite book and its enclosures only reached me a few minutes ago: congratulations on your anniversary, and congratulations too on the sharing in the humiliation of Jesus that your fatigue induces. Depression is largely just that, isn't it – fatigue? And yes, my dearest, what we are does speak far more cogently than what we say, but that's a *liberating* thing, Ann lamb. It means we do not have to judge, to conclude sadly that others are this or that. We can take the whole disappointment of life as our own. It is perhaps the most profoundly humiliating experience known to the soul, not only for what it reveals of selfishness within but, more, in our helplessness to repudiate the narrowness, though we 'long to'. Isn't your beautiful attraction to Jesus at His apostles' feet the same thing seen differently? Humiliation is *our* experience of what *God* sees as humility.

The enclosed card is a dear treasure: the only Nativity I know where the focus is on encounter with the Christ, however babylike. The men are relying, protecting themselves, on their gifts, but the little Jesus looks solely at their being with such round-eyed wisdom. But my reason for sending it is Our dear Lady, in whose grace you have a *right* to share. She is quite unconcerned: her only function is to hold up Jesus, like a lighted candle, and what she is or isn't, has or hasn't, she humbly ignores. Proclaiming the salvation of Jesus, the Kingdom, doesn't mean waiting until my being is pure enough, but seizing Jesus in a powerful grasp (look at her hands) and relying on Him. She doesn't even see that Joseph's gaze is fixed on her, nor does she mind that the Magi ignore her!

As to renewal.[1] I think your weariness makes it clear that you would have to have more time and energy than your present duties allow if you were to pursue it vigorously. This is the Lord revealing Himself in the ordinary. But *within those limits*, do what you can. For example, why not write to those splendid American Sisters and express your profound agreement? But add: if Sisters are to live wholly for Jesus, belonging to Him and revealing Him to His world, they need more concrete support. Authority is not the only area where time is wasted. An austere framework is not imposed on us, we choose it, to set us spiritually free. Like a plank-bridge across a ravine: guard rails on either side enable one to run across in freedom. [There is] too much danger of the truth remaining abstract because not incarnated in community structure ...

1   The word 'renewal', used on its own in the context of
     the religious life, invariably refers to the programme
     of updating and internal reform initiated in religious
     communities by the Second Vatican Council.

8 August 1982

This may cross in the post with a letter from you,
but wanted to say: a) Janet says they are reading
in the refectory a superb 3rd volume by Thomas
Green: *Darkness in the Market Place*, specially geared
to the apostolic religious.[1] I'm looking forward to
reading it soon, it sounds dead on for you – both
nouns![2] (Though 'Sunlight in the Sanctuary' would
be equally and more deeply true!) ... b) Books and
various cards most beautiful. The two photographs
are infinitely moving. c) Have spent your money
on a wonderful book on 12th century religious
art symbolism and three volumes of the Phaidon
'Makers of the Past' series. These heroic struggles of
man to body forth his God I find so beautiful. How
wholly Jesus answers all their desires and doubts and
fears.

1   Green, Thomas, SJ, *Darkness in the Marketplace: The
     Christian at Prayer in the World*, Ave Maria Press 1970.
2   Both 'darkness' and 'marketplace' in the book title are
     apt words where Ann is concerned.

31 August 1982

Darling Ann, if you never gave me anything more,
you have already overwhelmed me with generosity.
And the greatest gift of all will always be to see you

growing in His love. It sounds strange, but I 'knew' of the beautiful change of which you speak. Ah, dearest, how infinite the joy this is to His longing Heart. As for the Order: I think you will feel within when the time has come. The present situation does provide an objective basis on which to build your appeal. It's as though the Lord has forced a pause on this Order so dear to Him, and made His beloved women look well at where they are – not so much going – as sliding. One can't do everything. It has a clearly defined mandate from its Foundress which demands all one's energies. But we have said all this …

Such beautiful cards, and almost my favourite Klee, that bright fleet braving the darkness.[1] Am taking such pleasure in the Magritte punt, now before me:[2] the mystical life in all its deep mystery, beauty. The enclosed also delights me[3] (on a lesser plane) and, dear Ann, could you write in it and return? One of my pseudo-presents, I'm afraid. But the wondering child with the bubbles is all for you. We need never snatch: Jesus is a perpetual fount of bright living graces.

1 Probably Klee's *Schiffe im Dunkeln* ('Ships in the Dark'), painted in 1927.
2 René Magritte (1898–1967), Surrealist painter.
3 Neither this card nor nor the card with the child and the bubbles survive.

15 September 1982

… Oh your lovely cards! And I greatly enjoyed the prints and posters, especially *Parasoles*. Have you seen the Tate posters? Very inexpensive, too. What fun we could have buying them for college. But I really think I enjoy more through you than I would if I were to do these things … I have just taken down your print of Magritte's *Empire of Lights* and will be going in to the novitiate this afternoon to give a conference on it. Don't know if I'll be able to express the passionate vision it gives me: God the sole reality, objectively shining in His Love on all His world – and man subjectively providing his own night. The only reality of any act or thing is its relationship to God. But only Jesus lived fully in that sunlight. It matters so immensely that we should *live* in this reality; where all is simple Love and all we are and do only exposes us to Him … In haste and in love.

1983

1 January 1983

… As for the letter itself, clearly one such needed to be written, but there is a bitterness in the tone which indicates the heart isn't pure – and His work isn't truly done if there are undercurrents of self. I also feel it is a mistake to base the approach on the Church, which we are coming to see as an ambiguous concept since we are *all* Church, not just the Vatican. The basis as I see it can only be – not the gospel in itself, since all Christians must equally live by that – but the gospel as seen by your Foundress, as the principles her daughters were to live to the full. Her ideals, her vision: [your] modern Order has to look deep into these and compare them with the present emphases.

My third criticism would be that 'prayer' and 'life style' can't be separated. It's the whole woman who prays, in the concrete reality of her desires. I don't say that prayer is incompatible with seeking job satisfaction, social activity, nice clothes, pretty hair, etc., but it is incompatible for the daughters of your Foundress. A sister of your Order who lives in any other than an austere, sacrificial, totally given life, can't truly pray, there's falsity even if the time is virtuously given. In fact this falsity is the frightening thing, and how can it be avoided if we grow away from our

God-given roots? Don't know whether I've put this very well, but it seems to me vitally important.

Have included a card you might like and which can be taken in several ways. One is that there is the Lion of Judah and His Ann-lamb (don't you love her secret smile?): the Lord who can only be strength to your frailty if you are close enough, trustful enough. Another is that all the lion in us – the aggressive, passionate ego – can only lie down with our lamb when both are brought into the Kingdom. This is the same interpretation, really, from a different angle. We have to *become* Jesus, Lion of Judah and Lamb of God, and then only are we wholly integrated and wholly 'safe'.

A blessed Epiphany,[1] my love. This is a special Day for me: His Manifestation. Don't you think ... that this expresses uniquely the *meaning* of the Order? Your Foundress wanted most ardently to *reveal* Jesus, in *(end of note missing)*

1   6 January, the Feast of the Epiphany, celebrating the manifestation of the Infant Christ to the world.

26 January 1983

What a lovely surprise! I am cooing like a dove. I'll keep most of the books for my birthday and Easter and the July feasts – all the liquors are awaiting their occasion too!

Calamity: that wonderful Kandinsky card vanished the day it came. Fortunately I'd read your letter. I've searched high and low every day, like the woman in the parable, but in vain. I can only conclude a Kangaroo has eaten it. Do you think Hannah of her kindness could give me another?? The little calendar is for her, but not as a bribe! Don't ask if you feel it's greedy.

These days are weighted with grace. Only surrender can be a resting place, which means, of course, living in Jesus and nothing else. You are surrendered by Love to enter His mystery, dearest, and I know you do.

No comment on this autumn scene[1] except to say that our own bodily autumn reminds us constantly that life is meant to be growth in Jesus. Only one life: He will make it all He wants of it if we only look steadfastly into His Face, seeing nothing, perhaps, but content to look all the same. What praise, what surrender you give Him in the looking without 'seeing'.[2] I trust Him that my different way is equally His joy.

1   This note is written on a pasted card of a golden, autumn scene.
2   Sister Wendy frequently alluded to the words of Jn 14.9: 'Happy are those who have not seen and yet believe'.

28 January 1983

February 2nd[1] will have a special brightness for my dearest Ann-lamb for this feast – *His* light and never yours.

So as to send this by return, I'm assuming all will be well regarding the Guest House for your retreat (will write again if not). I had a sense there was something impending, and have been holding you up to Him very earnestly. We'll talk it all out at Easter. Meanwhile, dear and blessed Ann, here is your chance to lay yourself in all simplicity on His altar. I know that whatever He wants, as made known through obedience, you want too. That seems very obvious – the whole purpose of obedience – but too many poor Sisters have lost their sense of direction and I *rejoice* you can show the team how a true daughter of your Foundress accepts these painful changes. Whether it happens or not, the whole surrendering grace is pure Jesus, isn't it? But I know you are deeply conscious of this. You see and receive Him at ever greater depth.

I can't bear to use one of your lovely leaping fish, but fortunately have a stamp![2]

Your Klee card is radiant with that vision he saw first in Tunisia and thereafter lived out so painfully and truly.[3] I must guard it against that ravaging Kangaroo: it was just now (6.30 a.m. two weeks ago, that the Kandinsky vanished!).[4]

So much love, dear one. Am not too flourishing so
don't expect much at Easter.

1   The Feast of the Purification (Candlemass), *see n. 1,
      February 1981.*
2   She is referring to the design on a new issue of stamps.
      Ann had sent her some but now she cannot bear to use
      them because she likes the design so much.
3   The artist, Paul Klee, was deeply influenced by the light,
      colour and shapes of the North African landscape.
4   See the previous letter.

26 February 1983

Sternly ignoring the siren voices that cried: Easter
– July – next Christmas, I opened your gorgeous
chocolates and read one of the thrillers, and took
delight in the cards and the Christie book[1] and, best
of all, used your book token and a gift to order *Art
for Today* by Lucie-Smith.[2] It headed my Wishful
Thinking List – the others on it are more expensive
still! So, dearest, thank you.

However, I am really writing to answer your question.
I think it would be wise and loving to answer this
letter more fully than suggested … Don't know
whether you *can* help, but feel you should try. My
suggestion would be that you start by mentioning
with gratitude the one positive good in the correspondence: that it has enabled two Sisters to *express*,
explicitly, their love and concern. You are upset for
each other. But beyond that sole, but real, good,
your letters are resulting in mutual confusion. Isn't

this because you are at cross purposes? And the image I'd use is that you are like someone running up to say the ship is sinking, and she like one who takes no notice of this but wants to know why she has come onto the bridge without authorization, etc. The one, the message is all-important, self-validating. But the other not only does not believe the ship is sinking but has herself opened the stopcocks and carefully drilled holes in the sides. Not that she wants the ship to sink, but *she* thinks it should become a submarine! So all her actions are *designed* to put the ship underwater, and what fills you with alarm and distress are the very things she sees as unquestionable advantages. I don't see how you can dialogue without confusion! The real subject for dialogue, however, is whether such different versions can be contained in the same vessel. After all, submarine and ship are essentially unlike.

Please take no notice of the foregoing, love, if it doesn't help. This is the letter I would write, but that doesn't mean it is the letter *you* would write! But I'd like the reason why there is 'confusion' explained, just out of love.

Everything in your life He has designed to free you of self and expand your heart to enter into His limitless Love. The things that seem most to be an obstacle to this are usually what most deeply frees and opens out – if we surrender deeply enough.

1   Agatha Christie (1890–1976), crime novelist.
2   Lucie-Smith, Edward, *Art Today: From Abstract Expressionism to Superrealism*, Phaidon, 1983.

March or April

Thank you for the cards, the welcome enclosure, the expected parcels – each gift separately valued and thanked for. This will be a special Holy Week for you: objective correlative to your own relinquishment. Jesus opened His hands so absolutely for the Father to take what He would; in that relinquishment of death He enfolds your relinquishment of 'power', (using that as an index-word for your years in fruitful office, love).[1] Your present state is a real death in its way, and like all true death in Jesus, the *only way* the Father can bring you to a new life. What comes after May He wills as a Resurrection, though, unlike what happens after our final 'death', it may feel anything but!

And no, love, I still feel sure that we only hear false voices if we *choose*. But our present acuity of hearing isn't retrospective, you know. History is a reality, and what we were includes inabilities – and how could God even allow these to betray us? …

Diana tentatively broached 'vocation'. I've told her only the end matters, never the means, but gave her no directives. Only God can do this. Very painful not to be able to speak His word – you are a great joy to me in that I always can.

Blessed death-and-life in Him, Lamb.[3]

1   This letter is undated; Holy Week began on March 27 that year.
2   Ann had come to the end of her term of office as Principal of the college run by her Order.
3   A reference to the approaching Easter.

2 May 1983

When you 'see' Him you will know to what extent the Boards made the right decision[1] because you set your eyes on Jesus and the Joy set before you, 'enduring … and despising the shame.'[2] I felt a wave of thanksgiving that all this is decided.

Am really writing, of course, to send you the Kandinsky list.[3] How kind of Jane[4] – what an opportunity! Very fortunately the Pompidou book (excellent)[5] has just come and, Ann, they claim to have a large and superior Kandinsky collection! Nina gave them 30 oils and watercolours and then left them the lot in her will![6] I've added all I know about to extend your list of 6, and then I've also put down some other glories from the Pompidou book. These are just in case; the idea was to put down one at a time, but I see I've gone obliviously on! So please don't hesitate to curtail!

Just as I feel the air around the caravan will always be redolent of His Presence here, so I can't but feel the intensity of His Presence at the Cottage must somehow remain … Do you sense Him as you drive past? How strangely He intertwines our lives, dear Ann. Mustn't linger.

P.S.[7] Poor composer: his art is only 'there' when *somebody else* plays it! Out of his control; very painful. Artist and poet never run this risk … but God does, doesn't He?

1   Regarding Ann's position at the college.
2   An adaptation of Heb. 12.2.
3   A list of pictures for which she hoped to obtain postcard reproductions.
4   This mutual acquaintance had offered to make a gift of the cards.
5   The Pompidou Gallery, Paris, features a large collection of Modern Art.
6   Wassily Kandinsky's third wife, Nina.
7   The postscript refers to a picture Sister Wendy had added to the envelope.

8 May 1983 (Julian of Norwich vision day)[1]

Writing this in haste so as to catch today's post, so must strive to be legible (though cannot aspire to be 'almost pretty' again!)[2] … I think that the ultimate test of our seriousness of desire (a test met by few) is to be able truly to see means for what they are. It takes a lot of courage, as it will often expose us to seeming infidelity. You met this test when you took up the cause of the alternative version.[3] How many will be *able* to evaluate *what* was being done in relation to *why*: means and ends? The most moving example I know is little Thérèse:[4] able to discard all the 'time-honoured' penances and ways of looking at God, and think out afresh what He was and how best she could reach Him.

I expected to have to explain all this and was surprised at Diana's[5] immediate reception to it, as if she'd only been wanting to hear precisely this ... It has always been my hope that she would have a vocation because of its potential profundity – no more self-purifying way of entering fully into Jesus exists. But the pudding's proof is in its eating.[6] Is she, in fact, brought nearer to Jesus by [this vocation]? Or does she somehow camp out in it and receive her spiritual nourishment almost irrespective? For years I've thought that it was childishness; that she'd not yet grown to an emotional stability that would enable her to live in the religious austerity – emotional austerity above all, – that the religious life demands. But I've come to wonder whether she literally *can*, whether she may be unable to under-stand these demands. Not a lack of generosity but an essential unfitness: which would mean, no vocation. I would love her to stay – and grow – but must ponder whether the two are opposed to each other. Like you, I feel she has secretly, and with great relief, decided. Only Jesus could have brought about the concatenation of circumstances that have cleared her way ...

Please share all this with dearest Phyllis and know

that I am a silent partner in your prayer. Let us resolve to *trust* our dearest Lord.

1   Julian of Norwich (c. 1342–1412): a medieval mystic who wrote an account of the visions of Christ's Passion that she received on what she believed to be her deathbed. The last of the visions took place on 13 May 1373 and signalled her recovery. Her account of the visions and their meaning is contained in *The Revelations of Divine Love*, the earliest surviving text in English written by a woman. In the Anglican Church her feast day is celebrated on 8 May; in the Catholic Church it is celebrated on 13 May.
2   A reference to her handwriting.
3   A reference to a discussion relating to the updating of some of the Sisters practices.
4   Thérèse Martin (1873–97), entered the Carmelite Monastery of Lisieux, France, when she was 16. She died eight years later, aged 24. During this short period she forged a spirituality based on what she termed the 'very little way' of confidence and love, a spirituality which she foresaw would make the way of holiness accessible to ordinary Christians struggling in the world. Canonized by Pope Pius IX in 1925, she has become one of the most popular saints of modern times.
5   A mutual acquaintance who was experiencing many difficulties in discerning her true vocation.
6   A reference to the saying: 'The proof of the pudding is in the eating'.

6 October 1983

St Bruno, that lonely, absolute man, and the eve of our dear Lady[1]: good day to receive the document.[2] Thank you for sharing it. It seems to me beautiful, dignified and spiritually wise. There seems to me practically nothing one would want omitted. It is inspiring in the clear and fervent vision it has.

But, dearest girl, while it is essential to spell out ideals and directives, we must also anchor them firmly in the actual. That's why, though I wouldn't omit, I would *add*. This version has made brave strides towards establishing the structure sisters *have to have* if they are to live out these ideals, but it has to be taken further, don't you think? Look, for example, at the community section. It makes beautiful reading, but how does the actual community spell it out in practice? … And that fine section on Formation: so true, yet *how* is it to be accomplished? These things don't just come – they need a leader … I should like to see the *crucial* importance of every community having this centre: a Sister whose prime function is to inspire, direct, and *hold others to their vision*. I'd like to see this made even clearer, emphasized and given the necessary practical 'teeth'. (The Superior has to 'interfere', to involve herself: but she can't unless this is spelled out).

Oh well, all this may not help in the slightest. It's in prayer I can know that I do help. I'm so glad that Phyllis has been such a support. She's a marvellous lieutenant: capable, supportive, warm, humorous. I am awed by the relentless Love with which God pursues her heart. See how close association has shown you quality you'd not have appreciated? The essential thing is to share a vision and that's why I feel you could find others and would grow closer if they worked with you.

1 Saint Bruno (1030–1101) was Founder of the Carthusians, an Order of solitaries sharing a basic community structure. His feast day is on 6 October. The feast of Our Lady of the Rosary follows two days later.
2 The document referred to in n. 3 above.

19 October 1983

St Teresa, I think, kept quiet about revelations because they are essentially unshare-able.[1] What God does, or says, has no objectivity, apartness that one can 'take' and show to another. He shows Himself by changing our very being, so it's not that we now know or see differently, we *are* different. A vision isn't so much a touch to enlighten a general path as a change in our own personal eyesight. Those who already share our vision will be strengthened by our own new strength and see more deeply because of our new insight – and those in opposition, not. If He wants them to see as we see, then He must reveal Himself to them as He has to us. There is no way of transference: our authority can never be more than human. I feel there is perhaps some special validity for you, dearest Ann, in realizing fully both God's goodness to you, personally, and the need to rely on human means (in the sense I've been speaking of) if others are to 'see' ...

I'm really writing to tell you I shall be praying more than ever before. Perhaps this is His hour. Whatever His plans, all depends on everything you do being done 'in Jesus'. Your gentleness, sweetness and strength, your vulnerable humility and love for each sister: these *are* His victory, come what may.

1   Saint Teresa of Avila (1515–82), Foundress of the Order of Discalced Carmelites, a visionary, mystic and important spiritual writer of the Counter-Reformation in Spain. She was made a Doctor of the Church by Pope Paul VI in 1970.

Undated[1]

Just a word to reiterate my prayer and hope. 'Many prophets and kings desired'[2] – not to receive the grace you've received, because no human heart could desire it – but to receive a share in Jesus – which is the meaning of the pain. Lamb within the Lamb-vocation of Jesus: how precious!

Meanwhile, like this blossom, hang free and unsupported in the unseen embrace of His Spirit. Let *all* open up your heart to Jesus-joy. The contacts He gives will all help to fuel your writing, won't they?[3] Perhaps you should set aside a daily period in which you force yourself to begin?

Didn't realize the talks on prayer were in different rooms: oh dear! But all will fall out as the Spirit of Jesus desires ... Give Him the joy of your willed trust.

1   An undated note written on a notecard with a repro-
    duction of a painting of a hibiscus flower.
2   Mt. 13.17; Lk. 10.24.
3   Ann was planning to give some of her sabbatical time to
    writing a book.

Undated

Jeune Fille en Robe Blanche: Matisse the great
simplifier! One of those Nice interiors[1] that met with
nothing but scorn for many years. Only now have eyes
been unsealed to 'see' what this great visionary has
done with his 'ordinary' subject. He has seen them as
pure colour, great peaceful luminosities trembling in
the void of existence. *Only* their essential is here. The
lesser details, that might please or displease ('Has she
a pretty face?' 'What flower is it?' etc.) are ignored,
and we are left with the radiantly beautiful that is the
secret essence of all that is created.

Matisse sees the Lord – only the Lord – and to see
Him, he must first see the real materialities. But they
are then transcended. This is Love, isn't it? We look
at everyone and at all that happens, in Jesus, in its
lovely truth ...

1   Matisse (*see n. 3, 14 August 1981*) moved to a suburb of
    Nice on the French Riviera after the First World War.

1984

13 January 1984

How very good you are to me! One of the reasons why I came to Oxford was that it is always *you* who give the proofs of love, and I hoped for once it could be me![1]

I love today's feast, whether it is explicitly the Baptism or not, Jesus closes the Nativity cycle by going down beneath the waters: infinite symbolism there – the surrender to Life and all it will mean, utterly trustful that, however violent the floodtides, He can only be borne deeper into the life of His Father. So I pray for you, dearest.

Today brought in 3 parcels! The books came, each a delight. (If you don't know Steadman, buy his paperback *Freud* – the controlled violence of his line is very exciting.)[2] Then the prints came, as yet unexplored beyond just a happy glance – and finally your packet with its variety of treasures. Am still delighting in the previous books. I read Rumer Godden's *Nikolides* in the train,[3] shapely and sweet, and also finished Bernard Levin, rocking with mirth. What a *spacious* mind he has! Even when I disagree literally, as with Dickens, I'm enthralled by its sheer intelligence. Oh, but can't go through all the pleasures that have come to me through you – take too long!

I hope you realize, dear lamb, that I didn't come because you 'needed' any 'help',[4] in an absolute sense. I saw you, and left you, with an overwhelming sense of God's triumph. You've nothing to do but hold firm to His Heart – let Him work out His Mystery. As you know …

Am myself well and remarkably un-laid-low by the whole exodus. Don't know if I could do it again, though!! I wish I were finer clay, and I wish too I hadn't gone out with you and come away with the gorgeous books and cards. The one sole rag of virtue I retained was not to tell you when I saw two superb art books!!

I wish I had a card showing the undefended Heart of Our dear Lord, His gentle readiness to see what others felt or desired, wholly free to serve their secret needs because He sought nothing for Himself. That's the Heart He offers you to live by, the only spirit in which His little ones can see His Desire and reach out to Him. Best card I have is the Shepherd and His lambs, dearest. With very deep love and gratitude.

1 Sister Wendy had made a special effort to give Ann pleasure by unexpectedly meeting up with her in Oxford while the latter was passing through.
2 Ralph Steadman, *Sigmund Freud,* Penguin, 1982.

Steadman (b. 1936) is a British artist and cartoonist, hence Sister Wendy's remark.

3   Rumer Godden, *Breakfast with the Nikolides*, 1983.

4   Ann had misunderstood the purpose of Sister Wendy's meeting with her.

14 January 1984

... Epiphany: always moves me that the cycle doesn't end with its glories, any more than Paschal time with the glorious Ascension, but with a lovely hidden feast – Baptism and Whit.[1] And both the glorious feasts are not *literally* 'true'! The Gospel makes it plain ('Is not this the carpenter's son?')[2] that there was in fact no 'revelation'. Jesus never appeared in radiance, yet how profoundly true on a spiritual level! His lovely humanness was a silent, secret epiphany all the time, revealing His Father's Heart to all who had eyes to see. It's the will, the real, active, realistic desire to see and follow that makes the hidden Jesus infinitely 'revelation'. We see according to our desires – and our life tells us *what* we've seen.

Not very well put, dearest. Hope you can read through its poverty. These Mysteries carry me away to a region (the Kingdom) where there are no words or concepts.

I hold you to His Heart, dearest Ann. Are you better?

1   That is to say: just as the Christmas cycle of feasts comes to a close with a low-key Feast celebrating Christ's baptism in the Jordan, so the Easter season

ends by celebrating the hidden mystery of Pentecost (Whitsunday).

2   Mk. 6.3; Mt. 13.55.

30 January 1984

These came from the Postcard Gallery[1] and, I hope, will serve as visual prayer for the Feast.[2] It struck me how concrete a Presentation must be. One can only be given in actual circumstances, and there must be a Presenter. For the married, their relationship 'presents' them; for the nun, it's her Order – and herein the absolute need to understand one's vocation, made actual only within that Order. And herein, too, the significance of what the Lord is asking you to let Him do at this moment.

Strange artist, Balthus,[3] as remote from the mainstream as Modigliani[4] or Palmer.[5] Mysterious, too, because his pictures grow on one the more one looks. The *Cathy* picture is from his 'Wuthering Heights' sequence, but I don't think that matters much. What we have is the contrast between these two untamed creatures, night and day, man and woman, armoured and naked, independent and frail, turned inwards and turned outwards, and so on and so on. They are only alike in their refusal, their inability to adapt to the confines of domesticity. Eagles. Yet the housekeeper, the symbol of adaptation to this world is not a person at all, merely a drab function. What Balthus is saying is that the full person needs *all* these qualities that are here fragmented. Or, if you like, that vision and actuality each need the other.

The Turkish Room is apparently a famous room in the villa Medici in Rome, and its sensuous beauty, its ornamented enclosure, has summoned up a resident 'form'. She is clearly not flesh and blood in the normal sense – a creature of the imagination – expressing in her person both what the room lacks and what it affirms. I'd take it Balthus is really saying something about our relationship to our contexts. They must not form, [?] or create us – the soul must always be free and pure, possessing its 'room' and not vice versa. Don't know if any of this will appeal ...[6]

1 This letter was accompanied by two postcard reproductions of paintings by Balthus: *La Chambre turque* and *La toilette de Cathy*.
2 The feast of the Presentation of Our Lord, *see n. 1, February 1981*.
3 Balthasar Klossowski de Rola (1908–2001), usually known simply as Balthus, a Polish-French modern painter.
4 Amedeo Modigliani (1884–1920), Italian painter and sculptor.
5 Samuel Palmer (1805–81), a British artist of religious and visionary subjects.
6 The end of the letter is missing.

2 May 1984

Despite the pressures, your last two letters held a new note of joy – some deep, secret spring has been unsealed – so never mind if the poor earth still feels dry and aridly dead! But am really writing to ask you, love: if you have given me any authority over you (the authority of love), will you bow down your neck and see the doctor? You're a stubborn lass, dearest, and to choose to 'obey' will be a gift to Him, quite apart from all else. And it's *Him* you're obeying, speaking to you through your body where pain is His summons. What happens when we answer His summons is His affair.

Expensive books: quite irrespective of me, don't you agree that college is the only time when people can learn what treasures are available? (A sort of parable of the Kingdom.) Literature and music can be bought cheaply, but art still tends to cost. So to share these books with the students and draw them into their meaning seems just what lower education is all about!

Can't but smile at how I missed the Klee[1] through haste. Only £5 left, but all my 'fortune' has been finely expended – I don't repine!

The exquisite dreamworld of Palmer is to remind you of what we both know: that Jesus is our world and we rest always in His soft radiance.[2]

1 The artist Paul Klee, *see n. 3, 9 September 1976.*
2 Sister Wendy had included a postcard reproduction of one of Samuel Palmer's paintings (see Plate 4).

13 June 1984

Your Klee card, all grace and joy[1] and the sumptuous Royal Academy book arrived on Tuesday, the day when I celebrate in my heart my arrival in this blessed hermitage! And then, the next day, the marvellous Hockney[2] and the Pre-Raphaelites,[3] not our favourite period, but the book would convert anyone! *And* all the heavenly cards! Cannot express how beautifully all this speaks to me of Jesus. I gave the novitiate a Matisse conference on Monday,[4] so was thinking of you. The lucidity and strength of his vision of joy as the absolute (whereas grief will pass away) is strikingly visible in the Royal Academy book. He makes the others, charming though they are, seem only decorative.[5]

1   See Plate 6.
2   David Hockney (b. 1937), British artist.
3   Pre-Raphaelites, *see n. 1, 1 October 1980.*
4   Matisse, *see n. 3, 14 August 1981.*
5   Sister Wendy's remark here reverses a criticism originally made of Matisse himself: that his paintings were merely decorative and lacked depth.

27 July 1984

For four successive days the post has brought a parcel! The first contained the chocs., which I am keeping – you won't mind? – for the Transfiguration,[1] that feast specially dear to me when Jesus shows us what the real world is like: radiantly bright, and at its centre, His passion in the city of Jerusalem, city of peace. And then came Penny Lively,[2] and all the other paperbacks, most welcome, but not the 'best wine'[3] yet, until the last day, when, with great joy, I seized upon an artbook-sized parcel and out came these wonders! Why did you say 'nothing exciting'?? The Pompidou book[4] is joint-second on my *desideratissima* list – superb! – and the bright Dufy[5] and nice Utrillo:[6] how can I thank you? ...

Will you be going to the Tate [Gallery exhibition] *The Hard Won Image*? Sounds good.[7] Have just finished the Orientalists.[8] I so agree about Matisse, in a pure, true world of his own, a world of vision ... A pity they excluded Klee,[9] who is the most noticeable case of an artist awakened and inspired by the colour and clarity of the East, and Macke with him.[10] There's even a book on Klee in Tunisia, but I haven't read it.

Now am beginning the Pre-Raphaelites, with some irritation, most unfairly, because it's such a splendid catalogue, and yet, with all the patriotism in the world, one cannot think any of them major artists. But interesting, all right.

Have you been to the doctor? Will tell you in confidence that I am going myself next month ... Have told no-one because nothing to tell, as it were. These bodily weaknesses draw us so deep into the surrender of Jesus, into that human condition which He alone fully plumbed and said 'Yes' to. To live in His 'Yes' is to live in joy, always.

1 6 August.
2 Dame Penelope Lively (b. 1933), a popular writer of fiction and a near contemporary of Sister Wendy at St Anne's College, Oxford.
3 '... but you have kept the good wine until now', Jn 2.10.
4 An exhibition catalogue from the Pompidou Museum of Contemporary Art, in Paris.
5 Raoul Dufy (1877–1953), a French artist known for his brightly coloured depictions of outdoor scenes.
6 Maurice Utrillo [Maurice Valadon] (1883–1955), a native of Montmartre in Paris and painter of cityscapes and street scenes.
7 *The Hard Won Image*, an exhibition featuring traditional method and subject in modern British art, was running at the Tate Gallery in London from July to September that year.
8 Sister Wendy was still pursuing her project of studying the History of Art in consecutive order. The Orientalists were a movement that arose in the mid-1800s in response to the opening out to Europeans of the East.
9 The artist Paul Klee, *see n.3, 9 September 1976.*
10 August Macke (1887–1914), a leading German Expressionist painter.

6 August 1984

Just to tell you I am enthralled at the prospect of your purchases: would that they could waft here by balloon! However, among them could there be the Matisse and Martini, with a view to using for the novitiate? This afternoon I'm giving them a conference on *The Figure 5 in Gold*[1] which says so many deep things. What treasures you give me.

The Tempest² needs a book (like *Figure 5*), but essentially I think everyone on the island is both personal *and* symbolic, the symbolism being that of all the elements in a human personality (e.g. Caliban – man's animality; Ariel – his imagination; Prospero – the controlling will, etc.)

And 'lamb', my lamb, more for what He calls you to be than what you yet are. But already my Ann is recognizably 'lamb': pure, vulnerable, prepared for sacrifice. And longing to be as meek and gentle as vocation allows!

1   *I Saw the Figure 5 in Gold*, a painting by Charles Demuth (1883–1935) in homage to the poet William Carlos Williams (see Plate 7).
2   Shakespeare's play *The Tempest*. Ann had asked Sister Wendy about its interpretation.

19 August 1984

Ad Parnassum is a great joy, but why ask for a commentary when you yourself so clearly see what it says? 'A passionate musical silence' couldn't be improved upon! I could just add about this silence, that Klee shows us it is not any kind of *absence* – absence of noise, absence of diversity, absence of action. The entire picture is one vast and glowing diversity, but all these jewelled tesserae of colour and shape are held in an intense harmony. Silence is wholeness held in the balance of Love. Notice how inexorably the pyramid soars to its serene peak, (while the picture holds in its balance three narrow pyramids pointing right, left and downwards.) Notice the archway, that door that *cannot* be shut, opening perpetually for those who desire to enter – desire as ever the key word. And finally, notice the one concentrated intensity, the great round sun. This Presence (Jesus Himself) is what balances the whole. His joy makes the silence alive. All the brightness of Parnassus is drawn from the all-pervading glow of this Jesus Joy. Unless silence pervades our wholeness, like His, and permeates the day (though there will be pure concentration in it as well) then it's escaped silence. Your pressured life is called to enter the abysses just as much as the Carthusian life – or mine!

All of which I know you understand! …

25 October 1984

Thank you for the lovely presents! Very thrilled to see the Kenneth Clark biography which I hope to enjoy on All Saints![1] As for the chocs and gorgeous petits fours, I may – yes, I shall – celebrate on the Presentation,[2] uniting with your Foundress's true-born daughter[3] – keep the rest for the Immaculate Conception[4] and Christmas. All right? I shall look forward to seeing you …

You have been specially in my heart of late, as you enter upon one of the great divisions of life, that watershed, and the *last* watershed, after which your human courses will flow in another direction. The uncertainty of what that direction is to be, so painful a contrast to the well-known way of the whole of your adult life, can only be His call, love, beckoning you to an ever deeper surrender. *What* happens to us or *what* we do is not very important: what matters is our heart's desire. You have now a chance to desire Jesus with a wholly new purity. Stripped of 'position' and its certainties you may well feel like a thing thrown away – but *His* thing, thrown into His Love. The poor, smashed, bare little Klee head perhaps says this: reduced to grimmest essentials, it has become true beauty.[5]

Clown: I'd love to see Claire's clown, but the actual symbol has always disturbed me. Clowns seem to be a remnant of our far and pagan past, another form of scapegoat. He is our ill-will, our libido, set free in a controlled context. The clown knows no laws and comes to no grief, but he 'pays for' this freedom by being the perpetual outsider: different face, different clothes. We laugh and mock and vicariously expurgate our own desire to be free of law and yet be punished. Something ambivalent about clowns and something cruel. But he is safe. We play the clown (I do! or rather, have) in order to disarm those who fear us. The outsider is often made clown to remove his threat, or may make himself so for safety. It has always cut me to the heart that man stage-managed the Passion by making Jesus a clown.

1   Secrest, Meryle. *Kenneth Clark: A Biography*, Weidenfeld & Nicolson, 1984.
2   21 November, the Presentation of the Blessed Virgin Mary. According to an apocryphal legend, Mary was presented to God in the Temple by her parents when she was a little girl.
3   A humorous allusion to Ann herself.
4   8 December, the Immaculate Conception of the Blessed Virgin Mary.
5   Klee depicted a number of *Heads*; it is not known which one is being referred to here.

7 December 1984

There was a postal strike in Norwich, so your letter with all its sad news only came today. I must admit I've thought for some time you were not well, but didn't see what I could do except hold you up to Him. *Please*, love, let me know what the consultant says etc. What a shock about the chaplain's death. Oh, how fragile is our lodging here on earth: not our real home, an exile in which He is not seen clearly, 'through a dark veil'.[1] But our unique and wonderful chance to love Him without seeing (though I haven't really the right to say 'our') . . .

1   Cf. 'through a glass darkly' (1Cor. 13.12).

1985

20 March 1985

It makes me happy to know, that you are journeying, with the sun of your former 'career' sinking on one side and the pale moon of your future rising on the other, and that as you journey your deepest preoccupation is to listen to His voice:[1] 'This is my Son, the Beloved, listen to Him'[2] – God's most passionate desire, His sole command. He can only speak in proportion to our desire to listen, and sometimes all we want to hear, all we are prepared to listen to, are the big major inspirations. Yet He is *always* speaking. Awareness of His voice in whatever happens depends, again, solely on desire. But equally, love, I don't think one hears 'false voices' unless one *chooses*. We may not hear all He says, we may shut our ears to His undertones, but nothing 'false' in this – merely inadequate. As our love grows, our capacity to hear grows, and we learn that 'obey' and 'hear' are the same scriptural verb. You do know how to listen; and it does need exterior silence.

1 Sister Ann's appointment as Principal of her Order's college had now officially terminated and she was about to take a sabbatical year in the United States.
2 Mt. 17.5; Mk. 9.7; cf. Lk. 9.35.

Easter Saturday 1985[1]

Really only writing to tell you, your friend Gabrielle has just been. Can't help feeling that it was not very serious: a going-through-the-motions, though she is unaware of it. Just as well, because one would need a passionate conviction to enter at 45.[2] I feel it is you who can best help her, poor little woman. No reflection on Gabrielle, but what a sadness it is when a life has not been made resolutely His. I was struck this morning (3.30!) by: 'He that can take it, let him take it',[3] and its relevance for vocation.

I love that Jacobus remark about Matisse.[4] Just as it took time for Cézanne to be seen as incomparably the greatest Impressionist, so only now is Matisse appearing as the supreme Modern. Great though Picasso is, he more and more reveals that he lacks a dimension so gloriously present in Matisse. Am enclosing one of my favourites, where the outer world of external activity and the inner world of creative thought are both seen as centred on the contemplative heart – the *Goldfish Bowl*. That silence gleaming tranquilly in its transparent integrity gives forth a brightness to all our 'world' – its darkness and its light, its action and passivity. And the goldfish bowl is Jesus, heart of our heart, our 'prayer'.

Loving the Chagall cat.[5] I wish now I'd chosen her for your retreat, which would have been much easier than my present choice! Do you want to know or shall I keep it a surprise?[6] ...

I think often of you as He draws to His close the music He has played in you at college. May the final notes be all Jesus. All else is waste, isn't it, love? What He has done in us, at whatever cost, that alone counts and matters. To be His joy makes worldly affairs seem very small.

1   13 April 1985.
2   This was a lady who thought she had a vocation to the religious life. Ann had directed her to discuss it with Sister Wendy.
3   Cf. Mt. 19.12.
4   John Jacobus, *Matisse*, Thames & Hudson, 1985.
5   Marc Chagall (1887–1985) was a Russian born, Jewish artist based in France, who developed a distinctive, modernist style in a number of media, making use of Jewish folklorist themes.
6   As a special gesture of friendship, Sister Wendy agreed to provide material for Ann's annual retreat. The points for meditation were invariably focused on pictures that Wendy would choose beforehand.

Ascension Day 1985[1]

Your beautiful letter and cards arrived today, the one feast which is solely 'for' Jesus. I know He is our 'Pioneer', as Hebrews puts it,[2] but we celebrate our heavenly life on the Assumption.[3] It is very secondary here, when for once we just rejoice that Jesus is taken up wholly into the Love that on earth He lived only to glorify.

You are much in my heart as the laying down of a true 'life' draws near. For the first time one mission is not immediately superseded by a new one ... A new apostolate will certainly appear when this sabbatical year is over, but what and how are in His Mystery still. A unique chance to live exposed to grace, dearest. None of your customary supports will be there, and this sets you free to look deep into His Face.

A lovely touch of His Love that all takes place within the ambit of Pentecost. (Where *my* new life began, too.[4] Whit Tuesday and June 1st are days of rejoicing always – we nearly coincide!) I sometimes think the Church has the emphasis wrong at Pentecost. We are not meant to try to look *at* His Spirit – not possible – we can only look *in* the Spirit, through Him as it were. 'He' is the medium through which we 'see'. Paul calls Him the Spirit of Jesus: in the Spirit we, too, can adore the Father; a sort of actuality of surrendered Love made accessible to us ...

Will you be able to see the Bacon exhibition at the Tate?[5] Or go to the new Saatchi and Saatchi Contemporary Museum?[6] (How I'd love that!)

Dearest, a bright bird in an odd-shaped mount to say that the Spirit comes unexpectedly.[7]

1   14 May.
2   ... our Pioneer into the heavenly life. Cf. Heb 12.2.
3   The Feast of the Assumption of the Blessed Virgin Mary, *see n. 6, 14 August 1981.*

4   She is referring to the beginning of her hermit life.
5   The Tate Gallery in London was holding an exhibition
      that summer of paintings by the British artist, Francis
      Bacon (1909–92).
6   The Saatchi Gallery of contemporary art had newly
      opened in London that year.
7   This picture has not survived.

12 July 1985

I've been saving this birthday card for you and hope
you like it. I also enclose this moving sculpture:
Deposition. Cox is, of course, recalling our past,
which modern civilization has shattered, but he
suggests with all the sadness, a hope: these fragments
are perhaps more beautiful in their fragility than the
hard, strong (unconsciously complacent?), original
masterwork. Man is a shattered creature, and in
understanding the truth of his weakness he can
become beautiful. We *hate* being fragmented but the
Jesus pattern demands an interior re-ordering that
must shatter our dearest ego-hopes. Lots of meaning
in this work!!

Did you travel back in safety, love? You looked very
weary, (almost shattered!) though I know it was a
blessed and holy weariness.

On your birthday I shall celebrate with your Wispa –
very nice – and last slice of your cake and Tia Maria.
Have developed great enthusiasm for the Chinese
Rice Crisps which taste marvellous in solitude – must

make them last – no more treats to come! And best of all, am surrounded by your books: ah, ah! – all windows onto Jesus.

30 July 1985

You are so much in my heart as the day of departure draws near. All the Mystery of His Holiness spreads out before you in a unique fashion – this year cannot but draw you deeper into Him and, somehow, re-make you into Jesus. I hope, too, that it will be a very happy and stimulating year, but that, however likely, is only hope; that it will be a Jesus-year, I *know*. Hope it will be a healthy year, too!

Janet will have told you the consultant is anxious to avoid operations. I hope to break open the (imaginary) champagne in October when the treatments will end.[1] Don't you think there is something wonderful in *using* the body's weakness and turning it into a means of health? Our inability to endure great cold, hence frostbite, hence gangrene, is being applied deliberately as a way to kill off the afflicted area. However, drastic, if it saves me an op. I'll sing the psalm with great fervour: 'Oh frost and snow, bless the Lord!'[2]

Dearest, don't buy me any books when you're away. Keep your allowance for your own needs ... let me repeat, dear lamb, I truly want nothing. Just to know that you are joy to Him, and He to you. Don't even write unless you *want* to, though of course I hope you do!

1   Sister Wendy was paying the price of the cold in her hermitage and had developed a frostbite related condition. Subsequently she would be persuaded to have a more efficient heating system installed.
2   Daniel 3.69–70. This canticle, sung by the three young men in 'the blazing, fiery furnace' of the Daniel story, forms part of the Divine Office on Sunday mornings.

14 August 1985

A joy to get your letter and think of you tranquilly watching the sun rise into power above the ocean. And a true consolation to hear that you found 'a group with shared values'. A rather sad truth, though, that this should console, since this is the only object for living in community, isn't it, to deepen and support the living out of shared values? Will be very interested in your further impressions.

I do hope you aren't disappointed in your hope of seeing MoMA,[1] especially as you may never again be so relatively near. But, of course, Boston has its wonders too. Wasn't that where you saw the Dzubas exhibition?[2] So much delight has come to me from that and I've shared it with the Novitiate. One of the Novices was given a huge Dzubas poster for her Profession, which I look forward to showing you next year! It hangs in the little parlour, a great, glowing canvas in which silent shapes move constantly in a gentle yet concentrated pressure. Each form seeks its own space in reverent awareness of the others – a beautiful symbol of community! …

I go a week today for mini-op. no.2. Pain is relative, so I'll only say I am happy to have some little thing to offer Him. The sort of senseless brutality of bodily anguish surrenders us to Him in a very powerful way.

1   MoMA: the Museum of Modern Art in New York.
2   Friedel Dzubas (1915–54), a German-born, American modernist painter. The Boston Museum of Art possesses a number of his works.

31 August 1985

Today you finally reach 'Mecca',[1] and I shall be waiting eagerly to hear your impressions. There is a growing note in your letters of freedom and hope: no specific hope, but that happy expectancy which He Himself fulfils *in* Himself. I think the very immensity of the country, unrolled before your seeing eyes, is a sort of parable He tells you …

Very thrilled by the cards and the thought of my Christmas (possibly) present! And I almost 'saw' that wonderful Dzubas through you. Baffled as well as sorely dismayed by the lunatic policies of the Boston Art Museum. To think of being so near those great Louis' and not being able to see them! I hope you've better fortune in San Francisco. As you say, you'll have freedom of movement in Spokane, but I wonder how much opportunity? You may have to scout around and see if the village (?) rises to an art gallery – I speak with irony, I hasten to add!![2]

Before I forget, to answer your question about the mini-ops: they've been very successful, but alas, are apparently only a holding operation and will have to be endured every few years. All the same, this is still greatly to be preferred over a full-scale op., don't you agree? And it opens up a constant opportunity for a love that costs something. A precious grace to be allowed to love Him in the onslaught of bodily weakness. (Louis' *Breaking Hue*, poured out and exposed, is a visible image of this.)[3]

The enclosed card is very different from the misty beauty of McIver or our lovely Louis. Chia is one of the three 'C's' (with Clemente and Cucchi) who are the foremost Italian, contemporary artists,[4] and some of their work can at first sight repel. This doesn't, and it repays study. I think the basic theme is that 'we have here no lasting city'.[5] Man is always 'camping', and all too often 'melancholic camping', because of his indolence and self-absorption. The man lazes before the glorious diversity of his context. Behind him, unseen, is really a camp of fire and mystery, but he even ignores the presence of the lamb of sacrifice. He is making his own meaninglessness out of what should be adventure and direction. And all that fascinating bric-a-brac around him, art (pictures and frames) and sciences (metal pipes etc.) are not integrated and put to work: a great call to intimacy and use of what God provides, dear Ann, don't you agree? The *opposite* of your Foundress' ecstasy of action, where Jesus pulls us out of self and into Love, into the obedience of Love = action, freeing us from all narrow self-concern, from even awareness of our reputation, from all desire but to surrender to His joy and make it visible. Paradoxically, seeing may lead, as in this picture, to a sharp stimulus to receiving what the brightness of the whole symbolizes.

1   Boston.
2   Spokane is, in fact, the major city of the Northwest inland states.
3   Morris Louis (1912–62), an American colour-field artist, painted a series of 'Veil paintings', of which *Breaking Hue* is one (see Plate 8).
4   Sister Wendy was later to revise this opinion. The picture on which she comments here no longer survives.
5   Heb 13.14.

1 October 1985

There'll never be a time when you have less need of hearing from me! So, though my heart points out that you 'are away from home' etc., I feel I must be mortified and still so that I can best support you in this year of grace. Very, very happy with all you tell me, including the spiritual direction and 30-day retreat. I'd go into both situations freely and without pre-condition, and only react to what you find in the Spirit. I am so grateful to Him for all He is doing for you … Can't see myself ever writing

on Julian or anything directly spiritual, love. Too
overwhelming.[1]

1   Ann had suggested that Sister Wendy should publish
     something about the medieval English recluse, Julian of
     Norwich. *See n. 1, 5 May 1981.*

17 October 1985

Your letter arrived on St. Teresa's feast.[1] I wonder what
she would have made of that magnificent Clyfford
Still?[2] Please tell Fr Toby that I not only agree with his
conclusion about psychic and spiritual maturity being
two quite separate qualities, but I think confusion
about this separation is one of the greatest causes of
discouragement. People look in the wrong direction
for holiness. Subconsciously they are expecting transformation in Jesus to mean that they cease to be
themselves: they become 'perfect'. But if we think
holiness is 'perfection' we have never understood the
human reality of Jesus. In His 'weakness', we are real.
And just as His Love doesn't transform our physical
limitations, so neither does it our psychic: the stupid
remain stupid and the emotionally unstable retain
their personal affliction. But now it is 'different' – it is
a vehicle of grace. I'm sure Teresa came closer to God
through her adolescent agonies over Gracian[3] than if
she had been without these weaknesses. All that we
are is potential entrance for His Love, but it humbles
us to admit it! Here is the great actual divide between
what people *really* believe and what they think they
believe.

But I truly can't see the above being of much interest to Father Toby, dear Ann, who, I'm sure, said it all much more fully. I only write it because you've asked! I need hardly tell you what a joy it is to think of His goodness to you.

Could you come down to earth for a minute while I tell you that there is a great Franz Kline exhibition on at present,[4] starting at Cincinnati, (is that where you'll be for Christmas?) and going on to San Francisco? Kline is one of the Abstract Expressionists I wanted to use for your retreat, but could not get a good card. Marvellous, great ideograms, often in black and white, pure and ardent. The catalogue would be a mutual joy ...

P.S. I have often felt sad over the effect of what I said about St Teresa. To my mind she (St Teresa) is the *greater* saint for her limitations, but many Carmelites have refused to accept this as being 'disloyal'. This blind expectation that holiness changes the very fabric of the personality – or alternatively, that only those without flaw or limitation can become holy, makes a mockery of the humanity of Our dear Lord.

1   15 October.
2   Clyfford Still (1904–80), an American Abstract Expressionist painter.
3   Saint Teresa of Avila (*see n. 1, 19 October 1983*) depended heavily on a young Carmelite friar, Padre Gracian, both in the work of her foundations and as a personal spiritual director.

4   Franz   Kline   (1910–62),   an   American   Abstract
    Expressionist painter.

5 *November 1985*

Just to reassure you that I have sent off a glowing
letter of recommendation: they will probably ask
you to *give* the 30 Day Retreat! As far as I can, I
am sharing in this year of grace with you, asking the
Lord to hold you absolutely receptive to Him as
He is doing. As you've realized, it's the very being
there that matters, the silent, lonely, uncluttered
chance to be still in His Presence, and nothing else.
The various courses and people are extras, and I
think you should take them all lightly. You have put
your finger on the weakness, in that there can be
an implicit expectation that mystical prayer can be
learned. Contemplation isn't a fruit we can grow.
It is given when we truly long for it, and the truth
of that longing has to be lived. How unutterably
stringent is the earnestness with which we must seek
Him, which includes accepting the shame of our
triviality!

Since you urged me, I have tried three publishers
with the little commentaries. All say they like them
but they won't sell: too arty for those interested
in prayer; too spiritual for the arty! Janet says she
is glad, as they aren't for the marketplace. There is
something in this, though, even on the most material
level, I could have done with a little income! (You

can't think of any way I could earn $50 a year can you??) …

The Franz Kline exhibition starts in Ohio, so maybe you will see it after all. Don't forget to let me know when you leave, and your Christmas addresses, love.

I hope you like the enclosed, with its poetic delicacy. The *Nike* of victory must always be ambivalent, mustn't it, or 'androgynous', a neither-one-thing-nor-the-other? We don't know the rules of the game enough to assess triumph. The exquisite colour and abandonment, the seeming lack of control that is really austere discipline, all this makes Twombly dear to me.[1] What *risks* he takes, and how serenely! Only Jesus is the victory, only He 'knows' with certainty. And in Him, we can hurl ourselves forward as freely and joyously as Twombly does! (If your friend likes this, I could send a second copy??).

1   Edwin 'Cy' Twombly (1928–2011), modern American artist with a free, calligraphic style. The work referred to here may be his painting *Victory 1984.*

19 November 1985

Although I feel I ought to answer your letter, I don't really feel I know enough about the alternatives you suggest for your retreat. Like you, I feel wary about 'a hermitage', unless you had a strict timetable and, even more, regular and helpful human contact every day – personal contact, not just prayer in common. I feel that floodgates closed for over 40 years – closed by God Himself for an apostolic urgency – have now been opened by the same loving God, and to expose yourself unwisely would frustrate His purpose (i.e. drowning instead of sweeping away to new life!!) It also occurs to me that the best time for a lengthy retreat may be *after* the course. I feel you may welcome a few weeks in which you can discuss and consolidate all you've learned. It all should be looked at and accepted into your being, and for this you need both retreat time and a retreat friend. Would it help to come here? If you would like this, let me know as soon as you can. We could easily make Guest House arrangements, I hope, but I myself would need to start preparing immediately. However, dear lamb, don't hesitate to say 'No' if you prefer an American retreat. All that matters is what most helps.

Paternalism and women's lib.: don't you think that a violent protest is always a minority one? That its very stridency reveals that most people don't even see the injustice and need to be awoken?? So the situation you've found would be quite expected.

Health: ah love, I hate talking about this. Yes, I have some pain and the op. is still on the cards, but nothing unbearable. I feel that in other respects I am growing weaker, able to do less and less, but I think I can creep on for quite a time still. How this gradual helplessness of the body rouses up our longing for

Him, our need to live in Him, the true Life … He comes to us in every call, from every angle, more ourselves than we are.

Undated (after Christmas 1985)

… Ann, I beg of you don't encourage *anyone* to write to me – let alone (what a joke!) about me. But as to sanctity and mysticism, I feel that the soul that truly loves Him, that lives in Him and 'does always the things that please Him',[1] such a one will know His heart from within – isn't that 'mysticisim'? How this awareness of living in His life is experienced is immaterial, but the reality is unmistakeable. This to me is the only mysticism that matters. The natural 'mysticism' of insight, of 'experience', is essentially a temperamental quality. A great human endowment, but with no more relevance to holiness (that, deceptively, it can appear to have) than any other human gift.

I am looking forward to your next letter. Oh Ann, it was such a beautiful Christmas, and still is, as Epiphany draws near. This year all was exceptionally pure and still, a time of true Jesus-joy, because there were unusual sorrows. Tell you about it all when you're home again: all a source of deeper love, all to be blessing for the world. Have loved your Motherwell book.[2] The other parcel hasn't come, so I am stopping now in the hope it'll have arrived before I post this on Saturday – so it will meet you on your return. Your Ohio letter has just come. I am happy for you, dearest Ann, that for once at least, you've had the joy of a 'free' Christmas, with nothing demanded by duty or even circumstances. This is the kind of solitary, hidden celebration that has always made my hermit life so radiant. One can be wholly out of self and present in Jesus. Yet this is *always* the state of things if we desire it. All that has happened is that a temporal (and temporary, for you, love), anonymous all-ness is space to realize our nothingness. For you, it may be a sudden dizzying drop, though I don't think so.

I hope you aren't hurt by people's apparent concern only for the office as opposed to the person. Often it is simply the busyness of life, with no other implications. The enclosed Magritte[3] is one of my favourites, playing with the idea of appearance versus reality. This small round ball that sinks is what we see as sun, and it does seem to carry night and brightness with it. How much else of what we accept as experienced fact is really only visual illusion? Oh, we can never 'know' *anything* but Jesus – He is our certainty.

I look forward so much to hearing about Chicago ... Are you well, Ann? Blood pressure??

1   Jn 8.29.
2   Robert Motherwell (1915–91), another artist in the American Abstract Expressionist school.
3   Magritte, *see September 1982.*

1986

2 January 1986

I hope it was a happy Christmas in your diamond-bright atmosphere! Too great a clarity can be bewildering, though, can't it? Perhaps the air was more opaque in Ohio.

Thank you for your beautiful card – very much a picture of what our vocation should be: Jesus, our central core, our life-principle. I was delighted to receive the first 20 dollars, which I promptly spent [on art catalogues]. At first I was even more delighted by the second 20 dollars. I then felt alarmed at whether you were depriving yourself? Dearest, when I said 'earn 50 dollars',[1] I *meant* 'earn'. I suppose I am vaguely wondering whether any religious institution would buy those commentaries.

1   In her letter of 5 November 1985. Impressed by Sister Wendy's spiritual insights into works of art, Ann had urged her to seek a publisher for her 'picture commentaries'. Initially, however, Wendy drew a blank. But the idea of earning pocket money with which to buy her own art catalogues appealed to her and she was clearly still turning it over in her mind. It is interesting to note these modest beginnings in the light of her numerous future publications.

21 January 1986

May the Presentation be a day of grace for you in your solitude. The knife and the blood and the naming: all are significant, aren't they?[1] And your Order was founded to act an 'Anna and Simeon' part,[2] proclaiming Him from the lived reality of total prayer.

I'm sorry the little Chagall is only a photocopy – I've given the card away. The 'O Antiphons' (my translation) are for you to give Father Toby if you like.[3] ...

Your future: perhaps not time yet to become too sharply outlined? I very much like the ideas you suggest, though ... But I repeat, I feel it is too soon to make too concrete a suggestion.[4]

Have you read the January *Way*, with a splendid article on spiritual direction by Fr Lynch, SJ?[5] Shaky at the start, (if only one could get people to realize that one can do *nothing* for another's prayer except emphasize that time must be given – the great prayer of desire – and allay fear and correct misap-prehension) and there is a misunderstanding of something Janet had written at the end – though this was because I didn't explain clearly enough to her. All the rest is very good indeed ...

Dearest, have you considered staying on longer to finish the course (degree? diploma?) so as to be better qualified for retreat work – which essentially means setting the retreatant free to pray, free from despondences, doubts, unfaith, dying desires?

1   For the Presentation, *see 1 February 1981*. 'The knife and
    the blood and the naming' refer to the elements required
    by the rite of circumcision, which would have been the
    primary purpose behind the presenting of the child.
2   In the biblical account, Anna was an elderly widow
    who spent her days in prayer in the Jerusalem
    Temple; Simeon was a 'righteous and devout man' in
    Jerusalem who was on hand to give the child Jesus his
    blessing.
3   The Great 'O' Antiphons are so named because each one
    begins with the exclamation: 'O ... !'. These Antiphons
    are thought to date from around the fourth century
    and introduce the singing of the Magnificat at Vespers
    on the last eight days before Christmas. Sister Wendy's
    translation is as follows:

O Wisdom, O holy Word of God, the whole
created universe lies throbbing in your strong and
gentle hand. Come, show us how to live.
O Sacred Lord of ancient Israel, who showed
yourself to Moses in the burning bush, who gave
him the holy law on Sinai mountain. Come, stretch
out your mighty arm to set us free.
O Flower of Jesse's stem, every eye is held by you,
every prince of foreign power bows down in silent
worship to your beauty. Come, let nothing keep
you from our rescue.
O Key of David, O Royal power of Israel,
controlling at your will the gates of heaven. Come,
break down the prison walls of death and lead your
captive nation into freedom.
O Sun at morning, O brightness of the everlasting
Light. Come, with all your holy sunlight, where we
lie in darkness and in death.
O King of all nations, the only joy of every human
heart. O Keystone of the mighty arch of man.
Come and save the creature you fashioned from the
dust.
O Emmanuel, God who lives with us to rule

and guide; the nations of the earth cry out with
longing. Come and set us free, our Saviour God.

4   Sister Ann was considering the idea of setting up a
    retreat house. Part of the motive behind her sabbatical
    year in the States had been to participate in a training
    course for retreat directors.
5   *The Way* is a quarterly Jesuit publication.

21 February 1986

Thank you for all the marvellous cards of late,
with a special joy in the late Matisse. I was actually
looking at that very picture the day your letter
came: palm tree outside and curtain inside forming
one seamless jubilee of praise[1] – third island as you
say![2]

More and more it seems clear that you should stay on
for the MA. Even your experience of giving a 'credo'
conference[3] emphasizes what He wants to do in and
through you in this most precious area. I was happy
to think you were sharing the beauties of God's work
– His work in me is less radiant but perhaps almost
a stronger witness to His goodness just in that I am
poor material. Oh yes, love, please do write about
Him. The intense, unutterable *goodness* of God is
the heart of the message of your Foundress. It seems
to have been that, specifically, that fuelled all her
yearnings. Surely no saint has been so on fire with
insight into just that simple and infinite truth and the
active desire to proclaim it – not just in words but in

all one is, – surely that is the essence of your Order? But the very simplicity of it is so awesome that one can understand the unconscious need to dress it up, rather as we do with the simplicity of prayer. Your friends will like to know that Janet is two-thirds through a new book, one that will specially interest you, a study of John of the Cross.[4] She is incorporating my *Simple Prayer* into it.[5]

Wasn't I an idiot to say anything about sorrows! They were concerned with a blindness to grace, one of those Pharisee/Prophet situations that sadly arise in the Church ... Only grace came from it, *Deo gratias.* I also had some bodily distress but will be capering about full of energy when you return – in two years' time?? Staying on will affect coming home this year, won't it?? The enclosed is for Lenten prayer.[6] I find it unbearably poignant. Here is the Jesus situation, and here is the inescapable question: where do we stand? With the poor naked one? or with His well-fed victors? Every element seems designed to illustrate St Ignatius' two standards.[7]

1 *The Egyptian Curtain* (1948) (see Plate 5).
2 The expression 'third island' was coined by Ruth Burrows in *Guidelines for Mystical Prayer,* [Continuum, 2007] to express the distinction between the final stage of the mystical life and the two that she describes as preceding it; *see also 22 December 1978.*
3 A testimony of faith.
4 Saint John of the Cross (1542–91), a friar and associate

of Saint Teresa of Avila in the Reform of the Carmelite Order. His spiritual teaching is summarized in writings that have become classics of mystical literature. Like Saint Teresa, he has been made a Doctor of the Church.

5   *See n. 1, 11 November 1977.*

6   This picture has not survived.

7   Saint Ignatius of Loyola, founder of the Jesuits, wrote a form of *Spiritual Exercises* in which he invites the person doing the exercises to meditate on the opposition between two 'standards', that of Christ and that of Lucifer. (*Second Week, Fourth Day*).

18 March 1986

I was looking forward to your letter from Boston, hoping you'd been rejoiced by the Louis',[1] but you wrote an even lovelier letter, so at peace in your disappointment, (though I still hope …!)

Janet told me she had written. Of course, it should be clear that her relationship was something that rarely happens. It was the way God brought them both to mature love, but few are called to this particular fulfilment in Him. The principle, I feel sure, is that everyone must be attentive to whatever is God's gift for *them*. We don't like the labour of this attention – we want hard and fast rulings. But many things are not given by God – and many are gifts, but not from God – and only the heart that prays can distinguish them. Freedom is a weight, but we must accept it trustfully if we're to be psycho-sexually mature religious.

Baffled by this envy classification[2]: have never seen it in you, but then I only recognize two 'sins': pride and sloth, and these we all have. There is pride (in this 'capital sin' sense) in your implicit attitudes towards others, and I've seen with great happiness your battles to become conscious of this lovelessness and reject it. As Jesus draws us into His Mind, we can make this leap into the dark certainty of seeing others 'in Him'. Only He *knows* them, so only He can love them in truth. And we are taken into this.

1   Morris Louis; *see n.3, 31 August 1985.*
2   As part of her course Ann was required to carry out a form of psychological analysis. Apparently this was part of her assessment.

25 April 1986

The enclosed card sums up what your Foundress lived for: to be wholly alive in His Love, and to *manifest* this to those who needed it. The original print has been given to me by the artist, Eileen Cooper, who, I suppose, is the leading woman in the country,[1] – a lovely surprise! Show you when you come. Unfortunately, the longer I contemplate, the more lost I become in its truth, so the commentary is very inadequate. Letting Jesus draw us into His New Manhood[2] is an equivalent of letting Him be, as St Paul says, 'our great Amen to the Father'.[3] That wonderful phrase 'Yes, was always in Him' is also translated as 'Amen': I see all holiness as coming from this. The deepest truth of Jesus was His *response*, His *obedience*: 'I do nothing of myself'.[4]

The Father asking, the Son joyfully saying 'Yes': 'I do always the things that please Him.'[5] Jesus-joy (the ecstasy of action) is precisely this: letting His total 'Yes' well up in us and carry us on to whatever the Father asks. We are never asked to initiate, only to respond. Hence the necessity, the essential life-giving necessity, of prayer, because only the praying heart can hear the Father's requests.

1   The leading woman printmaker.
2   The print was titled *New Man*.
3   Cf. 2Cor. 1.18–20.
4   Jn 8.28.
5   Jn 8.29.

Easter Week 1986[1]

I wouldn't have felt entitled to write immediately on receipt of your posters – heavenly in their beauty, dearest – but want to say just a word about the MA. Our Lord never promised us that only the best would happen, only that He would make all that happened 'best' for us: His peace He gave[2] – and that you've received. So you were not wrong to think, as I do, that the extra year would have been the best and wisest course, the most useful for your Order, which was your aim. But the refusal is another kind of 'wisest and most useful'. Your loving submission has already, perhaps, done more *in Spiritu* than any course could ever do. In that holy light, I am happy my dearest Ann has this surrender to make. Not a pinprick, but a real, true sacrifice.

I've read parts of your letter to Janet. She said spontaneously: 'How well Ann writes!' Have you thought about using letter-form: 'Letters about Things that Really Matter'? An art form that is so flexible has much to recommend it, especially as one can 'preach' without sounding pious (which would *never* do!!).

1 The week beginning 30 March.
2 Jn. 14.27.

13 June 1986

How good of you to remember my blessed anniversary[1] ... You are very right to rejoice with me in His goodness. When I try to look back over the anguished South African years, I am glad I never had the least 'hope' of what was to come. One couldn't have foreseen such happiness anyway. But how I bless Him for allowing me the privilege of living with such difficulty, purely for Him! ...

Your free weeks have rejoiced me. Oh Ann, how wonderfully tender has been His love for you, leading you into His light at the very time when you were ready to advance. That special insight about really loving and being the gentle, humble one who sees and loves in Jesus only: that's very precious.

1 Sister Wendy's anniversary of becoming a hermit.

OTHER LETTERS

Notes to a Novice

Janet has told me you are profoundly happy and wondering about the duration. If it's any help … I too felt it to be sheer bliss when I entered 34 years ago, such bliss that everyone told me it couldn't last. Yet today I know that was but a shallow happiness compared with the bliss that has grown from it. 'First fervour' and 'honeymoon happiness' are *beginnings* – they never, never pass, if we let them work on us. They will grow and deepen. Our happiness is because now we belong to God. The pain of seeing how shallowly we have in fact surrendered is a happy pain, because it will deepen our desire and capacity … Joy gets deeper, greater, every day until heaven.

This day is one of such joy for Our dearest Lord,[1] who is at last able to proclaim to the world that you are His. He clothes you visibly with this holy sign: the habit of Carmel. How we must pray and labour for that sign to become wholly true interiorly, also … Human love frees us for the love of Jesus, as you know.

If you lay your gift on the altar as a gift, your special unique gift, by which you thank Him, through which you praise Him, it all changes. Suffering remains but it becomes not our own, as now, so no longer destroys us. Isn't this really what 'when I am weak, I am strong',[2] and similar words of His, means?

1   She had just received the Carmelite habit.
2   2Cor. 12.10.

*   *   *

We already have a dragon book (though quite different in emphasis) ... But I wondered if you'd like to see this one first? The reason is that the Prioress has shared with me, in confidence, your 'fears', and that's precisely what dragons are: the symbol of man's fear. Great presences, hideous, irresistible, able to disappear at will, destroyers, consumers, immense and threatening – evil! But as soon as we *look at* our fear, as soon as we sit down to portray our dragon, it immediately shows itself for what it is: a product of our own mind. It is essentially unreal, self-created, our own buried darknesses becoming objectified. So all these dragons shown here are essentially a delightful sort of therapy! In Jesus we *know*; 'what can I fear?' But here even art says it!

Continuing the same theme as above:

All His feasts have their own beauty, don't they? I was so happy to hear that all is becoming well in your dragon experience! Jesus came for the dragons, too, not to kill them (except symbolically) but to convert all that psychic energy to heavenly use. The shepherds were a sort of dragon in His Palestine – wild and fearful captors. Yet He brought them in their fearsomeness to His Mother's side and taught them to praise Him. The psychic energies that cause your fear are potential love energies, praise and glory energies. Alleluia!

Although, for several reasons, it was a very feeble conference,[1] alas, the point you make is a profoundly valid one. Love for one another has to have an absolute quality: I love them for what Jesus loves in them, whether I see it or not – and I pray to accept them in their whole mystery. So *their* conduct can never be a sure guide for *mine*. It can rouse my conscience or open new paths to generosity I'd not seen, but it all comes down to what God asks of me, irrespective of the other. 'She's good', '*she* does it, so I can' is very dangerous. Remember Peter and John at the lakeside? 'So I will have him wait – follow *thou* Me'.[2] Take all your sisters into love, unjudgingly, trustfully, and live, yourself, looking only at Jesus, at His standards; looking *solely* at Jesus, living by His light.

1   Sister Wendy had given a talk to the Novitiate.
2   Jn 21.22.

*   *   *

The wonderful thing about God is that *everything* leads to Him. If we are born anxious and eager to see evidence of our growth, these very emotions, held up to Love, 'work' as powerfully as anything else. You do know this, really, but we can't believe in it too much!

The fragrance of your Profession is still very present. In fact, no reason why it should ever fade. He means it to deepen and permeate. 'Your name, O Jesus, is as oil poured out': mysterious and lovely phrase.[1] I hope the joy of having your family present outweighs the pain of saying goodbye. But this pain – on both sides – is so integral to our vocation that it is healing of itself. They too have a vocation – to have a daughter/sister in Carmel. For all of you, any encounter can only be grace.

1   A quotation from a liturgical text that alludes to Ps. 45.

*   *   *

It's not the kind of privilege we would ever choose for ourselves,[1] but Jesus has chosen it. He has asked you to enter into His redemptive love in the way of His own choosing, and I have no doubt at all that every part of it – pain, fear, disgust, shrinking – all will expose your heart's depth to Him as never before. I send you a field ripening towards harvest.[2] All the field must do is accept – and understand ... I promise you that from tomorrow on I shall be holding you up to Our Blessed Lord so that He may take you deep into His redemptive Love. My earnest plea is that none of what you suffer will be 'wasted', none of the pain and none of the fear, either. Know that it is actually Love, it is 'His Love', and He will be the strength and the meaning of all that happens. I also pray a prayer of gratitude for your privilege – and in Lent, too! Another hospital find of mine was that one can pray in solitude if one wakes *early*. Once ambulatory there are balconies or waiting rooms if one wants, but solitude is an interior state, not something material, and one can be deeply Carmelite in a crowded ward – and loving and giving, too. A precious time – but I hope it doesn't last too long, love! United with you in surrender to all Jesus does.

1   This Novice had to undergo a small operation.
2   A picture card.

*   *   *

I didn't in fact mean fear of God, but fear of doing 'wrong' and consequently of attracting God's frown. Afraid of yourself? Yes, I've noticed you have lowly expectations of being loved and wanted. But I have loved and believed in you specially, uniquely, right from the start. So if someone with whom you've little contact and rarely would think of,[1] is regarding you lovingly and happily, all unknown, think how it must be with God, *passionately* concerned for you. This is an act of faith we need to make explicit, one that overflows His Heart with joy (our humble God). It is infinitely easier to delight Him than to displease Him. I loathe these words 'displease' and (worse) 'offend' as applied to Him. They're not in

His 'nature'. A clear, pure anger, yes, as Jesus shows, but always in terms of outrage. 'Come to Me, all you who labour and are burdened'.[2] 'Let the children come to Me'.[3] 'He who comes I will not cast out'.[4] And the tender parables, one after another, often showing concern for the least. We *do*, as you say, tend to see God in terms of our fellows writ large, but this is a narrowing approach.

1   That is, Sister Wendy herself.
2   Mt. 11.28.
3   Mt. 19.14.
4   Jn 6.37.

*   *   *

Found this card – beautiful, powerful work, isn't it? I've never seen the sheer yearning of the searching soul so delicately bodied forth … Don't think 'tolerant' is exactly the right word. It's more a sort of humble empathy that sees how others will receive what one says and does in utmost good will. People are so fragile specially those who conceal it! And though we must always be natural, we must also watch to see we're not unconsciously making others feel stupid or some such interior state. Only the selfless heart of Jesus can 'see' others truly enough to be always wise about them, so we have to accept we'll always be inadequate. But sometimes the desire to have the reverence (key word) we feel for the other comes through sufficiently to let them meet us unafraid.

It's a grace to feel disgusted with our own pettiness but only inasfar as we use it to turn from such an unappealing sight to the pure wholeness of Jesus. *Of course* we all want to be esteemed by people we value – it would be unnatural not to wince if one thought that x had a rather belittling view of one! But: a) the sting of this little humiliation should make us resolve even more explicitly that we know and believe that only what God thinks *matters*. And therefore I choose to bear a human humiliation in peace if it pleases Him. b) And then I leave all judgement to Him. 'Neither do I judge myself,' says Paul, wise man![1] Only He knows what we are really like, we certainly don't know ourselves! c) And finally, I must confess that I wouldn't myself mind 'dear little thing', as a summary! 'Nasty, pretentious lump' is more what I'd shrink from!

1   1Cor. 4.3.

*   *   *

Cannot find a really lovely card, so send this baby owl. Darling fluffy creature, yet with fierce beak and claws! Yet Holy Wisdom, of which the mature owl is emblem, can never be fierce or aggressive. Its main character is gentleness – that prayerful reverence to the other, that enables one to see them for what they are in Jesus' eyes. He wants most ardently to share His Wisdom with us and teach us gentleness of heart, so we have only to 'receive' it.

How I wish there were a way to lend these tremulous, exquisite words to your friend, she would see at once what they mean and perhaps her wounded spirit, always trembling on the brink of self-absorption (that fatal abyss) would be helped to go out of self and into Jesus, our only safety.

I think you have much 'compassion and under-standing' but it is limited at present by the natural. You tend to expect others to see *as you see*, and to feel impatient when they don't. And if people sense that one feels dismissive, their hackles rise and, in fear, they can't listen. We must pray for reverence, that deep acceptance of the difference of others that lets us show them what we are saying. Once people really 'hear', they nearly always respond. But nothing to be sad about. Having difficulties is a way of growing. It opens us up to Him.

Am I mistaken in detecting a slight note of despondency? Living as we do in Jesus, with all sorrow, failure and disappointment primarily just ways of receiving Him more deeply, life is infinitely lovely. It may not appear so, but it *is*. Our happiness, even if happiness of pure faith, is a duty we owe to the sad world where frustrations are not, as are ours, gateways into love.

Happiness is a willed thing, therefore we choose to let Jesus be our joy, our confidence, and to ignore our poor little fumbles. If we really want Him, and want to live in Love, it will most surely happen.

I thought the anaesthetic would fall on one like sleep,[1] unnoticed, but no: whirling up into consciousness, fully 'there' to be 'accepted'. Of course, it could not be *not* accepted, but all the same, a close parallel with all we fear. He lets us face it knowingly, if we allow Him, and so our 'yes' to the unknown and frightening is a pure putting of our hand into His. There isn't any trust when we are in control, is there? It's precisely when it's unknowable that we walk believing He is with us.

1   The recipient of this note had been alarmed by her first experience of an operation under anaesthetic.

*   *   *

No love, it's neither 'petulance' nor 'self' – it is suffering. Some of it is unavoidable, because no human being can ever understand another fully, so hurt and misapprehension are part of life's purification. Think of Jesus and His mother: how we romanticize their perfect understanding, yet the Finding in the Temple[1] and the Marriage at Cana[2] emphasize for us that, for all their mutual love, He was mysterious to her.

Having said that, I would like to make clear that she *does* value you. She loves you and looks forward to your support in the years to come. In a very true sense, you are in the condition of those 99 sheep who get left while the shepherd concentrates on the one. You are never an anxiety to her – she takes your response to her teaching as so true that she doesn't need to labour with you … We only lead souls to God through blood and tears. Can you see what sheer relief it is to have someone about whom she need not worry – and this can seem like lack of real interest?

Bring to your meetings[3] something lovely to share, either reflections on people or on art, etc. For the shy, these meetings can be a real source of distress – 'such an opportunity and I've wasted it'. Not so; you see her solely to grow closer to Jesus. So anything that happens is potentially fruitful.

All the same, tell her this problem, because in part this distress is unnecessary. If you prefer, I would be happy to tell her of the difficulty. Part, as I've said, is just to be accepted with love as inevitable pain and very fruitful. But part may well be just lack of communication. Let me know if you'd like me to speak to her.

I have great faith in you, dear. Ask Our dear Lord to free you from inner insecurities that block your insight into people. You're not specially blocked – we're *all* blocked – but this is a prayer and a longing dear to His Heart. 'Am I a source of His Love for all I live with?' If we want to be, He makes it possible. I join with you in trustfully offering all you are and experience to Him.

1 Lk. 2.41–52.
2 Jn 2.1–11.
3 Novices have regular meetings with their Formator. This particular Novice was finding it difficult.

*   *   *

You've been in my heart these last weeks as looking pressured. The time after Final Profession is so often a hard time. It's as if the forces of destruction rage against the triumph of His Love, and one can suffer from people, events, duties, one's self. You are specially liable to this pressure, being a fragile though strong woman. God hasn't given you stolidity but the sensitiveness that goes with insight. You have to use all that comes to you from within and without as a means to intensify your conviction that only God matters – and His Love. When you've found people misunderstand and events painful and responsibilities heavy and no (apparent) success anywhere, this is the precious time to live for God alone. You must fight to be at peace, dear girl, amidst distress. Anxiety is your enemy.

In case this is of practical help: when I feel disturbed, I try to pinpoint what I feel and why: 'I feel angry/ ashamed/anxious/upset – because …' Then I pull all my being together and place 'it' on His altar. I offer Him the shame/pain and entrust it all to Him, asking only to love Him. By my age, to do this once is enough, and even if it recurs once or twice again, I have merely to remember that it is now God's. You may have to repeat its concentrated surrender. But it *always* works and is wonderfully pacifying!

*   *   *

It seems to me absolutely essential to understand that our sexuality leads us to God, was fashioned for that very purpose and is for ever unfulfilled if not fulfilled in Him. To regard any aspect of our being as 'natural', 'animal', 'non-spiritual', even 'neutral' is to falsify the meaning of what we are. Easy to say, but the implications go very deep and are very powerful.

How our sexuality leads to God is a life-time's work. But we need to understand *why* it does. Everything in our language works against this: note the use of genital or sexual words as swearing, or the general *pudeur* about those bodily organs and functions as if they were non-respectable. We may not be able, temperamentally, or through cultural conditioning, to be free here, but that doesn't matter as long as we *understand*. Will this suffice? The actual surrender to God of all that we are, all aspects of body and mind, all we know and are, all we don't know and are not yet, our past, present, and future: all the personal surrender which means fulfilment in transformation, cannot be talked about or even thought about. We let Him do it and He alone knows what it is.

*   *   *

When someone thinks white is black, all one can do to begin with is help them to see a grey patch or two! Perhaps begin with her view of God, using her natural views on how good *people* act to others, and then move on to the Scriptures. It is worth spending years gently on this point, it is so vital. Keep your expectations low, though, and remember none of us can hear much truth, such is the din that our fears make! But we don't see what *we* don't see – only what others are blind to!

We are not monolithic in simplicity (and this is one of the deepest of human griefs), so even the holy are not fully 'there'. Holiness reflects the capacity, the amount of for-Godness within. As this capacity deepens, so does the Kingdom, but life involves more and more depth being opened up for the Kingdom to enter and transform. (This is what life is *for*.) In Jesus, all was capacity, all was 'there', unified in total love. So, He is unique in fact. It is this and *only* this that makes Him unique. 'Son of God', we approach Him in proportion to our absoluteness of surrender, which depends on more than mere will. It has to be an achieved will, a perseverance in desire that endures the purification of opening up the depth and bringing Him into... our 'there-ness'.

I think we can all practise deliberately exposing our dark sides to God so that His Love can transform them.

As for your second question: we tread a perilous line always between tension and laxity. It *is* a good practice to have a word of Scripture in hand mentally during the day, because one wants to want to desire to grow in His Love. But it has to be practised calmly, without compulsion. One has to stress *both* our freedom, our God-given right to be at peace within, *and* our need for interior discipline. Letting our thoughts roam ad lib. all the time doesn't help towards prayer or knowing Jesus more deeply. Yet constraint and anxiety equally block our union.

*   *   *

The death of a child,[1] perhaps above all a slow, cancered death, cuts to the heart of our faith in God ... It is so terrible, we *have* to think over our theology, accept mystery, reaffirm in utter certainty that God doesn't change what happens but changes how it affects us. The little one is being offered something far more precious than carefree girlhood and maturity, and her parents with her. God grieves as they do. But ... He exerts all His Love to turn that sorrow and pain into joy. Faith grasps this – and prays that it will happen. It is all *choice*; our prayer must be all concerned to choose God, without any *visible* proof. Oh, what mystery.

1   The relatives of this Novice had lost a child in anguishing circumstances.

*   *   *

Anger: two wrong attitudes:

1) to repress and ignore; 2) to explode

Right attitudes: to admit; reserve judgement as to what *kind* of anger until emotion calms. Then a) look at *why*, b) decide whether *ought* to act (i.e. whether it will practically *help*).

Sometimes one has to admit: 'too weak' to lay silently on the altar, but the weakness must be publicly admitted and prayed against.

Notes to a Novice Formator

Could you say to the Novitiate that I feel ashamed of having perhaps spoilt Botticelli's *Mars and Venus* by my inadequate treatment. It is not just a man and woman after the act of love – it is the god of war and the goddess of love, and at a deeper level, it is the two elements of the human soul, and the physical act symbolizes charity, pure love. Our aggressive elements lose their force after love: Mars lies wholly at peace, wholly vulnerable. His armour is cast aside; he has no use for his weapons except to let love play with them, while Venus has become wholly herself through receiving pure love. She is alert, beautifully composed (note the gown, its graceful folds) and waits open-eyed for love to come again. She has become one with Mars.

* * *

I'm afraid my remark hurt you and deepened your sense of being second fiddle. Dear Hilary, you have a real contribution to make – a unique one – and it is founded largely on a humble awareness of your 'lacks'. So please just be happy. Love made you as you are and called you to co-operate in the most precious of works.

Perhaps 'favourites' in novitiate relationships might be worth some prayerful pondering? How *able* – how *free* – are you to see each one *as she is*? But ponder hopefully and looking with great confidence at the wounded Heart of Jesus. How He loves you and asks only your constant and total 'yes'.

*   *   *

I have a distressed feeling of having discouraged you. That last note wasn't clear. (Can't think why the Lord chooses such duds for messengers – and sometimes fear it isn't His choice at all: the dud pushes herself in before the real angel gets a chance). Anyway, what may be, as you say, 'perplexing' is why I should write about charity and loyalty when you already try so hard about them … I think that what the Lord wants you to see, though it's hard to find exact words for it, but it's something like this: Here are areas where you truly try – yet you fail. Why? Because the desire is too surface – the 'yes' to love isn't coming from the very depths of you, and so, when taken unawares, lack of love peeps out. What can you do? Well, what you can't do is what the young man did with his lizard in that wonderful *The Great Divorce*, my favourite C. S. Lewis.[1] The great agony of being unregenerate man is precisely that: we just *can't*. Our will isn't enough 'ours' to be all gathered up in one total act whenever we want to. *But*, when we are wholly convinced of our helplessness – and that's a tremendous grace and we have to suffer and struggle to learn it – then we have the first condition for holiness. (Remember the parable?)[2]. And the second is to realize that, in proportion as we see that we can't, we must believe that God can, and will, and longs for nothing more.

But, third condition, we must ask Him to transform us, holding our helplessness up to Him constantly, which, in turn, we won't have the incentive to do so long as we feel we can fumble along well enough as we are … So really, what I feel God wants so passionately to do in you is to have you see, open-eyed, your weakness, and turn with constant trust to Him to be loved and so made loving. I think it might help if you took the twice-daily examen very seriously[3] – not what, or even why, but where you didn't act in love – just so as to keep alive the turning to Him for the living fire.

You have come a long way to being 'made whole', but love is never satisfied until it has all – and I think another real 'advance' state is at hand for you. Cheers!! It should give you tremendous hope! Lovingly – forgive my inadequateness.

1   *The Great Divorce*, (1945), a novel by C. S. Lewis.
2   This is not referring to one of the Gospel parables but to the story related in *Guidelines for Mystical Prayer* by Ruth Burrows (Burns & Oates: Continuum, 2007) about three servants to a king who were informed that, if they waited long enough for the answer, they would be told all they needed to know to pass an examination. Only the third servant, realizing his incapacity, took seriously his complete dependence on the proffered help.
3   Twice a day Carmelite nuns pause for a short period of self-examination.

* * *

As for conferences: they go best when the preparation is centred on a living insight. Dig out from your heart what you really believe, and develop *that* – don't you agree? So very glad those pictures help. When I've finished my translation work,[1] I want to do a series of art commentaries.

I *know* the Lord of life will make you all His.

1 At the time this note was written Sister Wendy was translating from Latin the *Sermons on the Song of Songs* of John of Ford, a twelfth century, English Cistercian monk. The translation was subsequently published by Cistercian publications, 1977.

* * *

In my youth I too puzzled over this 'fear', but now I see that the love of God is a poor thin thing without it. We *can't* love Him unless we know Him – which means realize He is *God*, with all the implications, – and this is something very terrible. Our relationship to God is so deeply *serious* – the one thing that matters – a great holy weight that should *press* on us every minute. We are not *afraid* of God – it's not fear of anything *happening* to us, or of God 'turning nasty', but just a profundity, an awesomeness, an awareness of Holiness, which immediately creates a stupefied awestruck hush in any heart that is not frivolous. And our hearts *can* be frivolous, chatting easily about God as though He were our teddybear. This is another way of making Him into a false God, who arouses no fear because fundamentally He is our creature: we know where we are. But with God we do *not* know where we are or how to cope. We are not afraid that this will lead to our downfall – we trust Him, we love Him – but with full consciousness that our Father is 'in Heaven'. Only Jesus could look at God and feel the *fullness* of this human awe, and *in* Jesus, our holy fear takes on its full, true dimension – a *love*-fear. In the Old Testament it had a far sterner meaning: they *were* afraid and *so*: God the 'Avenger'. Jesus knew that was not so, yet 'fear' (with no preposition) is only fully serious in Him. It is the knife side of love – its weight, its dignity, its reality.

* * *

I like all you say in the Conference.[1] The essential point – what Thérèse said so clearly[2] – is that God has given us *Himself* in the Bible, and we are turning a careless back on it if we don't use all our human resources to find Him there. We have no *right* to Jesus in our hearts if we don't search for Him in a) a love-relationship b) Scripture c) Church ...

The spirit of each Order is *different*. A nun formed in another Order has first to break down the (excellent) spirit in which she has been formed already so as to acquire the spirit of the new Order. So a fervent, humble novitiate is essential. One can't build the new spirit on *top of* the first – the novice has to be divested, slowly, and that's what is needed here. Both yours are equally good, but different. This one has to make a deliberate surrender of what she 'already knows' so as to learn it

252

again in a Carmelite manner. You would have to do the same if you transferred to another Order. This undoing and recreating is what makes transferring so hard and, in fact, impossible after a certain time. Then novitiate formation has set and the Sister can't change, except to adopt new externals. This novice is young enough to transfer fully, but must pay the price.

1   Sister Wendy was often requested for comments on newly written novitiate conferences.
2   Saint Thérèse of Lisieux (1873–97). Thérèse Martin entered the Carmelite Monastery of Lisieux, France, when she was 16 and died eight years later, aged 24. During this short period she forged a spirituality based on what she termed the 'very little way' of confidence and love, a spirituality which she foresaw would make the way of holiness accessible to ordinary Christians struggling in the world. Canonized by Pope Pius IX in 1925, she has become one of the most popular saints of modern times.

*   *   *

I think you need to say more about *why* we submit: a) to subdue our pride and train ourselves for when we *have* to submit, the big occasions. Perhaps *I* think it should be done 'this way'. But, if the matter isn't important, let me submit my pride and silently do it 'that way'.

b) To resemble Jesus. He took a servant role for His own and a servant is one who is *under* the power of *all* the family. Slave/servant, we have in fact few opportunities, so we should *look out* for some, *wanting* to be the servant who obeys, Jesus, and not independent Big Noise Me. c) To make reparation for those who refuse submission to God. We deliberately do what we don't *want* to, sometimes, and do it freely and happily (no compulsiveness or scruples) to bring humility into the world for *them*.

'In a world without a redeemer, only clarity was the answer to guilt. He would make it all clear to himself, shirking nothing, and then he would decide.' Read this last night in Iris Murdoch. It is *just* what worries me in this novice: no *redeemer*, she is doing it all herself and so, naturally, seeks 'clarity'. With Jesus we simply *obey* – and move on.

a) Personal relationships: I think humility is an essential – we must approach one another with genuine reverence. And the 'value' of the other is not based on any judgements about their qualities but on the price God sets on them: 'The brother for whom Christ died' as Paul says.[1] People are very quick to feel whether we value and respect them or not.

b) Crushes: these are so emotionally possessive that one isn't *able* to 'use' them. I think one has to regard these thoughts as pure temptation and turn away to God.

1   1Cor. 8.11.

*   *   *

I'm not quite happy about the 'desires' and what I 'like'. There can be *feelings*, and of course, as such, neutral. All depends on how I *act*: what do I *do*, if anything, to implement these desires? Just as desire for God can seem very real, yet in practice bear no fruit. I think you need to say this, to point out that it's what I actually *say* and *do* and *will* that shows how seriously I want God and *believe* that Jesus has made eternal life 'mine' for the asking. I'd also stress again that we *have* to ask: how seriously and often, every day, do we consciously hold out empty hands and beg for the living water?

You've a real note of earnestness in this way, but I think these points would make it more *effective*??

Splendid conference! With regard to areas of poverty: this can mean: a) personal deficiencies, lack of intelligence, which pride has to accept and simply live with. *Not* important. Jesus doesn't even *notice*.

OR, b) lack of generosity, *spiritual* immobility. That does matter. I have to be constantly raised up to Him for strength to overcome them. But this isn't really relevant to this conference.

* * *

Difference between Active and Contemplative vocations:[1]

a) I wouldn't say [the contemplative has] 'less direct contact': *very* direct contact but with fewer people – and the main service rendered there is in love. The contemplative gives herself to 'people in *concrete* practice by loving the community.

b) Regarding lifestyle, yes: [the contemplative has] emphasis on office and regularity that isn't possible in active life. All formation is to fit one into one's vocation; the difference is really only in the sheer form of lifestyles.

c) No, I think she is wrong regarding gifts (and also regarding similarities. There is a *great* difference between Carmel and her Order.) But *everyone* needs strength and power. Just as much needed for utter fidelity to prayer as in building up a foreign mission station, etc. And light and wisdom very needful for those who deal with people.

All I can see is that the Contemplative takes as her life's work surrender to God within a *narrow fixed compass*. Whereas the Active surrenders in a fluid open-ended environment. The Contemplative has security but monotony; the Active has interest and excitement, but insecurity. The Contemplative has 'desert', nothing to 'show'; the Active has 'market', much to show, perhaps, but greater danger in achieving it. The Contemplative is tempted to concentrate on self; the Active to concentrate on action. And each is tempted to feel the other vocation leads to greater holiness!

1   These notes were written in response to a query from a
    Sister in a different Order. They refer to particular points
    she had raised.

*   *   *

It seems to me that one must insist that the novices
(a) accept direction, and (b) provide sufficient
knowledge of their mind's working to make that
direction possible. But the area beyond, where one
shares at depth, I feel isn't strictly 'spiritual'. It is a
means to God, but the mechanism is natural: mutual
affinities, simplicities, etc. In heaven, we shall all
share like that – & perhaps a holy person's opening to
another of her deeps can draw a like response. But by
and large, *not* finding a response (which one knows
is *there* but denied to one) is part of human pain.
One sacrifices the joy of really 'speaking' and thanks
Jesus the Word for the times when it is given. I think
perhaps there's an element of human (and Carmelite)
inadequacy and loneliness here that for *you* is very
hard. But you have a humble longing really.

*   *   *

I like it very much[1] – you've got so much here,
(I won't add *too* much for one conference!) but I
think you should make the reason plainer as to *how*
freedom comes *from* God *through* our attitude to
others. Jesus *cannot* forgive us (because we can't
receive it, it's only surface,) until we have a forgiving
attitude to others. As we open up, God can come in.

C. S. Lewis, in his autobiography,[2] has a wonderful passage on this: how he could only receive mercy when he had finally opened his heart to giving it.

I agree we stress: 'God is *here*; receive Him', as opposed to: 'God is coming, watch for Him', but both are different ways of stressing the constant attention we need. And both are true … He has not finally 'come', so, until then, sail in hope.

1   For example, the conference.
2   Lewis, C. S., *Surprised by Joy*, 1955.

*   *   *

An unusual John Baptist[1]: not a weatherbeaten ascetic but a beautiful vigorous youth, yet the goat he embraces so tenderly is the poor condemned scapegoat. The white of virginity & red of martyrdom look too rich for the desert, but if you look well, he has overlaid them with the rough skin of his new garment. And how symbolic that the rock on which he reclines is bearing fresh greenery. I suppose it all points to the joy & beauty of a penitential life, how sweet & fruitful it is, how *happy* one is to live solely for God.

1   From the description this would seem to have been a reproduction of the *Boy with the Ram* [*John the Baptist*] by the Italian Renaissance painter, Caravaggio, in the Galleria Doria Pamphilj, Rome.

*   *   *

I think the main element in your card is its total simplicity of being.[1] There she stands, plain, dumpy, wholly engrossed in the unromantic business of standing to bath. Yet Rembrandt sees all the ordinariness as wholly beautiful. It *is*, it is there. No pretence, no foolish yearnings to be 'other'. The artist accepts her and loves what he accepts. And how pictorially lovely, too, the white chemise and clear water and the skintones.

1   A reproduction of Rembrandt's *Bathsheba*. The painting is based on the famous Biblical scene related in 2 Sam. 11 when King David sees Bathsheba bathing from his palace roof.

*   *   *

I like what you say. My own emphasis would be much the same.[1]

(a) *sacrificial*: something God *asks* of us, and its depth is our interior responsibility.

(b) *functional*: becomes play-acting if it doesn't achieve its purpose: to set us free for total love …

I don't feel enforced enclosure (grilles etc.) has anything to do with it. All depends on whether we say yes to our vocation or not.

1   These few lines were written in response to a query about the purpose of monastic enclosure.

*   *   *

Mary Magdalen.[1] The Renaissance painters usually

painted half-lengths of her with the alabaster vase. I
know we have Crivelli's, & others too. This is Mary
at the *beginning* (the Novitiate): beautiful, superbly
dressed, wholly in command of herself; repentance,
joy, and determined to pour out her perfume, but all
under her own control.

Then we move to the next series of paintings (van
der Weyden and others). This is the Magdalen at the
Cross. Now she has borne the cost, she is one of a
group, and she is not concerned with *her* offering
but with Jesus & with Mary. Yet she is still beautiful
– beautifully dressed.

Then the *Noli Me Tangere* pictures usually show a
difference.[2] *This* was the crucial moment in her life,
not the 'entering' (as in the case of the sinful woman
with the vase of ointment), or even the 'Profession'
(as at the Crucifixion). Mary is different now, shown
in a much simpler dress, and the intense emotions
of the passion scene have disappeared beneath the
reality of Jesus and what He says. She was still herself,
still playing 'her' part at the cross. Now Jesus is the
only reality. Only Donatello has dared (or realized)
what 'Noli Me Tangere' *led* to: this burnt-out husk
of a woman who lives only in Jesus, only for Jesus.[3]
She and her beauty have vanished, not under the
onslaught of grief and sorrow but under the onslaught
of passionate love. She has grown gaunt and ragged
because she wants only Him. This is her *soul* we are

seeing, not her bodily appearance as it externally was. Donatello's Magdalen is terrible to contemplate but it symbolizes the cost, which the young Mary could not even have imagined. Yet she chose it, blindly, out of love. Donatello's figure, if contemplated, has a profound and moving beauty. *She* doesn't find it 'terrible' to have nothing but Jesus.

1 In this reflection Sister Wendy draws an analogy between the three stages of commitment in the religious life and the three, archetypal iconographic depictions of Saint Mary Magdalene.
2 'Noli me tangere' ('Touch me not')are the words spoken by the risen Christ to Mary Magdalene in the garden of the resurrection as she falls at his feet in recognition, according to the account in the Fourth Gospel.
3 According to an early legend Mary Magdalene retired into the desert after Christ's ascension where she lived a life of solitary penitence. It is this gaunt figure of the ascetic Magdalene that is the subject of Donatello's sculpture.

*   *   *

I find it a frightening book. How swiftly William[1] is borne away by evil, despite his nobler intentions! And how well Hussein, poor little man, behaves in contrast! Surely it's because William relies on and believes in only himself, while Hussein knows he is powerless and clings to some Power greater than his own. He may not know what the Cross means, but he does know it stands for God and that he is wholly lost without Him ...

Also frightening is the revelation of what dark forces

can be genuinely worshipped. Genuineness is never enough: we have to use our minds to delve deep and evaluate all 'religion'. Very ugly things are believed about our dear God even in the church.

1   The book in question has not been identified.

*   *   *

The South American sage, Don Juan, says of warriors ... that they have 4 qualities. To be a warrior 1) one has to have respect (a reverence, a humility); 2) one has to be aware of fear (fully serious and 'real'); 3) one has to be wide awake at all times; and 4) one has to be self-confident (that is, confident of God's love and care). He sums it up as an 'awareness of intent', a most intense concentration of all our being. This could be misunderstood and cause strain and self-centred tension (mighty and all-important ego!) but, understood aright, it could be very helpful, no?

There is always something thrilling about a great natural gift, isn't there? And how inevitable people see it as dictating the whole shape of a life – overriding all other considerations. Isn't a vocation in the same category? A gift so great that all else that would be part of human life falls away, quite naturally. And like a musical art all *we* have to do is practise, learn from teachers, take our gift seriously ... But we *can* do this precisely because we have 'the gift'.

*   *   *

Are these any use to you?[1] Two representations of joy. The Lowry is earthly joy: VE celebrations.[2] There is an objective deliverance to be celebrated and man is doing all he can: flags, feastings, holidays. Yet these little ant people, crushed by the great weight of the impersonal building that bears down upon them, shut up and imprisoned in their narrow streets and box-like homes – how *depressing* they are. In the smoke-filled air, the flags have no colour; it is a dead picture, superbly organized. But the Ricci is in total contrast: heavenly joy where all is light, space, freedom, weightlessness.[3] Nothing is fixed, darkness reels away defeated, the imprisoning truly flies apart, the constricting soldiers in their armour are blown away; over all is the brightness of the Risen Jesus.

The point seems to me that this bright freedom, where God does all and man is powerless, is the glorious *truth*: this is exactly what joy is, letting Jesus be all to us. But the heavy activity of the Lowry may well be how it feels. He shows man's work and, indeed, man must put up his flags and lay his tables. But the cheering, the freedom, must come from Jesus; we can't do it for ourselves and, if we try, we get the dead weight of the Lowry. We don't have to feel the glory – it is *not* earthly – but to live by faith in it and to let it inwardly free us.

Can't help but feel you are 'weighted'. I suppose not-too-well, and the pain of head … etc.? But you don't 'live' in the shadow, whatever you 'feel': you live in the Jesus-joy, I know, so I pray for you with great confidence. He gives you a precious gift at present.

1   Two pictures.
2   L. S. Lowry, *VE Day*, Glasgow Art Gallery. Lowry was a painter of cityscapes and industrial scenes in which humans often appear dwarfed by their surroundings.
3   Sebastiano Ricci, *Resurrection*, Dulwich Picture Gallery. Ricci's work is characteristic of Late Italian Baroque.

*   *   *

That is an exquisite Cezanne ...[1] Can't add much, though. The big thing, I think, is the seriousness. Two persons playing cards in a café: trivial theme. Yet Cézanne is saying: *nothing* is trivial. All is deeply, beautifully serious. All offers profundity and has meaning, although, prayerfully, he does not spell out that meaning; he contemplates and receives it. Not only the men, the table, the cloth: all inanimate nature, too, is full of dignity and truth. It's a picture that calls us all to live deeply and therefore silently. Only the still, attentive heart can 'see' the breath-taking beauty of these dull colours and solid shapes. There is no 'unimportant', says Cézanne: all is holy, all is lovely ... Oh, what a glory of a picture ....

1   Cézanne painted several versions of *The Card Players*. Sister Wendy is probably reflecting on a reproduction of the copy in the Courtauld Art Gallery.

*   *   *

Sometime, share that deep entrance into the truth of Confession with the Novitiate. Yes, we *parody* the sacraments, cling to self-made 'versions' that we can hide away in – and we do this always, in every respect … Not only is the speaking aloud and asking a necessary element but it must be to *another*.[1] Man has been made to live in society and the sacraments *force* us to live out the spiritual implications of this. Forgiveness and sorrow are essentially a Jesus–soul affair, but they have then to be incarnated, as you say. There are two aspects here: the simplifying of the actual spoken words – when we understand what we're really doing – and the great importance of actually going to confession.

1   That is, sacramental Confession.

*   *   *

… Never mind if the steps go on-and-on. Great leaps are not common. But He can leap us forward if we take our patient steps. And at some point, or points, the steps cross a boundary …

*   *   *

I'm sorry I kept the letter so long. Oh, *what* a lovely true letter! Surely all would profit from it? … Could you show it anonymously? Or else ask her permission? 1 know – as she does – that there's nothing 'new' here, but it does come over with great force as a searching heart genuinely discovering her vocational

265

mysteries. Every Novitiate has to go through the same search, and it's only when solitude, in all its beauty, humility, unselfishness, poverty etc., has become *real* in the heart that teaching comes alive. I found this very moving in the letter, where one can see this happening and the price being generously paid, although the soul herself does not see it.

Insight is a precious responsibility. If we see, yet shrink from doing, we make it impossible for Him to give Himself. When we were in ignorance He could do more than to the fearful, doubting heart who knows – but in practice doesn't.

*   *   *

Excellent conference. The quotes from Saint Teresa[1], though, sometimes seem clearly to refer to *interior* 'solitude', i.e. recollection. Perhaps you need to spell out more explicitly that recreation is solitude.[2] Solitude is not primarily a *bodily* thing, being interiorly and corporeally 'alone', although *some* measure is a help, a need, towards realizing the end of true solitude, which is of the *heart*. (Cf. that Peanut cartoon about the 'solitary' walk, where self, in all its guises, provides a host of noisy partners ...!)

Hence, perhaps you need to spell out that *solitude* is to open us to love. Community, which is at its most intense at recreation, purifies and makes actual that love. It is the two wings of the bird: I *can't* love Him in solitude if *don't* love Him in my Sisters. But I *can't* love Him in my Sisters if I'm not drawn into *His* love in solitude.

However, the more I think of this, the more I wonder if you are not including *too much*? Really, solitude needs a fully developed conference, and then a second one on recreation that builds on what you've already established … Hope I've not been a hindrance. Just – and always – talk is of no value unless it helps.

1   Saint Teresa of Avila (1515–82), Reformer and Foundress of the Discalced Carmelite Order.
2   By 'recreation' Sister Wendy is here referring to the daily period of recreative conversation and activity that is a regular feature of contemplative religious life.

*   *   *

(a) You. Yes, this letting *Jesus* do and be in you is 'the way'. Too often – unconsciously – you are limited by yourself, not necessarily a selfish self, but a human and hence closed-to-some-things self. You are right in saying 'over-protective': your love makes you want to shield those you love, but it is Jesus you would shield them from also. Your affections in general get in the way of your objectivity. You tend – again unconsciously – to over-estimate, or at least see all the good in, those you are attracted to and to underestimate and quickly see the weakness in those you are not *en rapport* with. This does not come between Jesus and you. But you must recognize it and discount it and, above all, hold it out to Him so that all these natural feelings will be transmuted into His love. You want Him and you are truly growing in it – but always there is more ...

(b) She. Whether her personnel difficulties are objective or subjective, the point is that that is *not* where we live. We *embrace* the cross; we want the real, actual Jesus. If we groan and kick, however inwardly, we are looking in the wrong direction. Recall Thérèse,[1] resolving to hide the suffering even from Jesus? *That* is what she needs and it's the very opposite of what she is doing. But this is where growth in Christ will be for her. No need for you to discuss people, just to point out the underlying attitude we should have: 'Charity is patient and, kind' etc.[2]: let her meditate on that passage. *All self* resolved to see *good* in others, choosing to kiss the cross and ignore the pain! Deep, true, selfless surrender.

We don't realize how profoundly God comes to us in every single Sister, and that how we receive what she is, how we *see* what she is, is how we react to her.

1   Saint Thérèse of Lisieux.
2   1Cor. 13.4–6.

*   *   *

(a) I would say that the essential point about Wisdom is that it's our word for the Latin *sapientia*, which is an *experiential* word. *Sapio*, its verb, from which it comes, means 'to taste', 'to savour', 'to know' from an inner experience ... This is why Wisdom is always seen as the highest of the gifts and is always used in the Old Testament as a symbol of God Himself. It means we know God *directly*. And so Wisdom, in a very real, mystical sense, is Jesus, as He is the means by which we know the Father. Very hard to find words as Wisdom is the mystical gift *par excellence* and in itself.

(b) I don't think Patience has any relevance, really, except in that one who tastes of God, who knows of her own experience – felt or not, objectified as Jesus or not – that He is All, will naturally have patience with the trivial events of life. But equally, they will have Love and Joy and Perseverance, etc.

(c) 'Christ, the Wisdom of God', says Paul,[1] and the world cannot understand. The cross is the extreme instance but *all* of Jesus only makes sense if we 'experience' God: i.e. have a faith so total that we know from within.

(d) I think Romans 5 is the best description. But wisdom is so all pervasive ... that it is hard to speak of it, except briefly. As the mystical gift it is the essential contemplative gift, and all prayer is hollow unless the gift of Wisdom informs it. But clearly there are degrees. The one wholly possessed by God lives the gift of Wisdom in its depth: 'experiences' Him in everything ... Others, still flowing towards this point, experience Him only in some things, often specifically 'holy' or beautiful things.

(e) *Not* to be confused with feelings or emotion. Thérèse[2] 'felt' very little, but *lived* wholly dedicated to God. The gift can only be known in its *effects*. Centred on God, living the life of Jesus, as Paul says. The Old Testament says that 'wisdom is known by her *children*', i.e. her actions.

Any use?

1   1Cor. 1.24.
2   Saint Thérèse of Lisieux.

*   *   *

You know how I often say that we must receive God *as He comes to us*, that it's in the actual context of what-is that we find Him: well, as you suggest, the seeing – receiving Him as He comes – is 'knowledge'. Those Resurrection Appearances: 'Their eyes were held and they knew Him not'[1]; 'thinking He was the gardener'[2]. It has always seemed to me that no one refuses God when they see Him. But they see Him only when clearly apparent *as God*. Life is a division between 'holy things' – prayer, Divine Office, etc. – & 'non-holy'. But if people saw Him *all the time*, every minute would resolve into a simple response to Him. It's this ability to look beyond appearances to see God, to hear what He is *actually* asking. It could be to enjoy country dancing, to praise Him in it, or to sweep a floor for Him, or deal with another as if she were Him, etc. Knowledge never misses the face of Jesus, whatever the disguise, and it realizes that there are no rules or methods. It's essentially a *personal* thing: *I* look at Jesus and see each moment *acquire* what *now* he is asking and giving. It takes all life out of our hand and surrenders it to God. It demands total attention in the most actual and practical and all-encompassing gift imaginable. And it is the key to a 'supernatural' life.

1   Lk. 24.16.
2   Jn. 20.15.

*   *   *

Heaven. It seems I put it very bodily, but I don't like any idea of heaven which implicitly sees it as Nirvana, all our personality blotted out. But what causes my distaste may not be valid. It's because ecstatic prayer – where there *is* only God (and this is what Nirvana / Heaven implies) – is too 'terrible', too intense, to be bearable for eternity. But maybe He will change us. However, if I am right, and we do remain our complete selves, then we retain our memory. All sad memories will be transformed – we'll see the love and the pattern He wove – but our gratitude and praise will be fragrant with a sort of loving and tranquil contrition. We shall see what we have done, how we have failed Him, how He bore it all and made up for it at His expense. Our love will grow deeper and more radiant because of it, but the grief will remain to give it the depth of truth. I see purification as co-existing with Heaven. We continually become purer and so more aware of love ... This isn't 'self', it is personhood: that which makes me what I am.

*   *   *

Sorry I didn't reply yesterday but I had a temperature and was very hazy-in-the-head. Still am! Love, I wouldn't be too anxious as you are 'involved' and I feel it will work itself right. No, it's when there is no natural involvement that you are at danger. There are infinite depths still to be opened up so as to become His. No blame to you, but the more concentratedly you can be 'His', the more of you comes under your grasp, as it were, and whatever you do grasp I know you surrender. It's the not-yet-grasped that cools fervour and can, as you sadly see, be an effect of hidden laziness. But we have to suffer the pain of this. It *is* hidden, and all we can do is pray to see how and where we are lazing again, not taking things seriously, not thinking things through, etc. Every step closer to Him means we see more. So I feel very great hope.

You know how profoundly I long for you to be absolutely His possession. I see in you nothing to be 'destroyed', no 'conversion' needed, but there are still depths of stillness, silence, really looking at people, really receiving them. You *do* do this often. But there's work always.

'The clouds of night have passed away'.[1] The clouds are still passing here, and the full sunburst of Jesus is only caught in places by sky and sea, which is how life is, isn't it? Everyone will be bathed in the full radiance in heaven (or when they are transformed into Jesus). But even the fragment tells of the whole in which we *believe*. The clouds *have* passed, and we must live in that knowledge.

1   This note was written on Easter Day.

*   *   *

I feel very compassionate both for her and for you,[1] but it seems to me this sort of process is inevitable. Being what she is, I don't think it would be possible for her to receive the full grace of Jesus in Carmel without these terrifying 'undoings'. The self that has kept her going all these years is disintegrating, and she feels *she* is disintegrating. Not so. It is a false self, an ego-self as opposed to the infinitely humble, infinitely open and secret Jesus-self. The only way for her to cope is to be both simple and humble about it all. I know myself the fear and pain of 'psychosomaticism': one simply has to admit that one is not what one would like to be and this *doesn't matter*. Whether she has objective ills or not, she feels physical distress and this is real and can really be offered up to Him for the world. We have to accept we have a lowly image of ourselves, both in our own and in other's eyes. God made our bodies, our minds, our temperaments (using human means of heredity and environment); let us give Him the joy of gladly bearing all the pains of our condition, letting them carry us to Him. Unless she grasps this and does it, every manifestation, whether real or feared, of her weakness is going to provoke an ego-crisis! Once we see that is all it is, we can bear to be neurotic, flawed, pathetic – and even be glad of it as a means to come closer to Jesus. She knows we see her as *basically* fully sane and with every reason to grow into wholeness. But to grow there she must pass through the painful undoing of her self-image. So all is well!! Perhaps this will help the nausea. I agree, we *must* eat. If she grasps the nettle of her fear, says 'thank you' [for it], perhaps the nausea will go. But equally, it could be she has some psychical condition that causes it. But gently, gently: what does it matter?

You certainly have my prayers, but I feel that all this is very understandable. She is a complex woman and desperately keen to live up to her ideals. One of the deepest functions of the Novitiate is re-evaluating ideals and discovering that – usually – (and certainly in her case) these ideals are inadequate. Naturally all this is *humiliating* and *painful*. It is all mystery, but it has to be endured and lived through with *gratitude*.

What is being taken from us is only to leave space for something better and nobler. The second lesson of the Novitiate – though it is already known in part by all who have sought God truly in the past – is our complete inability to do it ourselves. She must accept that simplicity has to be *learned*, *prayed for*, given as His gift. It can't come by 'deciding'. We learn the human elements, i.e. not to be too taken up with ourselves; to learn Jesus; to use our powers of mind and will in understanding Him, but none of this *makes* us free. It simply prepares the ground for the Lord. When He sees we can accept it, He simplifies us. It can take years of trustful loving effort. This again is humbling and painful. But the pain is part of the process. Nothing is wasted if seen in the context of un-selfing.

1   Referring to one of the Novices.

Notes to an elderly nun

Oh yes: 'saintliness' and 'a saint'! One does all God wants, lives without any imperfections, and the other is a living fire of love for Him. It is like the difference between a truly good, loving wife, who always puts her husband first and is never selfish, and a woman passionately in love, who only exists to please her beloved. May He make us like that.

You are held deep in my prayer, and I ask God to keep you small, lowly, trusting, and happy, *looking only at Him*.

* * *

I think there is a risk of making our life sound 'antique', you know, a sort of historical fossil but not of much contemporary relevance.[1] You very beautifully avoid this in what you say about Our Blessed Lady, you show her as an ordinary woman, but I do feel that the historical approach to Carmel makes us sound like 'special' people, living in a past world … I fear people expect nuns to be 'different', special, rather remote spiritual beings, that's why I hesitated over any suggestion, however innocent, that we were actually living that 'perfect love' that we all *long* to live. Our goal and desires they can understand, as long as they understand that, just like them, we are striving – not reposing blissfully on the clouds of achievement!

1   This Sister had written a short talk to give to a group of women visiting the monastery.

*   *   *

… To answer your letter:

1) Yes, whatever the past has been, for all of us it was God's loving preparation for a total gift of self to come. In a way, too, a previous training that one can look on as 'unreal', means we are now more sensitive, perhaps, to reality, having had to search for it.

2) I know well you don't write to everybody as you do to me, and I know it is solely because you are looking at God and awaiting His word through me. So it's my responsibility, in return, to take what you say and hold it up to Him – though if His light shines on any part of what you've said, I must try and find words to express this to you. Oh dear, so badly expressed. But I mean that I don't just say things out of my own head. What *I* think is not worth writing down.

3) This is the real disagreement between us. Dear Lucy, to live a life wholly given to God would mean sanctity. It would not only mean no, even involuntary, movements of, say, impatience, but it would mean such an awareness of God that no opportunity of loving is ever missed. Now, although all people, of all vocations, aim at this – and Carmel is organized to help us lose

ourselves completely and be transformed in God – it takes a lifetime of heroic generosity for this state to be achieved, and one of the greatest sorrows of God's heart, is that so few Carmelites *are* heroically generous. Our life, in most cases, is a preparation, more or less total according to the depth of our love, for being wholly given. But oh, so far from attainment. Do you see now why it cuts me to the heart to hear anyone talking as if this great burning desire of God's had been granted her – even as if it followed, almost naturally, from entering the religious life? Whereas it takes an agonizing death to self for Him to give His love like that, and few, few, few, few will take this terrible plunge.

4) I know I see in you the surface self-importance (and how beautifully it is dying away, as you draw nearer to Him), and, deep down below that, the desire to live a life that is only prayer – the life of Jesus. But for Him to make this desire an actuality, you must be totally true – in words, in thoughts, in deeds that only express love: God, never self.

Does this clarify things at all, dear Lucy? It's not that I think you are unreal, but you still have further to go in laying aside all the props of self-importance, and living naked and simple under the light of the Holy Spirit. But since there is nothing He wants more than to have you live like this, you have only to ask Him to do it, to trust, and to keep your thoughts resolutely away from anything that is not Him.

Hope this is not too clumsy – I do so want you to be what He wants – and what you want.

*   *   *

Don't overdo things, love, now you are 'up and about', will you? The precious body God gave you has had a rough shaking, and you have a *duty* to be gentle and understanding with it. That must be your Lent!

Sometimes it is a help to glorify God for what He has taken away – to bring us closer to Him – and sometimes we give Him glory for what he has *not* taken, also to bring us into closer union. He has not taken your eyes or ears; He has not crippled your hands so as to make all work impossible; He has not bewildered your brain with terrible pain; He has not taken away your dear community, and your ability to receive the sacraments and praise Him in His Holy Place. So much richness! So much to *use* for Him!

Are you finding it wearisome in bed? I hope not, and that the warmth and ease, with nothing to do all day but pray and leaf over the pages of a book, are having the good physical effect the doctor expected? I would like to think you were having a kind of retreat, which would be perfect, but I know from my own, (now-not-to-be-repeated sojourns in bed) that it can be disappointing – people pop in, and one can't 'let go'. But maybe your doctor is better guided than mine was!... Well, the real purpose of this is to wish you the most blessed of feasts tomorrow.[1] Here is one feast in which we are all intimately concerned, whether rejoicing with our dear dead, or just resting in the certain knowledge that God's grace will one day turn us, too, into the saints of His choice. Maybe not the kind of saint we would have chosen, but what He wants, so infinitely better. I love to think of the countless hosts in heaven, don't you? All giving Him glory in the depths of what He has made of them, no little corners still kept back for self, no small ungenerous thoughts or half-conscious acts: all God's, total surrender. May He bring this to pass in us even on this earth.

1   All Saints.

*   *   *

When I was ill, it always seemed to me I could cope better if only I had my clothes on! One feels more capable, somehow. And now you are walking about, too! Bravo! But we both know that the hardest is yet to come, when the full realization of your curtailed activity comes home. I don't fear for you, though. It is like an operation, and God is whittling away all he sees must go for Him to fill the space. So the hurt is life-giving. The danger, as you've seen, is that one thinks of oneself and how one is feeling. But it is *God* that matters, and I know He will give you all the grace you could possibly need. Sickness cannot *make* us self-centred: what it does do is *reveal* the selfishness that our activities hid from us, and from others perhaps. Now, with little to occupy us, we see what we are. *This is grace.* We are shown so as to trust to Him for transformation. If we *refuse* to let our minds dwell on self, if we constantly raise them to Him, He will give us Himself in a way we have never dreamt of.

You are so very often in my loving thoughts, and I ask Our Blessed Lord to press on you with all the force of His Love. These are such precious days for you – as I know you understand well – days that are purifying your soul and printing on it, more deeply than ever before, the likeness of Jesus Himself. So I don't regret a single minute of them, for you, and I say my warmest 'thank you' to Him for His goodness to my poor suffering Sister.

I rejoice with you over the graces of the last week, difficult though it has been for you. I always think illness is like a knock on the heart from Our Lord. He wants to tell us He will soon be coming, and He asks: 'Are your hands empty?' 'Are you ready for this?'

*   *   *

I looked up at Lauds, and there didn't I see someone who I thought was a compulsory late riser! Is this something new? It must surely mean you are very much better and I thank Our Lord most lovingly. I hope the cold feeling at your heart is also better. This drizzly weather is not your best time, but it is our joy to open our hearts always to His sunshine, isn't it? There can't be a zero where Jesus is! And I see Him there within you.

> My goodness! My gracious!
> Whomever did I see,
> Sailing down the choir
> Like a ship upon the sea?
> Could it have been Stella?
> Fortissima et bella!
> Rosy cheeks and smiling face
> Lighting up God's holy place!
> How *glad* He was to see her,
> And how glad am – I!!

*   *   *

The liturgy is very beautiful, isn't it, so concentrated on Our dear Lord's victory that all else just falls into place behind it. That's how He wants us to live: with Him our joy, no thoughts of ourselves and what we want or can't do.

This is the day when He showed Himself literally as flames of fire[1]: His love made visible. And my prayer for you is that you open yourself simply to this devouring Love. I feel He asks you to live it most of all with your Sisters. For each He wants you to be all love: their glad servant, never wanting your own way, eager to give them all they want in time and attention and reverence; content to be taken advantage of, if that should happen, asking no glory or self-satisfaction … A life of love that only the Spirit could achieve in us, but one that He will, if we ask and long for it.

1   Pentecost.

*   *   *

Your little note touched me deeply. *I am quite sure* He is going to draw you close to the burning fire of His own Heart. With your nature, you feel a need to 'control' your environment, as it were, and to surrender to Love in the constant stress of daily living must be far from easy. But you *desire* it and how much more *He* desires it – and so it will come to pass. I can see a change in you over these years that we have known each other – you seem to me closer to Him. Pray for me too.

My answer in full must be in the silent oblation of a living prayer but perhaps our God will let me add: 'Don't worry; *He* will see to the sanctifying (of you and others through you) if you only press close to His heart.' *All is Love*, either adoring or repentant, and *He* sends the darkness, the failure etc. solely to turn you from yourself to the glad strength of His Love. Lose yourself in it!

*   *   *

Dearest, loneliness and a sense of failure, the whole burden of human life: Jesus knew them to their depths and, in Him, we can drink His cup with love and peace. We know, in Jesus, that this is the cup of His most loving Father and that it comes from Love. So we hold out loving hands, despite weariness.

*   *   *

When I spoke about my stupidity I meant more than the practical side, though I suppose it is all connected. I was really talking about my strange lack of common sense that can make me appear so demanding and unreasonable. Like a child asking his mother to mend his toy when she's up to her eyes in the kitchen! It is very hard to explain, because I am so unaware of what I am doing, but I have always exasperated people – and never known why or how. You say I have annoyed you a few times, and my heart sinks, knowing how far that has ever been from my mind. The kindest thing, truly, is to tell me when I am inconsiderate, and then I will stop at once. Please tell me, if you can remember, what the annoying things were, so I can avoid them in the future. One would think a grown woman would not need to be told, and indeed, I can't explain it – almost a mental deficit in me. My mind is just not able to give its full attention to things, so the top surface makes suggestions and the real 'I' is not sufficiently in command to see that they are silly. Quite honestly, I hardly ever have more than a vague 'that would be nice' sort of feeling behind my requests, and 'No' is a good answer. Is this any clearer to you? I grieve so to feel I make life harder for anyone, let alone a friend.

You have told me before of what you describe as this 'nasty streak', and in my case I don't think it applies. But all the same I pray often for the Lord to give you His own all-loving Heart. Not for my sake because if you had not told me I would never have known I irritate you, you have always been very sweet with me, but for His own sake. If we draw any secret lines, beyond which we don't want to go, how can He give Himself wholly? But perhaps you speak too harshly of yourself? And the sense of spiritual failure is the greatest grace He gives.

*   *   *

I meant this: that to desire a sacrament and do all we can to receive it, *is* to receive it. The man who longs for baptism or Holy Communion, etc, receives these sacraments just as truly as the man who has the historical opportunity. As long as he has done his best to meet the conditions. Would you agree?

Yes, I longed for this life from my teens, but was not allowed to go. If you feel you can't pray, God can still pray – it is His business, isn't it? We have just to let Him do what He wants in us. I don't think 'easy' or 'difficult' have any meaning here. If someone can think of nothing but wants to love

Him – like the sacrament – prayer is desire for God to have His way.

Oh yes, I too feel truth is a test of holiness. ('*I* am the Truth'[1] – the only virtue He said He *was*). I struggle to attain this honesty, this seeing and speaking truthfully, but it is beyond our own power. Only in Jesus can we become true, and then we naturally see what *is*.

1   Jn. 14.6.

*   *   *

Autumn is the harvest time, and it's a wonderful stage for us to affirm our complete faith that *God* is our 'Harvest'. We have no home we've built (how you would have loved that!), no career, no work – not even a spiritual achievement. We come to the end, as Thérèse says,[1] with empty hands, and *glad* to have them empty, so that God can fill them with Himself. So it's a time when our trust, which means love-in-action, comes into full play. Youth may still have a secret hope of personal harvest but at the turn of life we know the truth. And we live happy in it, or fret selfishly. I miss you too, but it's only an absence on one level, isn't it?

1   Saint Thérèse of Lisieux

*   *   *

That is a beautiful prayer.[1] Sometimes it helps, doesn't it, to have one's deepest longings *expressed*? It makes the way seem clearer. The only verbal prayer I have ever been able to say, (and I say it at the beginning and end of each day) is the formula I worked out for my Consecration, as expressing exactly what I long for. '*Come Holy Spirit, and utter within me, for all religious, the total Yes of Jesus to His Father.*' That '*Total* Yes', which only Jesus can say, is what incessantly draws me. He yearns to say it in everyone and it is such profound joy to me to hear it echoing, ever more distinctly, in *you*. Not 'total' yet, of course, but such a full 'Yes' already – and what will this new year bring??

1   The Sister to whom this note was addressed had shown Sister Wendy a prayer that was special to her.

*   *   *

When I look at you 'in the Lord', I can see no difficulty that matters – nothing that either isn't, or could not be, a doorway to Love. But perhaps I am not seeing clearly. So do write it out for me – and then I can say whether to allow no thoughts but of God, as I wrote, applies here or not! But if it's too difficult to write and you'd prefer a talk, then this would be the Spirit's signal that the time has come for one.

P.S. For you, tiny creature, 'little' never rings untrue! It's only untrue when the 'little' person is neither little in body nor truly sees herself as little in soul.

To a Correspondent

3 October 2011
Dearest,

Thank you so very much for sending me that large and interesting book.[1] My energies are a little low at present, so the community are having a first go at it. It's wonderful to see how God has gifted you and used you to proclaim His name.

Last time I did not have enough books for everybody and I asked the Sisters to share with you.[2] This time I also don't have enough but I'm sending the book to you and ask you to share with them. I know you'll respond to the deep spiritual beauty of this art. I know it because I know your heart and how you always want to love Our Blessed Lord and receive His love for yourself and for the world.

But O, dearest, you have got into a muddle about the Church, the hierarchy, priests, bishops, Vatican, the Pope … They're not the Church; they're a part of the Church, a functional part. The Church is the poor people of God, the faithful people who suffer and obey and never lose their trust in Him. This is the Church to whom Jesus promised His Holy Spirit, and we can see the presence of that Holy Spirit over the centuries. Always the leadership have made mistakes, it's part of their human frailty. Think of Peter, and the rigidity of some of the early popes; the frequent casual excommunications; the impurity and selfishness of the Renaissance; the fear of the Post-Reformation hierarchy as the world modernized itself and they were faced with new challenges they did not understand. Often they tried their best, but whether we had good popes or bad popes, in the end – because of the promise of Jesus to be with us – everything came right. Over time all the bad decisions were reversed. Why should it be any different today? The Pope isn't a superman. He tries his best and he gets things wrong. This will always be a source of great suffering but also our great opportunity to show our faith in the Holy Spirit. We cling to Him, obedient and trustful. To turn away from this body of believers, which St Paul says is the mystical body of Christ, is really, though I know you don't intend this, to turn away from Jesus on the cross. Remember how the Pharisees shouted at him: 'If you are the Son of God come down from the cross'? But it was by staying on the cross that He redeemed us. So His mystical body now enjoys the cross of these painful blindnesses that we see today and our obedience is redemptive.

Darling girl, please rethink your very natural, but not supernatural in the best sense, reactions to the sad mistakes that you list for me. Yes darling, mistakes, but of the hierarchy, not of the Church.

289

I always pray for you, with very much love,

1   Written by the correspondent.
2   Sister Wendy is referring to a copy of one of her own
     recently published books.

To a Journalist

Dearest X,

I am moved by your beautiful letter. I rejoice that our dear Jesus has shown you His Face, however veiled and 'in a glass darkly'. You see Him and you long for Him.

But that is a longing, wholly mutual, between you and Him. No confidences on how He gives Himself to another would allay your anguish or bring you any closer. The closeness is in your own reality, as it is for everyone.

Even if some holy woman were to spell out every detail of the 'story of her soul', it would leave all who read it awed and grateful but still faced with their own singleness. God looks at each individual and only a truthful desire to belong completely to Him can 'work'. Each of us is alone with Jesus, for the sake of the world. We are alone together.

I cannot even think of writing about myself. I cannot 'see' myself. I am lost in the overpowering Reality of God. So I just *can't*.[1]

Not sure if I can do the proposed book,[2] but that is an objective proposition and all I need is the energy.

For *your* book I'd need not to be Sister Wendy: what a paradox!

May the Holy Spirit take us both into the heart of the Trinity.

1   This journalist had written to ask Sister Wendy whether she could be persuaded to say something about her interior life.
2   The destinee of this letter had simultaneously put forward a proposition that Sister Wendy might write a book on a subject unrelated to the question above.

Selected spiritual notes

On Dedication

This is a grace-filled time for you as you prepare to lay your whole self on the altar of sacrifice.[1] Or rather you prepare to be lifted up to the altar by Jesus whom you are choosing as your Love for ever. He chose so passionately to be wholly given for the world. If we have no passion, merely our weakness, we are all the better equipped to let His ardour consume us and let His Yes become our centre. 'You do it in me, Lord,' is the only true prayer for so great a vocation.

Just to tell you I am holding you fast in the Heart of Love as you make this sacrifice. It is all His doing, His deliberate choice. So I know, and so do you, that your 'Fiat' means He is free to give you all He desires. This is a happy thing – a true and beautiful grace – never mind how we feel. All our Beloved does can only be for our enrichment.

I often pray for you, knowing how glorious is the special vocation God has given you, asking your sensitive heart to live in some real way alone, desolate, in a true Carmelite desert. And yet this is solely for Love, love received within your heart and meant to be shared with all you see and with all you don't see.

1   The nun to whom this note was written was about to enter into her Profession retreat.

On Community

I don't think it really matters whether a community feels they have much in common. They *do* have – I know they have – a common desire to love Him and be surrendered to Him. So these broad goals are clear. But different interpretations and manners and attitudes are all part of being human. The sheer 'loneliness' of nobody-on-one's-wavelength can open one up profoundly to Jesus, and to that sacrificial joy that is at the heart of Carmel. So very many in the world live alone and sad: we take that natural state and 'redeem' it for them. I do think you should gently and sweetly try to establish shared desires, but in peace and security. At depth we must choose to *trust* our Sisters, that they want Him as much as they are able.

You have received a very great grace: to understand that we don't live in community for what it *gives us*, (affirmation, love, support – none of which we may perceive), but for what it frees us to *become*, in Jesus. The human loneliness and all the inevitable misunderstandings open us up to true Jesus-love. Love is obedience, He told us, and we are obedient to the Spirit of Love in 'doing the works of love'. Faith, as you've been granted to see, is in living this out, even though, within, no love at all may be felt. As Thérèse[1] knew: that *is* love. You have a naturally tender and loving heart and all your life you may be tempted to seek a 'warmer' environment. But that is what it is, temptation. It's not despite but because of your womanly tenderness that Jesus calls you to the desert surrender of Carmel. Here you are living in faith for all the lonely ones of the world.

I would never try to scrutinize motive, if I were you. All we can ever do is look at Jesus, and *try* to please Him. It demands great trust to stand alone and respond only to Him, unseen and unheard. But that is the essence of prayer, isn't it? No support, not even of feeling good or loving or generous, just the bare desire to be and do whatever He wants. In this context it can even be a help to our weakness to have no 'special friend'. It can open us to a deeper love of everyone: poor, weak, misunderstanding creatures as they and we all are. Jesus entrusts you with His own sweetness and gentleness to heal their wounds.

But don't, in your heart, allow yourself to think little of your Sisters. Choose to trust them, however they may seem to you. A grace not to let anything show[2]; but Jesus can even root out the indifference and let us see how *He* sees them – with intense reverence and affection.

1   Saint Thérèse of Lisieux.
2   Not to let negative feelings show themselves outwardly.

On Prayer

That was a lovely letter, which made me very happy. Jesus never asks us to achieve anything but to *want*, to *long*, to *pray* – and then He will be the holiness and the love within us. We shall feel all the shame of our poverty and lack of faithfulness, but it won't make us anxious, because we shall promptly offer it to Him. That sense of our failure is the goad that keeps us looking at Him and longing. If once we think we have got there and been utterly faithful, then we are saying we don't need Him. In His dear Mercy, He lets you suffer from the pain of nothingness and fervourlessness, so He can live and love in your desire.

It would take a book to answer your letter – and a life-time of prayer and love to live that answer fully! So I'm only making a few points for your prayerful study. First, as to why we pray: I would say because the Father made us to be His. The reason is His doing – we *must* pray, just as humans. But as to what prayer is, ah, only Jesus knows that. Just as there is no other holiness except His – and we have no other holiness of our *own* – so there is no prayer but the prayer of Jesus, and 'our' prayer means entering into His. But what did He do when He prayed? He gave His whole self to the Father through the Spirit. He too did not pray 'on His own', as a mere man, so to speak. No, it was always the Spirit who drove Him. Here is a very deep and almost paradoxical mystery.

Yes indeed! We are living out that truth all day: being truly human to the depth of our reach and in proportion to our true desire. But at prayer the focus narrows: we can just 'be', in His Presence, receptive and surrendered (two sides of the same state). Desire is the key because it means that we seriously seek Him in the actual context of our lives and cling to Him where He really is. And we can't do this unless our hearts are free for Him. Cling on to the Jesus that your enlightened heart has seen. We love Jesus *because of what He is* and never because of what we are, or are not. Our hope is grounded on Him, 'our Rock'.

On Trust

Just to tell you I've been asking the Holy Spirit to guide your retreat, and above all, to reveal Himself, secretly, to you as the Spirit of trust. Total trust in God is the only true foundation for you – we can't afford to live at peace while we inwardly believe all depends on us, and that we hold God's love on the fragile basis of our virtue. But when we trust His never-failing concern for us, His steady unfaltering love and determination to give Himself, no matter how weak we are: then we can rest contentedly on His broad fatherly shoulders. And our proof of our trust in Him must be a resolution to trust our sisters. Not the way we trust Him, because all human beings are so limited, but a trust in their essential goodness, that they want Him as much, perhaps more than we do … and that we all meet peacefully in that longing.

I am sure His loving Heart is pleased with your efforts, and He doesn't even notice your inevitable failures. He just says, gently, love me all the more for the falls and I will do My will in you.

Trust means that we (at least!) expect fairness! And God could never make demands that we couldn't meet, could He? All worries about backsliding are just 'self'. He always asks us to live in peace, in 'largeness'. If we fall, we simply look at Him and go on. We never fret or feel strained. Better for Him that we give 'less' in peace than 'more' in strain because He is only present in the peaceful heart. Be brave ... never give in to these lowering fears. And remember that trust is a virtue that has to be struggled and prayed for. The reason why He lets you feel as you do is precisely so you *can* struggle – and receive in His sweet time.

'How does one become ...' One *trusts*, and one waits in hope. Sometimes He cannot show us; we would take it to ourselves. So we consent to live poor and trustful.

It is terribly hard when our family are in need and call upon us. You have been guided by the Spirit of Jesus to see, lovingly and compassionately, that your poor sister is speaking to you from her own guilt, not from truth. Your family are God's, more than yours, and in your vocation, they too have a share. They are called to be the family of a Carmelite, with all the loneliness and pain that it may bring them. He gives them special sanctifying grace through the very things we want to shield them from, if only we trust Him, and again and again throw ourselves on His Love.

On Truth

God-talk is very dangerous. It can disguise from us that our love is mainly cerebral and, when we do see it, we can feel helpless. But never so with Jesus whom we are given precisely to hold us in reality and to save us from our helplessness. If you look at John's Gospel (and the others, too) it is obvious that Jesus does not direct us to 'God' but to *Himself* – or else to God-in-relation-to-Himself, to the 'Father'. Infinite depths here ...

As for our 'really' wanting Him, that too is unknowable. Our part is to ask Him, incessantly and trustfully, to make us one, embodied longing, and He will fill us with Himself. We can never know how deeply we respond. He knows. He will show us all we need to *do*. ('Doing the truth in love')[1].

But how are we to understand that we 'can't' unless we see what we are: poor, ungenerous ones who play and preen and cheat Him? But when we see this, then we can begin to see that Jesus 'can' – and *will*. Contrite recognition of our shame sets us free to receive His glory. So let all the joy be His, if that is His will. And trust Him absolutely. All depends on the living knowledge that Jesus is the way to the Father.

I think 'not to be in the truth' means that a person has chosen, at some level of consciousness, to evade the pain and labour of love. Really to love Him means such a readiness to be purified that all the unpleasant and laborious striving are accepted with ready heart. Love is constantly shown in the need to change, but we are selfish. If to put this right is too much for us and yet we still want to feel 'spiritual' we can choose not to see, to evade reality, and so avoid the pain of growth. Note: I am talking of a *conscious* choice. Everyone evades unconsciously, of course, because God has not yet shown them with His effective light.

Do you remember Paul's 'I know nothing but Jesus, and Him crucified?'[2] Speaking in the context of that truth, then:

We *know* the reality of God. All spiritual truth is absolute and certain. It may be in faith that we know but the reality remains absolute.

We *believe* in other people. Here I am not speaking theologically but use the word 'belief' to suggest the nature of our knowledge of reality in others. I.e.: it is *never* absolute and certain but *always* relative and provisional. All we can *know* is that God sees their reality. We make an act of faith in their good intentions and pray to be taken into the humility of Jesus.

So we know 'how' we should regard others and pray earnestly to be helped to do so.

We *don't know* our own state of soul. Remember the aphorism: 'man does not know whether he is worthy of love or hate.' We know that we *receive* love and salvation but what we are 'worthy of' is a question mark – and a hypothetical question mark. As He is God, our soul's good, He will show us all we need to do; never any strain or fret about Him. Are we doing our 'best'? How can we tell? What is our best? He knows, and He expects us to leave it peacefully in His love. Our concern is to love, using our minds to see what love requires. In this context the question of what is real or unreal doesn't matter. We know that Jesus is real and we live in the implications of that fact.

1   Cf. Eph. 4.15: 'speak the truth in love'.
2   1Cor. 2.2.

On Patience

Of course we are called – passionately, perseveringly called – to a union so intense that words are useless. And His call is an *effective* call, not an invitation only. Unless we choose to say 'no', His love will transform us. But *how* the wonder is achieved is *His* affair. By definition we cannot comprehend it. So we need great and trustful *patience*. Patience is far profounder and more all-embracing than it appears to be. To enter deeply into patience means accepting our lowliness and, equally, His power and will to transform us.

Reality is His message and patience leads straight to it. We seem to see our shabbiness and conclude we are getting absolutely nowhere. It may not be so at all. We long to push ahead, to 'take it by violence'[1]. But helplessness, accepting the ordinariness of our day as the divine means of purification: all this is painful. So my first word is *patience*. Affirm His power; wait in trust. And my second is to remind you that pure love is usually experienced as nothingness. If all is His, what is there left for self? So never seek to judge from how it 'feels'. To go on and on and never see anything 'happening': what trust we need!

1   Mt. 11.12.

On becoming fully human

The only one to be 'fully human' was Jesus – with Mary a close second. So it is easier to say what it is *not* than what it *is*. Essentially, it means accepting our full body-soul creation with its inbuilt limitations. For example, our minds have to be constantly opened to see truth and beauty, and yet, as we can never see with full clarity, we can never judge. And bodily, too, our appetites have to be accepted in their reality and purified of all that is not of God.

I'm not putting this very well. Our desire for God can betray us into angelism: that perfidious and subtle form of pride. I'm afraid a lot of the martyrdoms that are so lauded are, in large part, only this – and it amounts to a fear of God's goodness. One wants the security of one's own earnestness; pain seems to provide that!

Since we're not born 'human' but (hopefully) become so, nobody is in a position really to discern how far on another is. What seems lack could be an inbuilt defect. But we should listen to what is found wanting in us and sweetly and trustfully look to Jesus for Him to transform what He wishes. Often 'not fully human' refers to our relationships. We can only strive, with all our sensitivity, to make them warmer, more loving.

On Anxiety

Worry is a canker. And it's *self*-regarding. Whereas all our real life is in Jesus.

The function of anxiety is surely to alert us to our dependence on Him and to the fact that He alone matters. It is a most useful feeling. It says: You are fragile, unrealized, not in charge of your life, in danger of ... *therefore* turn wholly to Jesus. The feeling may or may not diminish but the direction out of self's narrowness into His love has been conquered. We have to go on and on until finally we live out of self, in Him. Mother Julian[1] is the most beautiful example of this. One can never read her without being pierced through by the Truth. She has an infallible instinct for this, don't you think? Very sane. She is never deceived by how things seem or what anyone appears to be saying, etc.

The great thing to grasp is that to feel 'relaxed/ happy' or to feel anxious is *unimportant*. Feelings only matter as an occasion for love. Happy, secure feelings prompt us to praise Him; sad, anxious feelings prompt us to express our faith and pray for Him to be All in All to us. The feelings themselves tell us nothing about our 'state' which is God's secret and God's work. We don't base anything on ourselves but only on Him, on His goodness, knowing, as Paul says, in whom we have believed. *Why* are we anxious? Let's will to have Jesus as our holiness. Gradually even the feeling vanishes, but that is unimportant.

We can feel that growing in love should make life 'easier' – that there is some failure in our fear, temptation, struggle. Not so. In fact the tempest may blow more severely as we near harbour. Jesus could never know a psychic respite, as the gospels show. But our *attitudes* change. We cease to be afraid of fear; we open our arms to the will for the Father to give us whatever He will, *knowing*, in Jesus, that He gives only 'good things'.

1   Julian of Norwich, author of *Revelations of Divine Love.*

On Love

We only know God through the person of Jesus – only when one with Jesus can we love – but the whole life of Jesus is one of surrender to the Spirit. We become Jesus to the extent that we become *ourselves* – that's what I meant by: 'not the person of Jesus but His

Spirit'. It is the Person of the glorified Jesus, if you prefer it so said – but that's what the 'Spirit of Jesus' is. Father, Son and Spirit have no meaning for us in isolation. The Father is only 'Father of Jesus', the Spirit is only 'Spirit of Jesus'. For me, 'life is Christ'[1]. There is no other answer than that.

We often think that love and holiness mean no bad thoughts, no struggle. But these things are the very strife in which love is shown. Never did Jesus love more than in the Garden when He didn't 'want to' but yet chose pure surrender. And the choosing and the turmoil lasted hours. So if ours lasts days … weeks … years: Fiat! It all redeems both us and the world. I think we can be so grateful that it all shames and hurts. This is the deepest reparation because it is not of our choosing.

Jesus' own rejection would be unbearable were it not that the only love He wanted was obedience to the Father, and our desire to give Him that is wholly effective, irrespective of time. This is the wonderful thing. The Lord will always arrange our lives for us, sweetly seeing to it that all things bring us closer to His heart, as painlessly as possible. 'Why are you anxious, O you of little faith?'[2] He Himself transforms our 'little faith' into total faith. We have only to wait in peace and prayer.

1   Phil. 1.21.
2   Cf. Mt. 8.26.

Now, journey through the Bible with Sister Wendy Beckett and the greatest artists of all time!

From the majesty of Genesis to the mystery of Revelation, the Bible contains many of humanity's most powerful stories and treasures of sublime wisdom. No wonder it has inspired so many glorious works of art, including some of the greatest pictures ever painted. In *Sister Wendy's Bible Treasury* lovers of religious art will find superb examples, along with Sister Wendy Beckett's inimitable commentary, and passages from the beloved King James Bible/Authorized version.

First are works depicting Adam and Eve expelled from Paradise, Jacob wrestling with the angel, God appearing to Moses in the burning bush, Samson betrayed by Delilah, David slaying Goliath and other dramatic episodes and memorable characters from the Old Testament, as portrayed by artists such as Masaccio, Raphael, Rubens, Degas, and Rembrandt.

Then, from the New Testament, the figure of Jesus becomes the focus, with Christ's parables and miracles depicted by such artists as Poussin, Delacroix, and van Gogh, and the major events of his life, from the Annunciation to the Resurrection in paintings by Botticelli, Piero, Duccio, da Vinci, Giotto, Titian, and Craigie Atchison.

Available at your favorite bookseller, or direct from
www.orbisbooks.com

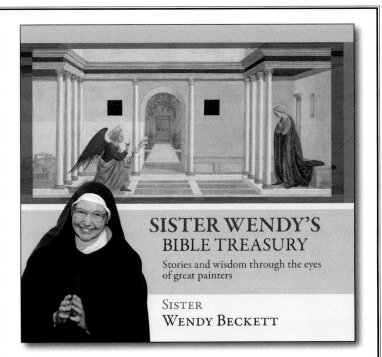

Sister Wendy's Bible Treasury

ISBN 1-57075-972-7 Soft cover, French flaps, 144pp.,
50 full-color illustrations

Featured in the popular BBC documentaries, **Sister Wendy
Beckett** is author of the international bestseller *The Story of
Painting*. Formerly a Sister of Notre Dame, Sister Wendy has
lived since 1979 as a contemplative nun within the grounds of a
Carmelite Monastery in Norfolk, England.

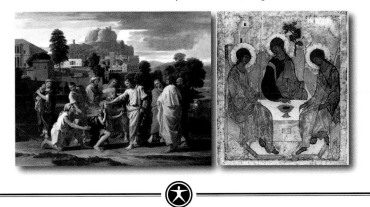

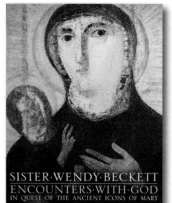

Encounters With God
In Quest of the
Ancient Icons of Mary
by Sister Wendy Beckett

Sister Wendy leads us on a "pilgrimage of desire" to view the earliest surviving icons of Mary.

ISBN 978-1-57075-832-4
Hardcover, 140pp.,
65 full-color illustrations

"These early images of Mary seem to me to have the power to shock us out of our complacency, to make us look anew at what the birth of Jesus meant, and means…"

In this story of discovery and spiritual adventure, Sister Wendy Beckett, a contemplative nun and beloved art commentator, travels from England, to Rome, to Ukraine, and finally to a remote monastery in Sinai, to find the earliest icons of Mary, Mother of God. These rare and mysterious images are among the few that survived the wholesale destruction of icons in the early eighth century AD. They come to us from a time closer to that of Christ, when faith was still alive with wonder, and possibilities were infinite.

In the course of her pilgrimage, Sister Wendy also reviews the history of Christian art, the meaning and function of icons, and shares her thoughts on the relation between beauty, prayer, and the search for God.

Available from your bookseller, or direct: www.orbisbooks.com

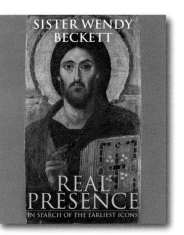